CW01659292

RECOGNISING ACHIEVEMENT

Intermediate Tier

GCSE Exam Revision
Mathematics

Howard Baxter

Mike Handbury

John Jeskins

Jean Matthews

Mark Patmore

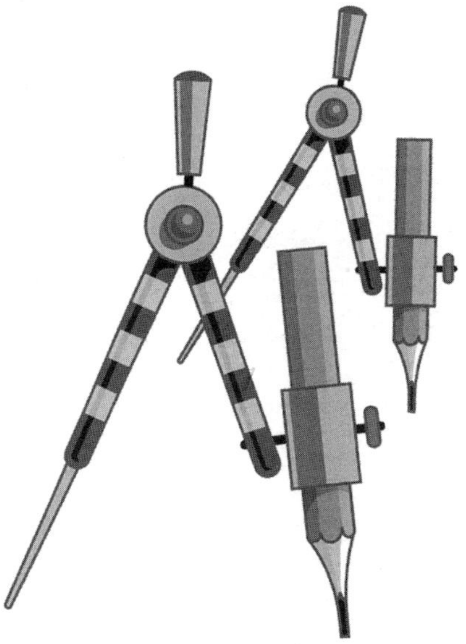

Series editor

Brian Seager

Hodder & Stoughton

A MEMBER OF THE HODDER HEADLINE GROUP

Orders: please contact Bookpoint Ltd, 130 Milton Park, Abingdon, Oxon OX14 4SB.
Telephone: (44) 01235 827720, Fax: (44) 01235 400454. Lines are open from
9.00–6.00, Monday to Saturday, with a 24 hour message answering service.

British Library Cataloguing in Publication Data
A catalogue record for this title is available from The British Library

ISBN 0 340 85613 0

First published 2002

Impression number	10	9	8	7	6	5	4
Year	2008	2007	2006	2005	2004		

Cover illustration by Mark Oliver.
Typeset by Pantek Arts Ltd, Maidstone, Kent, ME14 1NY
Printed in England for Hodder & Stoughton Educational, a division of Hodder Headline Plc,
338 Euston Road, London NW1 3BH by Hobbs The Printers

Introduction

This book is intended to help you prepare for the final examinations in GCSE Mathematics. It does not matter if you have taken tests at an earlier stage, this book covers all you need to know for the terminal examination. It is suitable for any OCR specification and it may also be used in preparing for any other GCSE Mathematics examination, as all the specifications' contents derive from the same National Curriculum.

The topics from the specification have been left in their original groups: Number; Algebra; Shape, space and measures; Handling data. Each topic has been introduced in the same way: a reminder of definitions and techniques; one or more worked examples; a short exercise for each part. Finally, there is an examination question, together with a model answer, and then some examination questions for you to try. The answers to all the questions are at the back of the book. For full model answers to the exam questions, go to http://www.hoddermaths.co.uk. Throughout, there are explanations and tips to help you understand and make the most of your knowledge and understanding in answering questions in the actual examinations. Most of the topics are completed on two facing pages. A few that involve many diagrams continue to three, four or six pages.

How to use this book

There are many ways of using the book. You could use it for reference when doing work from a different book. You could use it by opening a page randomly and checking that you can do the questions. The most satisfactory way, however, will be to use it systematically as part of your planned revision. Whether you choose to work through it in order or jump between topic areas, you can keep a check on your progress by using the Revision record at the front of the book.

Once you have chosen a topic, see if you can remember how to tackle the various parts. You can either work through the reminder sections and worked example first or try to answer the first question for yourself, to test if you can remember what it is about. Whichever way you do it, make sure you work through all the exercises and examination questions, as practice reinforces your learning. When you have completed a topic, don't forget to tick the box in the Revision record. If you know that your understanding is worse in certain topic areas, don't leave these to the end of your revision programme. Put them in at the start so that you will have time to return to them nearer the end of the revision period.

This symbol next to a question means you are not allowed to use a calculator. These questions would appear in the non-calculator paper/section. Here they always come first.

This symbol next to a question means you need to use your calculator. These questions would appear in the calculator paper/section. Here they always come second.

If a question has neither symbol, you can choose whether or not to use your calculator but it is unlikely to be required to answer the question. These questions could appear in either paper/section. Here they always come last.

Examination tips

Examination papers all have a formulae sheet on the second page. Make sure you know what is on it. If a formula is not there, you will have to remember it. The formulae sheet for the Intermediate tier has the formulae for the area of the trapezium and the volume of a prism.

Make sure you read the instructions carefully, both those on the front of the paper and those in each question. Here are the meanings of some of the words used.

- **Write, write down, state** – little working out will be needed and no explanation is required.
- **Calculate, find** – something to be worked out, with a calculator if appropriate. It is a good idea to show the steps of your working as this may earn marks even if the answer is wrong.
- **Solve** – show all the steps in solving the equation.
- **Prove, show** – all the steps needed, including reasons, must be shown in a logical way.
- **Deduce, hence** – use a previous result to help you find the answer.
- **Draw** – draw as accurately and carefully as you can.
- **Sketch** – need not be accurate but should show the essential features.
- **Explain** – give (a) brief reason(s). The number of features you need to mention can be judged by looking at the marks. One mark probably means only one reason is required.

As well as this book, there are a lot of websites that will help you revise. Go to http://www.m-a.org.uk/assoc/links/index.htm for a list of links.

Brian Seager, 2002
Series editor

Revision Record

☑ Tick the boxes to keep track of your progress

Number

Integers (pages 2–3)

- Multiples ☐
- Factors ☐
- Prime numbers ☐
- Prime factors ☐
- Highest common factor (HCF) and lowest common multiple (LCM) ☐
- Reciprocals ☐
- Negative numbers ☐
- **Exam questions** ☐

Powers and roots (pages 4–5)

- Indices ☐
- Multiplying and dividing with indices ☐
- Using powers and roots ☐
- Standard index form ☐
- **Exam questions** ☐

Fractions (pages 6–7)

- Mixed numbers and top-heavy fractions ☐
- Adding and subtracting fractions ☐
- Multiplying and dividing fractions ☐
- Increasing or decreasing by a fraction ☐
- **Exam questions** ☐

Decimals and percentages (pages 8–9)

- Changing between fractions, decimals and percentages ☐
- Recurring decimals ☐
- Finding *A* as a percentage of *B* ☐
- Finding a percentage of an amount ☐
- Finding an amount before a percentage increase or decrease ☐
- **Exam questions** ☐

Ratio (pages 10–11)

- Writing as a ratio ☐
- Mixing in a ratio ☐
- Simplest form ☐
- Sharing in a given ratio ☐
- **Exam questions** ☐

Mental methods (pages 12–13)

- Squares, square roots and cubes ☐
- Rounding to a given number of significant figures ☐
- Standard index form ☐
- Mental shortcuts ☐
- **Exam questions** ☐

Written methods (pages 14–15)

- Repeated proportional change ☐
- Repeated percentage change ☐
- Direct proportion ☐
- **Exam questions** ☐

Calculator methods (pages 16–17)

- Calculating with negative numbers ☐
- Calculating with fractions ☐
- Reciprocals ☐
- Powers and roots ☐
- Brackets ☐
- Standard form ☐
- Trigonometric keys ☐
- **Exam questions** ☐

Solving problems (pages 18–19)

- Some common money problems ☐
- Compound measures ☐
- Checking your work ☐
- Accuracy of answers ☐
- Trial and improvement ☐
- **Exam questions** ☐

Algebra

Use of symbols (pages 20–21)

- Manipulating algebra ☐
- Multiplying brackets by single terms ☐
- Common factors ☐
- Substitution ☐
- Indices ☐
- **Exam questions** ☐

Linear equations (pages 22–23)

- Solving equations ☐
- Brackets in equations ☐
- Dealing with the 'unknown' ☐
- More than one set of brackets ☐
- Fractions in equations ☐
- **Exam questions** ☐

Formulae (pages 24–25)

- Substituting in formulae ☐
- Writing your own formulae ☐
- Rearranging formulae ☐
- Powers of the subject ☐
- Subject in twice ☐
- **Exam questions** ☐

Simultaneous equations and inequalities (pages 26–27)

- Simultaneous equations ☐
- Inequalities ☐
- **Exam questions** ☐

Quadratic equations (pages 28–29)

- Multiplying out brackets ☐
- Factorising quadratic expressions ☐
- Solving quadratic expressions by factorising ☐
- **Exam questions** ☐

Numerical methods (pages 30–31)

- Trial and improvement ☐
- **Exam questions** ☐

Sequences (pages 32–33)

- Term-to-term rules ☐
- Common sequences ☐
- Position-to-term rules ☐
- **Exam questions** ☐

Shape, space and measures

Handling data

Integers

Multiples

The multiples of a number are the numbers in its times table.

Example

Find the multiples of 6 up to 30.

6, 12, 18, 24, 30

Now try these:

1 Find the first six multiples of:

(a) 4 (b) 9 (c) 15

Factors

The factors of a number are the numbers which divide exactly into it.

Example

Find the factors of 36.

1×36 2×18 3×12 4×9 6×6

The factors of 36 are 1, 2, 3, 4, 6, 9, 12, 18 and 36.

It is easier to find factors by looking for pairs of numbers that multiply to give the number.

Now try these:

2 Find the factors of:

(a) 24 (b) 40 (c) 32

Prime numbers

Prime numbers are numbers which have only two factors; 1 and the number itself.

Example

Find the first five prime numbers.

2, 3, 5, 7, 11

Prime factors

Prime factors are factors which are also prime numbers.

Example

Write 48 as a product of prime factors.

Keep breaking the numbers into factors until you end up with prime numbers.

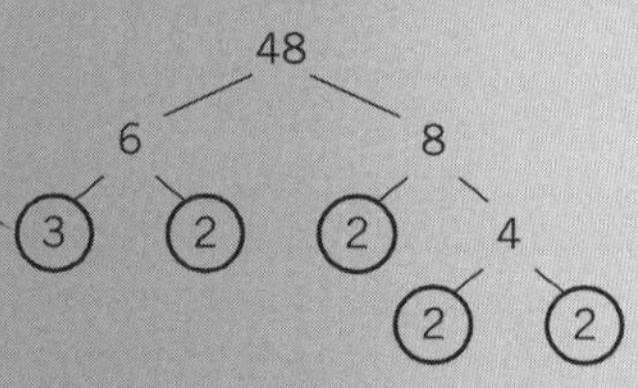

$48 = 2 \times 2 \times 2 \times 2 \times 3$ or $2^4 \times 3$

Now try these:

3 Write the following as a product of prime factors:

(a) 36 (b) 140 (c) 84

Highest common factor (HCF) and lowest common multiple (LCM)

- HCF is the largest number that will divide into each of the given numbers.

Example

Find the HCF of 120, 36 and 84.

Express each as a product of prime factors.

$120 = (2) \times (2) \times 2 \times (3) \times 5$

$36 = (2) \times (2) \times 3 \times (3)$

$84 = (2) \times (2) \times (3) \times 7$

Choose the factors that are **common** to all three numbers.

$HCF = 2 \times 2 \times 3 = 12$

- LCM is the smallest number that can be divided exactly by each of the given numbers.

Express each as a product of prime factors.

Choose the largest number of primes from each number.

Example

Find the LCM of 120, 36 and 84.

$120 = (2) \times (2) \times (2) \times 3 \times (5)$

$36 = 2 \times 2 \times (3) \times (3)$

$84 = 2 \times 2 \times 3 \times (7)$

$\text{LCM} = 2 \times 2 \times 2 \times 3 \times 3 \times 5 \times 7 = 2520$

Now try these:

4 Find the HCF and the LCM of:

(a) 15 and 24 **(b)** 12 and 40 **(c)** 90, 54 and 36

Reciprocals

- The reciprocal of x is $\frac{1}{x}$.
- The reciprocal of $\frac{a}{b}$ is $\frac{b}{a}$.

Example

Find the reciprocals of:

(a) 4 **(b)** $\frac{2}{3}$ **(c)** 0·1

(a) $\frac{1}{4}$ **(b)** $\frac{3}{2}$ or 1·5 **(c)** $\frac{1}{0{\cdot}1}$ or 10

Now try these:

5 Find the reciprocal of:

(a) 5 **(b)** $\frac{1}{9}$ **(c)** $\frac{3}{4}$ **(d)** 0·2 **(e)** $2\frac{1}{2}$

Negative numbers

- When multiplying and dividing or when two signs follow each other then use the rules:

+	+	=	+
−	−	=	+
−	+	=	−
+	−	=	−

- Combine the signs and numbers separately. A number with no sign is always +.

Example

Work out:

(a) $3 - (^{-}7)$
(b) $^{-}4 \times 3$
(c) $^{-}12 \div {^{-}6}$

(a) $3 + 7 = 10$
(b) $^{-}12$
(c) $^{+}2$ or 2

Now try these:

6 Work out:

(a) $6 + (^{-}4)$ **(c)** $^{-}10 + (^{-}6)$ **(e)** $^{-}5 \times 3$ **(g)** $16 \div {^{-}4}$

(b) $^{-}4 - (^{-}3)$ **(d)** $9 - (^{-}2)$ **(f)** $^{-}20 \div {^{-}5}$ **(h)** $^{-}8 \times {^{-}3}$

Here is an exam question ...and its solution

Write 30 as a product of prime factors.

$30 = 2 \times 3 \times 5$

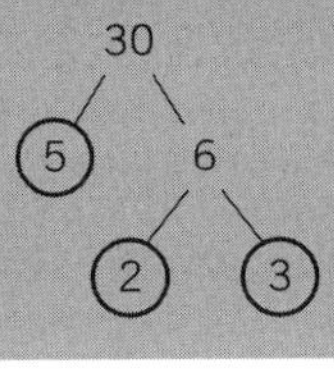

Now try these exam questions:

1 From the numbers from 10 up to 20, choose:
(a) a multiple of 7
(b) a factor of 36
(c) a prime number.

2 Write 264 as a product of prime factors.

3 Find the HCF and LCM of 12 and 16.

4 Find the HCF and LCM of 10, 12 and 20.

5 Find the value of 4 multiplied by the reciprocal of 4. Show clear working to explain your answer.

6 Find the value of $(^{-}5)^2 + 4 \times {^{-}3}$.

Powers and roots

Indices

Indices (or powers) give a short way of writing numbers multiplied by themselves.

Now try these:

Find the value of:

1 3^4
2 3^0
3 3^{-2}
4 10^0
5 6^3
6 2^{-3}

The 4 in 2^4 is called an index or power.

Examples

$2^4 = 2 \times 2 \times 2 \times 2 = 16$
$2^3 = 2 \times 2 \times 2 = 8$
$2^2 = 2 \times 2 = 4$
$2^1 = 2 = 2$

Continuing the pattern:

$2^0 = \quad = 1$
$2^{-1} = \frac{1}{2^1} = \frac{1}{2}$
$2^{-2} = \frac{1}{2^2} = \frac{1}{4}$

Don't forget that $n^0 = 1$ and $n^{-a} = \frac{1}{n^a}$ for any non-zero value of n.

Multiplying and dividing with indices

- Multiplying: $n^a \times n^b = n^{a+b}$ — Add the powers.
- Dividing: $n^a \div n^b$ or $\frac{n^a}{n^b} = n^{a-b}$ — Subtract the powers.
- Powers of powers: $(n^a)^b = n^{ab}$ — Multiply the powers.

Examples

$3^2 \times 3^4 = 3^6$ ($2 + 4 = 6$)
$2y^4 \times 3y^5 = 6y^9$ ($4 + 5 = 9$)

Example

$3^5 \div 3^3 = 3^2$ ($5 - 3 = 2$)

Example

$\frac{a^2b}{ab^2} = \frac{a}{b}$ ($2 - 1 = 1$, $1 - 2 = {}^-1$)

Example

$(2^3)^4 = 2^{12}$ ($3 \times 4 = 12$)

Remember, this only works with the same base number. $m^2 \times p^3 \neq mp^5$.

For adding and subtracting, indices are not so helpful. There is no shortcut rule.
Example $3^2 + 3^3 = 9 + 27 = 36$

Now try these:

Simplify the following:

7 $5^2 \times 5^8$
8 $6^5 \div 6^2$
9 $4a^6 \times 2a^3$
10 $\frac{12a^5b^2}{2a^3b^3}$
11 $(c^2)^5$
12 $(2x^4)^3$

Using powers and roots

- You are expected to know the squares of the counting numbers up to 15. You need also to be able to recognise the square roots of these numbers.

Number n	1	2	3	4	5	6	7	8	9	10	11	12	13	14	15
Square n^2	1	4	9	16	25	36	49	64	81	100	121	144	169	196	225

- You are expected to know the cubes of the counting numbers up to 5, and 10.

Number n	1	2	3	4	5	10
Cube n^3	1	8	27	64	125	1000

Examples

$6^2 = 36$ $\sqrt{36} = 6$ $3^3 = 27$ $\sqrt[3]{27} = 3$

Know how to use the square root and power buttons on your calculator.

Now try these:

Write down the value of:

13 11^2
14 $\sqrt{49}$

Use your calculator to find

15 $\sqrt{848}$, correct to 1 d.p.
16 36^3

Standard index form

- This is used for large or very small numbers.
- They are written in the form $a \times 10^n$, where n is an integer and $1 \leq a < 10$. For example, a can be 9·8 but not 11·7.
- To multiply or divide numbers in standard form without a calculator, use the rules of indices.

Example

(a) $3\,500\,000 = 3{\cdot}5 \times 10^6$
(b) $0{\cdot}000\,42 = 4{\cdot}2 \times 10^{-4}$
(c) $(3 \times 10^6) \times (5 \times 10^8) = 15 \times 10^{6+8}$
$= 15 \times 10^{14}$
$= 1{\cdot}5 \times 10^{15}$

Don't forget – to enter standard form on a scientific calculator, use the **EXP** key, not **×** **1** **0**
Example To enter $3{\cdot}5 \times 10^6$, press **3** **·** **5** **EXP** **6**

Many calculators display numbers in standard form as if they were powers. You need to interpret your calculator display and write down the number correctly in standard form.

Now try these:

Write the following as ordinary numbers:

17 $3{\cdot}72 \times 10^5$ **18** $4{\cdot}8 \times 10^{-4}$

Write the following in standard form:

19 0·000 058 3 **20** 75 600 000

Work out, without a calculator then with one:

21 $(8 \times 10^5) \times (1{\cdot}5 \times 10^8)$ **22** $(5 \times 10^7) \div (2 \times 10^{-3})$

Here is an exam question ...and its solution

This question tests the rules of indices and standard form without a calculator.

(a) Simplify the following:
(i) $y^3 \times y^4$ **(ii)** $\dfrac{pq^3 \times p^2}{p^5 q}$

(b) Write these numbers in standard form:
(i) 41 000 000 **(ii)** 0·000 062 9

(c) Calculate, giving your answer in standard form:
(i) $(3 \times 10^{-9}) \times (7 \times 10^{11})$
(ii) $\dfrac{6 \times 10^4}{2 \times 10^{-4}}$

Solution

(a) (i) y^7 — $3 + 4 = 7$
(ii) $p^{-2}q^2$ or $\dfrac{q^2}{p^2}$ — for p: $1 + 2 - 5 = -2$; for q: $3 - 1 = 2$

(b) (i) $4{\cdot}1 \times 10^7$
(ii) $6{\cdot}29 \times 10^{-5}$

(c) (i) $21 \times 10^2 = 2{\cdot}1 \times 10^3$ — $7 \times 3 = 21$, $-9 + 11 = 2$; $21 = 2{\cdot}1 \times 10^1$
(ii) 3×10^8 — $6 \div 2 = 3$, $4 - -4 = 8$

Now try these exam questions:

1 Write the following as whole numbers or fractions:
(a) 4^3 **(b)** 4^{-2} **(c)** 4^0

2 Write down the square root of 81.

3 (a) Simplify, writing each number as a power of 3:
(i) $3^4 \times 3^5$
(ii) $\dfrac{3^3 \times 3^5}{3^6}$

(b) Work out, writing each answer as a whole number:
(i) $2^3 \div 2^2$
(ii) $\dfrac{2^5 \times 3^2}{4^2}$

4 (a) Work out $(3{\cdot}0 \times 10^4) \times (6{\cdot}0 \times 10^3)$, writing the answer in standard form.

(b) A terawatt is 10^{12} watts. A power station produces $1{\cdot}2 \times 10^8$ watts. Write this in terawatts.

5 Calculate $\sqrt{31}$. Write your answer to 2 d.p.

6 (a) Find $\sqrt{470{\cdot}89}$
(b) (i) Work out $8{\cdot}7^4$, writing down all the figures on your calculator display.
(ii) Write your answer to (b) (i) correct to 3 s.f.

7 Calculate the difference between 5^{-2} and 2^{-5}. Give your answer in standard form.

8 Simplify: **(a)** $3a^2b \times 4ab^3$ **(b)** $\dfrac{14a^3b^2}{2ab^3}$

9 Here are the population figures for 1998 for five countries.

Australia	$1{\cdot}9 \times 10^7$
Botswana	$1{\cdot}4 \times 10^6$
China	$1{\cdot}2 \times 10^9$
Denmark	$5{\cdot}3 \times 10^6$
Egypt	$6{\cdot}6 \times 10^7$

(a) Write these populations in order of size, smallest first.
(b) How many times larger was the population of China than the population of Egypt?

Fractions

Mixed numbers and top-heavy fractions

- To change a top-heavy fraction to a mixed number, divide the denominator into the numerator and write the remainder over the denominator as a fraction.
- To change a mixed number to a top-heavy fraction, multiply the whole number by the denominator and add on the numerator. Then write this number over the denominator.

Example

$\frac{14}{5} = 2\frac{4}{5}$ $\quad$ $14 \div 5 = 2$ rem 4

Example

$3\frac{5}{8} = \frac{29}{8}$ $\quad$ $3 \times 8 + 5 = 29$

Notice that the denominator does not change.

Now try these:

Change to mixed numbers.

1 $\frac{11}{4}$ **2** $\frac{16}{5}$ **3** $\frac{29}{6}$

Change these to top-heavy fractions.

4 $1\frac{3}{4}$ **5** $3\frac{1}{6}$ **6** $4\frac{3}{8}$

Adding and subtracting fractions

- Change the fractions to the same 'type' i.e. with the same denominator, and add or subtract the numerators.

Example

$\frac{1}{6} + \frac{3}{4}$

$= \frac{2}{12} + \frac{9}{12} = \frac{11}{12}$

Change both to denominator 12. Multiply $\frac{1}{6}$ by $\frac{2}{2} = \frac{2}{12}$ and $\frac{3}{4}$ by $\frac{3}{3} = \frac{9}{12}$.

Example

$\frac{4}{5} - \frac{2}{3}$

$= \frac{12}{15} - \frac{10}{15} = \frac{2}{15}$

Change both to denominator 15.

- When mixed numbers are involved, deal with the whole numbers first.

Example

$2\frac{2}{3} + 1\frac{3}{8} = 3 + \frac{2}{3} + \frac{3}{8}$

$= 3 + \frac{16}{24} + \frac{9}{24} = 3\frac{25}{24} = 4\frac{1}{24}$

- If, in subtraction, the first fraction part is smaller than the second, change a whole number to a fraction.

Example

$3\frac{1}{4} - 1\frac{2}{5} = 2 + \frac{1}{4} - \frac{2}{5}$

$= 2 + \frac{5}{20} - \frac{8}{20} = 1 + \frac{20}{20} + \frac{5}{20} - \frac{8}{20} = 1\frac{17}{20}$

Now try these:

7 $\frac{1}{4} + \frac{2}{3}$ **10** $1\frac{2}{3} + 3\frac{4}{5}$ **13** $3\frac{4}{5} - 2\frac{1}{4}$

8 $\frac{2}{5} + \frac{1}{3}$ **11** $\frac{3}{4} - \frac{2}{3}$ **14** $4\frac{2}{5} - 1\frac{5}{6}$

9 $2\frac{3}{8} + 3\frac{1}{6}$ **12** $\frac{5}{7} - \frac{1}{2}$ **15** $\frac{3}{8} + \frac{3}{4} - \frac{1}{6}$

Multiplying and dividing fractions

- When multiplying fractions, multiply the numerators, multiply the denominators and then simplify.
- When multiplying by a whole number, just multiply the numerator by that number and simplify.

Example

$\frac{4}{5} \times \frac{5}{9} = \frac{20}{45} = \frac{4}{9}$ $\quad$ $\frac{4}{5} \times \frac{5}{9} = \frac{4}{1} \times \frac{1}{9} = \frac{4}{9}$

You can simplify (or cancel) before multiplying. Here divide top and bottom by 5.

Example

$\frac{5}{6} \times 9 = \frac{5}{2} \times 3 = \frac{15}{2} = 7\frac{1}{2}$

- When dividing fractions, turn the second fraction upside down and multiply.
- When mixed numbers are involved, first change to top-heavy fractions.

Example

$\frac{3}{5} \div \frac{7}{10} = \frac{3}{5} \times \frac{10}{7} = \frac{3}{1} \times \frac{2}{7} = \frac{6}{7}$

Example

$2\frac{1}{2} \times 1\frac{2}{5} = \frac{5}{2} \times \frac{7}{5} = \frac{1}{2} \times \frac{7}{1} = \frac{7}{2} = 3\frac{1}{2}$

Example

$3\frac{3}{4} \div \frac{1}{2} = \frac{15}{4} \div \frac{1}{2} = \frac{15}{4} \times \frac{2}{1} = \frac{15}{2} \times \frac{1}{1} = \frac{15}{2} = 7\frac{1}{2}$

Now try these:

16 $\frac{3}{4} \times 16$

17 $\frac{4}{5} \times \frac{3}{8}$

18 $2\frac{1}{3} \times 4\frac{1}{2}$

19 $\frac{3}{5} \div 2$

20 $\frac{3}{10} \div \frac{4}{5}$

21 $3\frac{1}{3} \div \frac{1}{2}$

Increasing or decreasing by a fraction

To increase or decrease an amount by a fraction,
(i) add or subtract the fraction to or from 1 and then
(ii) multiply by the new fraction.

Example

Increase 18 by $\frac{1}{3}$.

$18 \times \frac{4}{3} = 24$

$1 + \frac{1}{3} = \frac{4}{3}$

Now try these:

22 Increase 20 by $\frac{1}{4}$

23 Decrease 15 by $\frac{2}{5}$

24 Increase 84 by $\frac{1}{6}$

25 Decrease 54 by $\frac{2}{9}$

Here is an exam question

Work out the following. Give your answers as simply as possible.

(a) $\frac{2}{3} + \frac{4}{5}$

(b) $2\frac{2}{5} \times \frac{5}{6}$

...and its solution

Change to a common denominator, add the numerators, change to a mixed number.

(a) $1\frac{7}{15}$ $\quad \frac{2}{3} + \frac{4}{5} = \frac{10}{15} + \frac{12}{15} = \frac{22}{15} = 1\frac{7}{15}$

(b) 2 $\quad 2\frac{2}{5} \times \frac{5}{6} = \frac{12}{5} \times \frac{5}{6} = \frac{2}{1} \times \frac{1}{1} = 2$

Change to a top heavy fraction, cancel down, multiply out.

Now try these exam questions:

1 Work these out, writing the answers as fractions:

(a) $\frac{1}{4} + \frac{3}{8}$ **(b)** $3\frac{2}{3} - 2\frac{1}{2}$

2 Work out the following. Give your answers as fractions as simply as possible:

(a) $\frac{3}{5} \times \frac{4}{9}$ **(b)** $1\frac{1}{4} + 2\frac{3}{5}$

3 **(a)** Work out $\frac{3}{7}$ of 35 kilograms.

(b) All the prices in Helen's shop are reduced by $\frac{1}{5}$ in a sale.
What is the sale price of a jumper that cost £27·50 before the sale?

4 **(a)** Put these fractions in order of size, smallest first:

$\frac{3}{4}, \frac{7}{10}, \frac{3}{5}, \frac{5}{8}$

(b) Work out the sum of the four fractions.

5 Work these out, giving your answers as fractions in their lowest terms:

(a) $2\frac{3}{8} - 1\frac{1}{2}$ **(b)** $\frac{2}{3} \div \frac{4}{5}$

Decimals and percentages

Changing between fractions, decimals and percentages

- To change a fraction to a decimal divide the numerator by the denominator.
- To change a decimal to a percentage multiply by 100.

Example

Change $\frac{4}{5}$ to (a) a decimal (b) a percentage.

(a) $\frac{4}{5} = 4 \div 5 = 0{\cdot}8$ (b) $0{\cdot}8 \times 100 = 80\%$

Recurring decimals

When some fractions are changed they give recurring decimals, that is decimal numbers with a repeating pattern.

Example

Change (a) $\frac{1}{3}$ (b) $\frac{5}{11}$ to (i) decimals (ii) percentages.

(a) (i) $\frac{1}{3} = 0{\cdot}333$ written as $0{\cdot}\dot{3}$
(ii) $33{\cdot}\dot{3}\%$

(b) (i) $\frac{5}{11} = 0{\cdot}4545$ written $0{\cdot}\dot{4}\dot{5}$
(ii) $45{\cdot}\dot{4}\dot{5}\%$

Now try these:

1 Change these decimals to percentages:
 (a) 0·34 **(b)** 0·27 **(c)** 0·356 **(d)** 1·428

2 Change these fractions to **(i)** decimals **(ii)** percentages:
 (a) $\frac{3}{5}$ **(b)** $\frac{9}{40}$ **(c)** $\frac{5}{8}$ **(d)** $\frac{4}{9}$

Finding *A* as a percentage of *B*

- To work out *A* as a percentage of *B*, first write *A* as a fraction of *B*, then change to a decimal and then a percentage.

Example

Express £30 as a percentage of £80.

$\frac{30}{80} = 0{\cdot}375 = 37{\cdot}5\%$

- To find an increase or decrease as a percentage, use the original value.

Example

A coat is reduced in price from £75 to £69. What percentage reduction is this?

$\frac{75 - 69}{75} = \frac{6}{75} = 0{\cdot}08 = 8\%$

Make sure units are the same.

Now try these:

3 Express £14 as a percentage of £40.

4 Express 4 m as a percentage of 32 m.

5 Express 15 litres as a percentage of 25 litres.

6 David's wage increased from £160 to £180 a week. What percentage increase was this?

Finding a percentage of an amount

- To find a percentage of an amount, change the percentage to a decimal and multiply.

Example

Find 24% of £80.

Decimal 0·24.

$0{\cdot}24 \times 80 = £19{\cdot}20$

- To find a percentage increase or decrease add or subtract the percentage from 100 and then work as before.
- If an amount increases or decreases by the same percentage each year, work out the new amount at the end of each year.

Example

£3500 is increased by 2% per year.
(a) What is the amount after one year?
(b) What is the amount after three years?

100 + 2 = 102%

Decimal 1·02.

Multiply by 1·02 for each year.

(a) After 1 year: $1{\cdot}02 \times 3500 = £3570$
(b) After 2 years: $1{\cdot}02 \times 3570 = £3641{\cdot}40$
After 3 years: $1{\cdot}02 \times 3641{\cdot}40 = £3714{\cdot}228$
= £3714·23 (to the nearest penny)

Now try these:

7 Work out: (a) 15% of £48 (b) 37% of 46 m

8 Increase: (a) £84 by 7% (b) £6300 by 2·5%

9 Decrease: (a) £12 by 10% (b) £5900 by 3%

10 Find the value of £2000 when it is decreased by 5% each year for three years.

Finding an amount before a percentage increase or decrease

To find the original amount before a percentage increase, add the percentage to 100, change to a decimal and divide. If it is a decrease, subtract instead of adding.

Example

The price of a skirt was £27·55, after a decrease of 5%. What was the original price?

Decrease so new is 100 – 5 = 95% of original.

To find the original divide by 0·95.

Original = $27{\cdot}55 \div 0{\cdot}95 = £29$

95% = 0·95.

Now try these:

11 A quantity is increased by 3%. It is now 61·8. What was it before the increase?

12 A wage is increased by 6% and is now £8692. What was it before the increase?

13 An amount is decreased by 2·5% and is now £1170. What was the amount before the decrease?

Here is an exam question ...and its solution

(a) Jenny used to go to the village hairdresser. A trim there cost £4. The hairdresser left and she went to a salon in town. A trim there cost £30. What percentage increase is this?

(b) Since going there prices have gone up several times. The last increase was 6% and she now pays £37·10. How much did she pay before the last increase?

(a) 650% — Increase = £26. Original was £4. Percentage increase = $\frac{26}{4} \times 100$

Find fractional increase and multiply by 100.

(b) £35 — New is 106% (1·06) of previous. Previous is = $37{\cdot}10 \div 1{\cdot}06$

Previous is wanted so divide by 1·06.

Now try these exam questions:

1 Annabel bought a motorcycle for £5595. She later sold it for £4795. Calculate the percentage loss.

2 A calculator was sold for £6.95 plus VAT. VAT was 17·5% at that time. What was the selling price of the calculator including VAT? Give the answer to the nearest penny.

3 The Candle Theatre has 320 seats. At one performance 271 seats were occupied. What percentage of the seats were occupied?

4 All clothes in a sale were reduced by 15%. Mark bought a coat for £68 in the sale. How much did it cost before the sale?

5 My computer cost £899. It decreases in value by 30% each year.
(a) What is its value after one year?
(b) Show that, after four years, it is worth less than a quarter of its original cost.

6 In 1997 Mrs Patel earned £16 640 for a 52-week year. At the start of 1998 she was given a rise of 3%. Calculate how much she earned per week in 1998.

Ratio

Writing as a ratio

If two quantities are in proportion to one another so that for x parts of the first there are y parts of the second then the ratio is x to y, which is written as $x:y$.

Mixing in a ratio

- If two substances are mixed in a ratio $1:n$ then to find the second amount the first must be multiplied by n.
- To find the first from the second the second must be divided by n.

Example

To make grey paint, white and black paint were mixed in the ratio 1 part white to 2 parts black (1:2).

(a) How much black paint needs to be mixed with 4 litres of white paint?
(b) How much white paint needs to be mixed with 12 litres of black paint?

(a) Black paint = 4×2 litres = 8 litres. (Multiply by 2.)
(b) White paint = $12 \div 2 = 6$ litres. (Divide by 2.)

- If two substances are mixed in a ratio $m:n$ then to find the second amount the first must be multiplied by the fraction $\frac{n}{m}$.
- To find the first from the second the second must be multiplied by the fraction $\frac{m}{n}$.

Example

In a recipe, flour and fat are used in the ratio 5:2.

(a) How much fat is needed when 480 g of flour are used?
(b) How much flour is needed when 300 g of fat are used?

(a) Fat = $480 \times \frac{2}{5} = 192$ g. (Multiply by $\frac{2}{5}$.)
(b) Flour = $300 \times \frac{5}{2} = 750$ g. (Multiply by $\frac{5}{2}$.)

Now try these:

1 The ratio of the lengths of the sides of two triangles is 1 : 4.
  (a) The shortest side of the first triangle is 4 cm. What is the shortest side of the second triangle?
  (b) The longest side of the second triangle is 28 cm. What is longest side of the first triangle?

2 To make cookies, flour and butter are mixed in the ratio 8 : 3.
  (a) How much butter is needed with 200 g of flour?
  (b) How much flour is needed with 90 g of butter?

3 Green paint is made from blue and yellow paint in the ratio 2 : 3.
  (a) How much yellow is needed with 5 litres of blue?
  (b) How much blue is needed with 9 litres of yellow?

Simplest form

- To write a ratio in its simplest form both parts of the ratio need to be in the same units. They can then both be divided by the same number.
- To write as $1:n$, divide the second part by the first.

Example

Write these ratios
(a) in their simplest form
(b) as $1:n$.

(i)	**3:6**	**(iii)**	**50p:£4**
(ii)	**4:14**	**(iv)**	**5 m:40 cm**

(a) (i) 1:2 (Divide both sides by 3.)
(ii) 2:7 (Divide both sides by 2.)
(iii) 50:400 = 1:8 (Change to pence and divide both sides by 50.)
(iv) 500:40 = 25:2 (Change to centimetres and divide both sides by 20.)

(b) (i) 1:2
(ii) 1:3·5 (Divide by 4.)
(iii) 1:8
(iv) 1:0·08 (Divide by 25.)

Now try these:

4 Write these ratios
  (a) in their simplest form
  (b) as $1:n$.
    (i) 4 : 12
    (ii) 24 : 9
    (iii) 400 m : 2 km
    (iv) 80p : £2

Sharing in a given ratio

To share in a given ratio, first add the parts of the ratio together. Divide the amount to be shared by this total. This is the multiplier for each of the parts.

Example

£150 is shared in the ratio 2:3:5. How much is each part?

Total of ratios is 10.
Multiplier is 150 ÷ 10 = 15.
Parts are £30, £45, £75.

Multiply each part by 15.

Example

A sum of money is divided in the ratio 3:8. The larger share is £44. How much is the smaller share?

8 parts is £44.
3 parts is $\frac{3}{8} \times 44$ = £16·50.

You do not need to work out the total amount.

Now try these:

5 Share £18 in the ratio 4 : 5.

6 To make pink paint, red and white are mixed in the ratio 2 : 5. How much pink paint can be made if 6 litres of red paint are used?

7 Share £150 in the ratio 1 : 2 : 3.

8 A gardener divides his garden between vegetables and flowers in the ratio 2 : 5.
The area for vegetables is 50 m^2. What is the area for flowers?

Here is an exam question ...and its solution

Helen, Jessica and Rebecca are left £13 500 to be shared in the ratio of their ages.

Helen is 20, Jessica is 15 and Rebecca is 10.

How much does each get?

Ratio is 20 : 15 : 10 = 4 : 3 : 2 in simplest form.

Total is 9, so multiplier is 13 500 ÷ 9 = 1500.

Helen gets 4 × 1500 = £6000.
Jessica gets 3 × 1500 = £4500.
Rebecca gets 2 × 1500 = £3000.

Multiply each part of the ratio by 1500.

Now try these exam questions:

1 A recipe uses 240 g flour to make 30 date cookies.
How much flour is used to make 50 of these cookies?

2 The Winder and Gower families had a meal together. They agreed to share the cost in the ratio of the sizes of their families.
There are two people in the Winder family and three in the Gower.
The Gower family paid £10·80.
How much was the total bill?

3 Eau de Parfum is made from three parts flower extract, eight parts water and nine parts alcohol.
(a) How much water does a 250 ml bottle of Eau de Parfum contain?
(b) How many litres of Eau de Parfum can be made with 45 litres of flower extract?

4 To make a map, a scale of 5 cm : 2 km was used.
(a) Aberville and Banchester are 7 km apart. How far are they apart on the map?
(b) Write the ratio 5 cm : 2 km as simply as possible.

5 Alison used this recipe to make a fruit drink:
9 parts orange juice, 4 parts lemon juice and 2 parts grapefruit juice.
She wants to make 2 litres of the drink.
How many millilitres of orange juice does she need?

Mental methods

Squares, square roots and cubes

- You need to know the squares of all the whole numbers (the integers) from 2^2 up to 15^2 and their corresponding square roots.
- You need to know the following cubes: 2^3, 3^3, 4^3, 5^3, 10^3.

Example

Write down the answers to:

(a) $\sqrt{5^2 + 12^2}$ **(b)** 3^3 **(c)** $2^2 + 3^2 + 4^2$ **(d)** $10^3 \div 5^3$

(a) $\sqrt{5^2 + 12^2} = \sqrt{25 + 144} = \sqrt{169} = 13$
(b) $3^3 = 27$
(c) $2^2 + 3^2 + 4^2 = 4 + 9 + 16 = 29$
(d) $10^3 \div 5^3 = 1000 \div 125 = 8$

Now try these:

1 Write down the values of:

(a) $\sqrt{121}$ **(b)** $\sqrt{225}$ **(c)** $\sqrt{64}$

2 Write down the values of:

(a) $(5^3 + 5^2) \div 10$
(b) $14^2 + 13^2$
(c) $(6^2 - 5^2)^2$

Don't forget to work out the brackets first.

3 Which of these numbers cannot be squares of whole numbers and why?

(a) 124 **(b)** 169 **(c)** 200 **(d)** 289

Rounding to a given number of significant figures

Remember, when rounding, that zeros are kept in their places to show the size of the number.

Example

Write the following numbers correct to 3 s.f.:

(a) 3·6583 **(b)** 0·5432 **(c)** 95 770 **(d)** 0.050 43

(a) 3·66 **(b)** 0·543 **(c)** 95 800 **(d)** 0·0504

Now try these:

4 Write the following numbers correct to 2 s.f.:

(a) 5·384 **(b)** 12·049 **(c)** 0·3142 **(d)** 45 300

5 Write the following numbers correct to 1 s.f.:

(a) 23·99 **(b)** 123·99 **(c)** 0·695 **(d)** 1·345

Standard index form

Standard index form is used to write a large or small number as a number between 1 and 10 multiplied by a power of 10.

Example

Write these numbers in standard index form:

(a) 16 000 **(b)** 432 **(c)** 0·314 **(d)** 54 320 000

(a) 1.6×10^4 **(b)** $4{\cdot}32 \times 10^2$ **(c)** $3{\cdot}14 \times 10^{-1}$ **(d)** $5{\cdot}432 \times 10^7$

Example

Write these numbers out in full:

(a) 4×10^3 **(b)** $2{\cdot}74 \times 10^4$ **(c)** $5{\cdot}3 \times 10^{-1}$ **(d)** $4{\cdot}68 \times 10^{-4}$

(a) 4000 **(b)** 27 400 **(c)** 0·53 **(d)** 0·000 468

Now try these:

6 Write these numbers in standard index form:

(a) 46 000 **(b)** 0·0484 **(c)** 3 600 000 **(d)** 5965

7 Write these numbers out in full:

(a) 8×10^6 **(b)** $9{\cdot}4 \times 10^3$ **(c)** $7{\cdot}7 \times 10^1$ **(d)** $3{\cdot}03 \times 10^{-4}$

Mental shortcuts

You need to be able to 'see' short-cut methods to help you calculate without using a calculator. For example:

- to multiply by 25 multiply by 100 then divide by 4

Example

Find 36×25.

$36 \times 25 = (36 \times 100) \div 4 = 3600 \div 4 = 900$

- when working out an answer add to or subtract from an easier calculation

Example

Find 64×24.

$64 \times 24 = 64 \times 25 - 64 = 1600 - 64 = 1536$

- use doubling and halving

Example

Find 18×16.

$18 \times 16 = 18 \times 2 \times 2 \times 2 \times 2 = 36 \times 2 \times 2 \times 2 = 72 \times 2 \times 2 = 144 \times 2 = 288$

- understand place value – be able to multiply and divide by powers of 10.

Example

If $4{\cdot}7 \times 3{\cdot}6 = 16.92$ then what is $0.47 \times 0{\cdot}36$ and $470 \times 3{\cdot}6$?

$0.47 \times 0.36 = 0{\cdot}1692$
$470 \times 3{\cdot}6 = 1692$

Example

Find $0{\cdot}46 \times 0{\cdot}08$.

Write it as
$(46 \times 8) \div (100 \times 100) = 368 \div 10\,000 = 0{\cdot}0368$

Now try these:

8 Work out:
(a) 1.6×26 **(b)** 84×24 **(c)** 12×24

9 Work out:
(a) 17×32 **(b)** 45×16 **(c)** 143×16

10 If $9{\cdot}4 \times 4{\cdot}9 = 46{\cdot}06$, find the value of:
(a) $0{\cdot}94 \times 4{\cdot}9$ **(c)** $94 \times 4{\cdot}9$
(b) $94 \times 0{\cdot}49$ **(d)** $0{\cdot}094 \times 0{\cdot}49$

Here is an exam question

(a) The Astronomical Unit (AU) is used to measure large distances between stars. One Astronomical Unit is $1{\cdot}496 \times 10^{11}$ m. What are 100 Astronomical Units? Give your answer in standard form.

(b) Light travels at $2{\cdot}998 \times 10^8$ m/s. Write this as an ordinary number.

...and its solution

(a) $1{\cdot}496 \times 10^{13}$ m

$1{\cdot}496 \times 10^{11} \times 10^2$
$= 1{\cdot}496 \times 10^{13}$ m

(b) 299 800 000 m/s

$2{\cdot}998 \times 10^8$
$= 2{\cdot}998 \times 100\,000\,000$
$= 299\,800\,000$ m/s

Now try these exam questions:

1 There are 4.546 09 litres in a gallon.
(a) Round 4·546 09 to 3 d.p.
(b) Round 4·546 09 to 3 s.f.

2 The attendance at a World Cup match was 54 682. The TV commentator stated that 55 000 people were there. To how many significant figures (s.f.) was the commentator's figure?

3 A radar transmitter sends out a beam of radio waves at a frequency of 24 thousand million pulses per second.
Write this figure in standard form.

4 Amy is trying to estimate the number of seconds in September, October and November. She writes down the following calculation:
$100 \times 24 \times 60 \times 60$
What answer does this estimate give?

5 Write down the values of:
(a) **(i)** $\sqrt{144} \times (\sqrt{25} - 1)$
(ii) $4^3 \div 2^3$
(b) Given that $1{\cdot}4 \times 23{\cdot}7 = 33{\cdot}18$ write down the values of
(i) $0{\cdot}14 \times 2{\cdot}37$
(ii) $14{\cdot}0 \times 237{\cdot}0$

Written methods

Repeated proportional change

- To increase a quantity by say $\frac{1}{5}$, one way is to multiply by $\frac{1}{5}$ and add the result on to the original. A quicker way is to multiply by $1 + \frac{1}{5} = \frac{6}{5}$ or $1{\cdot}2$.
- If this is repeated then it is equivalent to multipying by $\left(\frac{6}{5}\right)^2$ or $1{\cdot}2^2$. So to increase a quantity by $\frac{1}{5}$ four times you multiply by $\left(\frac{6}{5}\right)^4$ or $1{\cdot}2^4$.
- Similarly to reduce a quantity by $\frac{1}{12}$ you multiply by $1 - \frac{1}{12} = \frac{11}{12}$. So to reduce a quantity by $\frac{1}{12}$ three times you multiply by $\left(\frac{11}{12}\right)^3$. In this case since $\frac{11}{12}$ is a recurring decimal it is best to use fractions.

Remember the power button on your calculator is y^x or x^y or ^

Example

A company promised to increase the value of an investment by $\frac{1}{12}$ every year. If this promise is kept how much would an investment of £500 be worth in five years?

Value $= 500 \times \left(\frac{13}{12}\right)^5 = £746{\cdot}07$

Example

In a town's road safety campaign the aim is to reduce accidents by $\frac{1}{10}$ every year. If there were 400 accidents in 2000, and the campaign is successful, how many should there be in 2004?

$400 \times \left(\frac{9}{10}\right)^4 = 262$

Repeated percentage change

This is done in a similar way.

- To increase by say 6% for five years you multiply by $1{\cdot}06^5$.
- To decrease by 15% four times in succession you multiply by $0{\cdot}85^4$.

Example

Sheila invests £600 at 4% compound interest. How much will the investment be worth after 10 years?

Value $= 600 \times 1{\cdot}04^{10} = £888{\cdot}15$

Example

A car depreciates in value by 12% per year. If it cost £12 500 when new, how much will it be worth after five years?

Value $= 12\,500 \times 0{\cdot}88^5 = £6596{\cdot}65$

Now try these:

1 What value do you multiply by to increase by:
(a) $\frac{1}{7}$ **(b)** $\frac{3}{8}$ **(c)** 7% **(d)** 32% **(e)** $17\frac{1}{2}$%?

2 What value do you multiply by to decrease by:
(a) $\frac{1}{7}$ **(b)** $\frac{3}{8}$ **(c)** 7% **(d)** 32% **(e)** $17\frac{1}{2}$%?

3 Insurance premiums reduce by $\frac{1}{5}$ every year if no claims are made. If the original premium is £350 per year, what will the premium be after three years if no claim was made over the three years?

4 A headline reads 'Violent crimes going up by $\frac{1}{10}$ every year'. If there were 18 000 violent crimes in 1995, how many does this suggest there were in 2001?

5 Gina invests £2000 at 3% compound interest. What will this be worth:
(a) after three years **(b)** after ten years?

6 A car depreciates by 13% per year. If it cost £9990 when new in 1998, what will it be worth in 2004?

7 An antique increases its value by 60% every five years. If it was worth £300 in 1980, what will it be worth in 2005?

8 The number of a certain species of bird has been decreasing by $\frac{1}{20}$ every year. If there were 20 000 in 1990, how many were there in 2000?

Direct proportion

- If quantities vary in direct proportion it means that: if you double one quantity, you double the other; if you treble one quantity, you treble the other; if you halve one quantity, you halve the other; and so on.
- If x and y vary in direct proportion the graph of y against x will be a straight line passing through the origin. In this case the equation will be in the form $y = kx$.

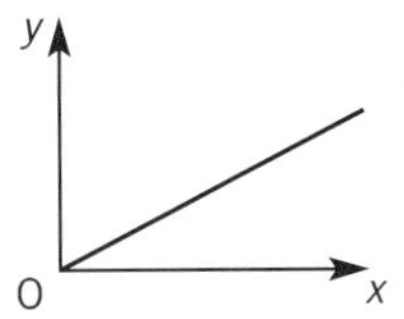

Example

The total cost of books is directly proportional to the number of books bought. If 30 books cost £240, how much will (a) 120 books (b) 15 books cost?

(a) $120 = 4 \times 30$
so 120 books cost $4 \times £8 = £960$.

(b) $15 = \frac{1}{2} \times 30$
so 15 books cost $\frac{1}{2} \times £240 = £120$.

Alternatively you can work out the cost of one book (= $240 \div 30 = £8$) first and then multiply by the number of books.
So $C = 8n$ is the equation connecting the number of books (n) and the total cost in pounds (C).

Now try these:

9 The time taken to mark students' homework is directly proportional to the number of students. If it takes two hours to mark 16 students' homework, how long does it take to mark **(a)** 4 **(b)** 32 **(c)** 40 students' homework?

10 A recipe says that to serve four people you need 300 ml of milk and 100 g of flour. How much of each do you need to serve **(a)** 2 **(b)** 12 people?

Here is an exam question ...and its solution

The recipe below is for cheesecake for eight people.

Wheatmeal biscuit crumbs	160 g
Butter	50 g
Cream cheese	640 g
Caster sugar	70 g

(a) Calculate the amount of butter required to make a cheesecake for four people.

(b) Calculate the amount of caster sugar required to make a cheesecake for 12 people.

(a) 25 g $\frac{50}{8} \times 4 = 25$

(b) 105 g $\frac{70}{8} \times 12 = 105$

Now try these exam questions:

1 Kelly invested £450 for three years at 6% per year compound interest. Calculate the total amount that the investment was worth at the end of the three years.

2 In 1995 Mr and Mrs Mann paid £160·48 for their house insurance. The cost of insurance has risen by 2·5% each year. How much should they pay in 1998?

3 Here is a recipe for chocolate pudding for four people.

100 g	flour
75 g	plain chocolate
50 g	butter
300 ml	milk
65 g	sugar
$\frac{1}{2}$ tsp	vanilla essence
2	eggs

Nadia is making the pudding for six people.

(a) How many eggs will she need?

(b) Find the amount of milk she needs.

(c) Find the amount of vanilla essence she needs.

4 Mrs McCabe invested £300 in National Savings certificates in 2000. She will keep them for five complete years and will receive compound interest of 9·5% per year.
Calculate the amount, correct to the nearest penny, that she will receive for the certificates in 2005.

5 It takes 100 g of flour to make 15 shortbread biscuits.

(a) Calculate the weight of flour needed to make 24 shortbread biscuits.

(b) How many shortbread biscuits can be made from 1 kg of flour?

Calculator methods

Calculators vary. The position and symbols used on the buttons are different depending on the make and model of calculator. The order in which the buttons have to be pressed can also vary. Make sure you know how **your** calculator works. Don't borrow a different calculator or change your calculator just before an exam.

Calculating with negative numbers

Use [(−)] or [+/−] to make negative numbers.

Don't get [(−)] and [−] confused.

Example

Work out **(a)** $^-3 \times {}^-5$ **(b)** $5 - ({}^-3)$

(a) [(−)] [3] [×] [(−)] [5] [=] 15

or, on some calculators,

[3] [+/−] [×] [5] [+/−] [=] 15

(b) [5] [−] [(−)] [3] [=] 8

Now try these:

1 Work out:

(a) $5 \times {}^-2$ (b) $^-6 + ({}^-3)$ (c) $^-30 \div 4$ (d) $^-6 \times {}^-6$ (e) $7 - ({}^-5)$ (f) $^-9 + 5$

Calculating with fractions

Use the [ab/c] button.

Example

(a) Write $\frac{25}{100}$ as a fraction in its simplest form.

(b) Find $1\frac{2}{3} + \frac{3}{4}$.

(c) $\frac{2}{5}$ of £12.

(a) [2] [5] [ab/c] [1] [0] [0] [=] $\frac{1}{4}$

(b) [1] [ab/c] [2] [ab/c] [3] [+] [3] [ab/c] [4] [=] $2\frac{5}{12}$

(c) [2] [ab/c] [5] [×] [1] [2] [=] £4.80

Notice how the answer of 4⌟4⌟5 or 4.8 becomes £4.80.

Now try these:

2 Change these fractions into their simplest form:

(a) $\frac{20}{35}$ (b) $\frac{21}{27}$ (c) $\frac{31}{42}$

3 Work out:

(a) $\frac{4}{5} + \frac{2}{3}$ (b) $4\frac{5}{6} - 2\frac{1}{4}$ (c) $1\frac{1}{2} \times 3\frac{3}{8}$ (d) $2\frac{2}{3} \div 2\frac{2}{5}$

4 (a) Work out $\frac{3}{4}$ of £124.

(b) How many pieces of pipe, each $2\frac{3}{4}$ metres long, can be cut from a 55 metre length?

Reciprocals

Use the [1/x] or the [x^{-1}] button.

Example

Work out the reciprocal of:

(a) 0·1 **(b)** $1\frac{2}{3}$

(a) [0] [·] [1] [1/x] = 10

(b) [1] [ab/c] [2] [ab/c] [3] [1/x] = $\frac{3}{5}$ or 0·6

Now try these:

5 Find the reciprocal of:

(a) 8 (b) $\frac{4}{5}$ (c) 0·04 (d) $2\frac{3}{4}$

Powers and roots

- Use [x^y] or [^] for powers.
- Use [$x^{1/y}$] or [^] with [ab/c] for roots.

Your calculator may require you to press [+/−] or [(−)] after 2.

Example

Work out:

(a) 6^7 **(b)** $4^5 + 3^4$ **(c)** $100^{-\frac{1}{2}}$

(a) [6] [x^y] [7] [=] 279 936

(b) [4] [^] [5] [+] [3] [^] [4] [=] 1105

(c) [1] [0] [0] [$x^{1/y}$] [(−)] [2] [=] 0·1

Now try these:

6 Work out:

(a) 5^4 (b) $6^4 - 4^6$ (c) $81^{\frac{1}{4}}$ (d) $\sqrt[5]{243}$

Brackets

When doing complex calculations with a calculator, be safe and introduce brackets. Remember for every [( ] there must be a [ )].

Now try these:

7 Work out:

(a) $\frac{3.6 \times 5.9}{2.47 - 1.98}$ (c) $5.8 \times 1.7 + 3.5 \times 4.4$

(b) $\sqrt{3.2^2 - 2.2^2}$ (d) $\frac{26.9 - 7.8}{\sqrt{8} + 1.95}$

Example

Work out:

(a) $\frac{2.3 + 4.5}{5 \times 3.2}$

(b) $6.4 + 7.2 \times 8$

(a) [( ] [2] [·] [3] [+] [4] [·] [5] [ )] [÷] [( ] [5] [×] [3] [·] [2] [ )] [=] 0·425

(b) [6] [·] [4] [+] [( ] [7] [·] [2] [×] [8] [ )] [=] 64

Standard form

Use [EXP] or [EE]

These are **in place of** [×] [1] [0] in a standard form number.

Now try these:

8 Work out:

(a) $4.25 \times 10^{-2} \times 1.72 \times 10^{-3}$

(b) $(3.7 \times 10^5)^2$

(c) $\frac{3.4 \times 10^6}{5 \times \sqrt{0.0289}}$

Example

Work out:

(a) $2.3 \times 10^6 + 5 \times 10^7$

(b) $\frac{6.2 \times 10^8 - 7.5 \times 10^7}{1.5 \times 10^3}$

Your calculator may not give the answer in standard form.

(a) [2] [·] [3] [EXP] [6] [+] [5] [EXP] [7] [=] 5.23×10^7

(b) [( ] [6] [·] [2] [EXP] [8] [−] [7] [·] [5] [EXP] [7] [ )] [÷] [1] [·] [5] [EXP] [3] [=] 3.63×10^5

Trigonometric keys

Use [sin] [cos] [tan] keys.

Before using these always check that your calculator is in degree mode, [DEG] or [D]

Now try these:

9 Work out:

(a) $5\cos 60°$ (c) $10\cos 47° + 25\sin 43°$

(b) $\frac{50\sin 30°}{\sin 80°}$

Example

Work out:

(a) $\sin 30° + \cos 60°$ (b) $\frac{4 + \tan 45°}{5^2}$

(a) [sin] [3] [0] [+] [cos] [6] [0] [=] 1

or, on some calculators,

[3] [0] [sin] [+] [6] [0] [cos] [=] 1

(b) [( ] [4] [+] [tan] [4] [5] [ )] [÷] [5] [x^2] [=] 0·2

Here is an exam question ...and its solution

Work out the following. Give your answers to 2 d.p.

(a) 4.2^4 (b) $\frac{3.9^2 + 0.53}{3.9 \times 0.53}$ (c) $\sqrt{3 + 5\cos 40°}$

(a) 311.17 (b) 7·61 (c) 2·61

Now try these exam questions:

1 Find:

(a) $\frac{3}{5}$ of 200 g

(b) $2\frac{3}{4} - 1\frac{4}{5}$

(c) $\frac{4}{7}$ of £26·60

2 Work out the reciprocal of 3^2.

3 (a) $\frac{18.6 - 2.75}{3.5 + 1.043}$ (b) $\frac{316.5 \times 0.54}{47.4 - 19.65}$.

4 (a) $\frac{4.2^5 - 1.7^4}{1.25^2}$ (b) $\sqrt{3^2 + 2.7^3}$

5 Work out:

(a) $6.3 \times 10^9 + 5.8 \times 10^{10}$

(b) $\frac{9.52 \times 10^{14}}{8 \times 10^{-3}}$.

6 Work out:

(a) $6(\cos 27° + \sin 27°)$

(b) $3 - 4\sin 28.7°$.

Solving problems

Some common money problems

You need to be able to:

- assess value for money
- deal with other ratio problems
- calculate currency exchange
- calculate tax/insurance
- work out percentage problems.

Make sure you know what the percentage is 'of'.

Example

Which size of cornflakes is the better buy: 500 g for 99p or 750 g for £1·42?

1500 g costs $3 \times 99p = £2·97$ or $2 \times £1·42 = £2·84$. So the 750 g size is cheaper.

Example

A spade costing £13·60 was reduced by 15% in a sale. Find its sale price.

Sale price = 85% of £13·60
= $0·85 \times £13·60 = £11·56$

Always show enough working to make your methods clear.

Now try these:

1 A pack of cheese cost £1·56 for 250 g. How much was this per kg?

2 Two families share the cost of a meal in the ratio 3 : 5. The total cost of the meal was £72. How much did each family pay?

3 Jenny had to pay 10% tax on £1520 of her income, and 22% tax on £1435. How much tax did she pay altogether?

Compound measures

Examples are:

- speed
- density
- population density.

The units tell you which way to divide, so density measured in g/cm^3 means grams (mass) divided by cm^3 (volume).

Now try these:

4 Pali drives 270 miles in 4 hours 30 minutes. Find his average speed.

Change the time into hours.

5 A gold ring has a mass of 15·44 g and a volume of 0·8 cm^3. Find its density.

6 A town has a population density of 2530 people/km^2 and an area of 87 km^2. Find the population of the town.

Checking your work

Use the following methods:

- common sense – is the answer reasonable?
- inverse operations – work backwards to check
- estimates – one significant figure is often easiest.

Example

Pat calculated $\dfrac{67·4 \times 504·9}{12·3}$ and got the answer 418 572·2. Use estimates to show her answer was wrong.

$\dfrac{70 \times 500}{10} = 3500$. Her answer is far too large. (In fact, Pat had multiplied by mistake instead of dividing.)

Accuracy of answers

- Sometimes you are asked to round to a given accuracy, either to a given number of decimal places, or to a given number of significant figures.
- Sometimes you need to work to a reasonable degree of accuracy.

If the value of the first digit being ignored is 5 or more, round up.

Look at the context and the accuracy of the information you have been given.

Now try these:

7 Use 1 s.f. estimates to find approximate answers, showing your estimates:

(a) £792 ÷ 19 **(b)** $\frac{5857}{62 \times 20{\cdot}3}$

8 Round these to 2 d.p.:
(a) 30·972 **(b)** 4·1387 **(c)** 24·596

9 Round these to 3 s.f.:
(a) 5347 **(b)** 61·42 **(c)** 3049·6

Trial and improvement

Only use trial and improvement if there is no exact method. Show your trials and their outcomes clearly. For each trial, think what the outcome has told you to try next.

Now try these:

10 The difference of two numbers is 5. Their product is 32·19.
Use trial and improvement to find the two numbers.

Here is an exam question ...and its solution

In June 1998 the speed limit on the Kingston bypass was reduced from 70 m.p.h. to 50 m.p.h. The bypass is 7·3 miles long. How much longer does it take to drive along the bypass at 50 m.p.h. than it did at 70 m.p.h.? Show your method clearly and give your answer in minutes to 1 d.p.

Read the question carefully and break the problem down into steps:
- What do I know?
- What do I have to find?
- What methods can I apply?

Time = $\frac{\text{distance}}{\text{average speed}}$

At 70 m.p.h., time = $\frac{7{\cdot}3}{70}$ = 0·1042... h

At 50 m.p.h., time = $\frac{7{\cdot}3}{50}$ = 0·146 h

Difference = 0·146 – 0·1042... h
= 0·0417... h
= 0·0417... × 60 minutes
= 2·5 minutes to 1 d.p.

Now try these exam questions:

1 Three friends had a meal together. They had three 'chef's specials' at £8·99 each, two drinks at £1·45 each, one drink at £1.75 and two puddings at £2·49 each. They agreed to share the bill equally.
How much did they each pay? Write down your calculations.

2 The table shows the prices of different packs of chocolate bars.

Pack	Size	Price	
Standard	500 g	£1·15	
Family	750 g	£1·59	
Special	1·2 kg	£2·49	

Find which pack gives the best value for money. You must show clearly how you decide. You may label and use the spare column in the table if you wish.

3 **(a)** Mrs Duncan took 43 pupils to London on a school trip. The train tickets cost £20·25 each. She worked out the cost of the tickets to be £770·75. Do a rough calculation to show this answer must be wrong.
(b) The next year the cost of the ticket was £21·87. By what percentage had the cost of the ticket increased?

4 The table shows the population of three countries.

Country	Population
Spain	$3{\cdot}92 \times 10^7$
Denmark	$5{\cdot}14 \times 10^6$
Luxemburg	$3{\cdot}73 \times 10^5$

(a) Calculate the total population of the three countries. Give your answer to a reasonable degree of accuracy.
(b) The area of Denmark is 16 600 square miles. Calculate the average number of people per square mile in Denmark.

Use of symbols

Manipulating algebra

When simplifying algebraic expressions, only the same type of terms can be added or subtracted.

Example

Simplify:

(a) $3ab - 2ac + 4ab + ac$

(b) $a^2 - 2a + 3a + b^2 - 2a^2 + 3b^2$

(a) $7ab - ac$

(b) $a - a^2 + 4b^2$

The *ab* and *ac* terms are each collected.

The a^2, *a*, and b^2 terms are each collected.

Now try these:

Simplify:

1 $x + 4x - 3y + 4y - 2x + 3y$

2 $2ab - 3ac + ab + ac$

3 $a^2 - 2ab + 4ab - 3b^2$

4 $4x + x^2 - 2x + 2x^2 - x^3 + 4x^3$.

Multiplying brackets by single terms

When expanding brackets, multiply every term within the brackets by the term immediately in front of the bracket.

Example

Expand and simplify $3(2a + 3b) - 2(a - 2b)$.

$6a + 9b - 2a + 4b = 4a + 13b$

Multiply out the brackets, note $^-2 \times {^-2b} = {^+4b}$, then collect like terms.

Now try these:

Expand and simplify:

5 $a(2a - 3) + 2a(3a + 2)$

6 $4(2x - 3y) - 2(x + y)$

7 $3x(2x + 3) - 4x(x - 3)$

8 $3x + 2x(x - 2)$

Common factors

Look for every number and letter that is common to every term and write these outside a bracket. Write the terms in the bracket needed to give the original expression when expanded.

Example

Factorise:

(a) $3a + 6$

(b) $2x^2 - 3xy$

(c) $4a - 8ac + 16a^2b$

(a) $3(a + 2)$

(b) $x(2x - 3y)$

(c) $4a(1 - 2c + 4ab)$

Note that $4a = 4a \times 1$ so 1 must be in the bracket.

Now try these:

9 $5x - 25$

10 $3ab - 2ac$

11 $2a^2b - 6ab^2$

12 $4abc - 8ab + 2a$

Substitution

When substituting numbers in expressions or formulae be careful with negative numbers.

Remember that $3a^2$ means $3 \times a \times a$ not $3a \times 3a$.

Examples

Given $P = 3a - 5b^2$, work out the value of P when:

(a) $a = 8$, $b = {^-2}$ **(b)** $a = 3{\cdot}5$, $b = 1{\cdot}5$

(a) $P = 3 \times 8 - 5 \times {^-2} \times {^-2} = 24 - 20 = 4$

(b) $3 \times 3{\cdot}5 - 5 \times 1{\cdot}5 \times 1{\cdot}5 = 10{\cdot}5 - 11{\cdot}25 = {^-0{\cdot}75}$

Notice $^-5 \times {^-2} \times {^-2} = {^-20}$.

A calculator is needed in (b).

Now try these:

Work out for the values given:

13 $A = 2pq + 2q^2$ when $p = 2$, $q = {}^-3$

14 $B = a^3 - 2ab$ when $a = 3$, $b = {}^-2$

15 $C = 3a(2b - c)$ when $a = 2$, $b = {}^-3$, $c = {}^-4$

16 $A = 2pq + 2q^2$ when $p = 1{\cdot}2$, $q = 2{\cdot}3$

17 $B = a^3 - 2ab$ when $a = 3{\cdot}5$, $b = {}^-2{\cdot}5$

18 $C = 3a(2b - c)$ when $a = 2{\cdot}5$, $b = 3{\cdot}2$, $c = {}^-2$

Indices

- The rules of indices are:
  $a^m \times a^n = a^{m+n}$ $a^m \div a^n = a^{m-n}$
  $(a^m)^n = a^{m \times n}$ $a^0 = 1$
  $\frac{1}{a^n} = a^{-n}$.
- These need to be used to manipulate expressions involving letters and numbers.
- Remember $a = a^1$.

Example

Simplify these:

(a) $3a^2b^2 \times 4ab^3$

(b) $\frac{5a^2b \times 4b^3}{12a^3b^2}$

(c) $(2a^2b)^3$

(a) $12a^3b^5$

The numbers are multiplied and the indices added.

(b) $\frac{5b^2}{3a}$

Numbers are $5 \times 4 \div 12 = \frac{5}{3}$. Letters are $a^{2-3} = a^{-1}$ or $\frac{1}{a}$ and $b^{1+3-2} = b^2$.

(c) $8a^6b^3$

The number is cubed and the indices are multiplied by 3.

Now try these:

Simplify:

19 $2abc^2 \times 4ab^2c$

20 $(4a^2)^3$

21 $\frac{14a^2b^3}{2a^3b}$

22 $\frac{4a \times 3b^2}{2a^2b}$

Here is an exam question ...and its solution

Sometimes an exam question will include several parts covering different aspects of the topic.

(a) Expand the brackets and write as simply as possible $2(3x - 4) - 5(x + 3)$.

(b) Factorise completely $3a^2 + 6ab$.

(c) For the formula $H = 17 - 0{\cdot}5a$, work out the value of H when:
(i) $a = 12$ **(ii)** $b = {}^-4$.

(d) Simplify $2a^4 \times 4a^2$.

Solution

(a) $x - 23$ $6x - 8 - 5x - 15 = x - 23$

Take care with the signs. ${}^-5 \times {}^+3 = {}^-15$.

(b) $3a(a + 2b)$

$3a$ is common to both terms.

(c) **(i)** $H = 11$ $17 - 6 = 11$
(ii) $H = 19$ $17 + 2 = 19$

(d) $8a^6$

Multiply the numbers and add the indices.

Now try these exam questions:

1 Factorise completely $12p^2q - 15pq^2$.

2 Multiply out and simplify $2(3x + 1) - 4(x - 3)$.

3 **(a)** Simplify $\frac{12p^2q}{3p} \times 2q^2$.
(b) Factorise completely $3a^2 + 6ab$.

4 **(a)** Given that $v = u + at$, calculate the value of v when $u = 2$, $a = 3$ and $t = 6$.
(b) Multiply out the brackets $2(m - 3)$.
(c) Simplify the expression $3a + 2b - a - 3b$.

5 For the formula $S = at + bt^2$, work out the value of S when:
(a) $a = 3$, $b = 2$, $t = 5$ **(b)** $a = 2$, $b = 3$, $t = {}^-4$

6 Simplify $\frac{3a^6 \times 4a^2}{2a^3}$.

7 For the formula $F = a^2 - 3b$, find the value of F when: **(a)** $a = 8$, $b = 2$ **(b)** $a = {}^-4$, $b = {}^-2$.

8 Simplify **(a)** $3a^2b \times 4ab^3$ **(b)** $\frac{14a^3b^2}{2ab^3}$.

9 **(a)** Simplify $\frac{4a^3b \times 3a^2}{2a^4b}$.
(b) Factorise fully $4a^2 - 2a$.

10 $S = 3p^2 + 2p$.
Work out the value of S when $p = {}^-1{\cdot}5$.

Linear equations

Solving equations

Always perform the same operation on the **whole** of each side of the equation.

Now try these:

1 $5x + 6 = 31$

2 $4p + 4 = 12$

3 $3m - 9 = 0$

4 $7y - 6 = 50$

Example

Solve the equation $3x - 4 = 20$.

First add 4 to both sides giving:

$3x - 4 + 4 = 20 + 4$

$3x = 24$

This line can be left out.

Then divide each side by 3 giving:

$x = \frac{24}{3} = 8$

Brackets in equations

If the equation has brackets multiply out the brackets first.

Now try these:

Solve the following equations:

5 $2(m - 4) = 10$

6 $5(p + 6) = 40$

7 $7(x - 2) = 42$

8 $3(4 - x) = 21$

The answer is negative in question 8.

Example

Solve $3(x + 4) = 24$.

$$3(x + 4) = 24$$
$$3x + 12 = 24$$
$$3x = 12$$
$$x = 4$$

Dealing with the 'unknown'

If the 'unknown' is on both sides of the equation rearrange to collect the numbers on one side and the unknown on the other side.

Now try these:

Solve the following equations:

9 $7x - 4 = 3x + 8$

10 $6x - 2 = x + 8$

11 $3x + 2 = 8x + 1$

12 $5x + 2 = 7x + 10$

The answer is negative in question 12.

Example

Solve $5x + 4 = 2x + 19$.

First subtract 4 from each side:

$5x = 2x + 15$

Then subtract $2x$ from each side:

$3x = 15$

$x = 5$

More than one set of brackets

If there are more than one set of brackets multiply them out first.

Now try these:

Solve the following equations:

13 $6(x + 4) = 4(x - 3)$

14 $7(m - 2) = 5(m + 4) + 12$

15 $4(p + 2) = 5(p - 5) - 9$

16 $3(4x - 4) = 4(2x + 8)$

The answer is negative in question 13.

Example

Solve $5(2x + 1) = 4(x - 2) + 10$.

$$5(2x + 1) = 4(x - 2) + 10$$
$$10x + 5 = 4x - 8 + 10$$
$$10x = 4x - 8 + 10 - 5$$
$$= 4x - 3$$
$$6x = {}^{-}3$$
$$x = \frac{{}^{-}3}{6}$$
$$x = \frac{{}^{-}1}{2}$$

Fractions in equations

If the equation has a fraction in it multiply both sides of the equation by the denominator.

Example

(a) $\frac{3x}{4} = 12$ **(b)** $\frac{2}{3}(x + 2) = 4$

(a) Multiply both sides by 4 giving:

$3x = 48$

so $x = \frac{48}{3} = 16$

(b) Multiply both sides by 3 giving:

$2(x + 2) = 12$

$2x + 4 = 12$

$2x = 8$

$x = 4$

Now try these:

17 $\frac{x}{4} = 4$

Don't be tempted to divide by 4.

18 $\frac{3x}{4} = 6$

19 $\frac{1}{2}(x + 7) = 4$

20 $\frac{1}{5}(2x - 1) = 3$

21 $\frac{1}{2}(3x - 1) = 3(2 - x)$

Here is an exam question ...and its solution

Solve the following equations:

(a) $2(3 - x) = 1$

(b) $\frac{5x + 8}{3} = 6$

(c) $4(x + 7) = 3(2x - 4)$

(a) $x = 2\frac{1}{2}$

$6 - 2x = 1$

${}^{-}2x = {}^{-}5$

$x = 2\frac{1}{2}$

(b) $x = 2$

$\frac{5x + 8}{3} = 6$

$5x + 8 = 18$

$5x = 10$

$x = 2$

(c) $x = 20$

$4(x + 7) = 3(2x - 4)$

$4x + 28 = 6x - 12$

$40 = 2x$

$x = 20$

Now try these exam questions:

1 Solve $3x = x + 1$

2 Solve $3p - 4 = p + 8$

3 Solve $\frac{3m}{4} = 9$

4 Solve $2(y + 3) = 5y$

5 Solve $4(x - 1) = 2x + 3$

6 Solve $4(x + 2) + 2(3x - 2) = 14$

7 A rectangle has its longer side 2 cm more than its shorter side.
Its perimeter is 36 cm.
Let x cm be the length of the shorter side.
(a) Write down an equation in x.
(b) Solve your equation to find x.
(c) Find the area of the rectangle.

8 Tom is five years older than Maureen.
In two years' time, Tom will be twice as old as Maureen.
Tom's age now is x years.
Write an equation in x and solve it to find their ages now.

Formulae

Substituting in formulae

When substituting in formulae remember:

- expressions like ab mean $a \times b$
- multiplication and division are done before addition and subtraction unless brackets tell you otherwise
- expressions like $3r^2$ mean $3 \times r^2$, that is you square r and then multiply by 3.

Don't forget $3x^2$ means $3 \times x^2$.

Now try these:

1 If $A = 3x^2 - 5y^2$, find A when $x = 4$ and $y = {}^-3$.

2 If $y = \frac{(a + b)h}{2}$, find y when:

(a) $a = 2{\cdot}3$, $b = 5{\cdot}2$ and $h = 1{\cdot}9$

(b) $a = \frac{1}{2}$, $b = \frac{3}{4}$ and $h = {}^-3$.

3 If $s = ut + \frac{1}{2}at^2$, find s when $u = 30$, $a = {}^-10$ and $t = 5$.

Example

(a) If $C = 6b + 3a^2$, find C when $b = {}^-3$ and $a = 5$.

(b) If $y = \frac{3a - 2b}{c}$, find y when:

(i) $a = 2$, $b = {}^-5$ and $c = 3$

(ii) $a = \frac{1}{4}$, $b = \frac{3}{4}$ and $c = 2$

(a) $C = 6 \times {}^-3 + 3 \times 5^2 = {}^-18 + 75 = 57$

(b)(i) $y = \frac{3 \times 2 - 2 \times ({}^-5)}{3} = \frac{6 + 10}{3} = 5\frac{1}{3}$

(ii) $y = \frac{3 \times \frac{1}{4} - 2 \times \frac{3}{4}}{2} = \frac{\frac{3}{4} - 1\frac{1}{2}}{2} = \frac{\frac{^-3}{4}}{2} = \frac{^-3}{8}$

Writing your own formulae

When writing your own formuale:

- make sure you define your letters carefully, including any units
- make sure you use brackets if you want addition and subtraction to be done before multiplication and division
- use a fraction line not a ÷ sign for divide.

Now try these:

4 To convert from the Fahrenheit scale to Celsius, you subtract 32 and multiply by $\frac{5}{9}$. Write this as a formula.

5 Write a formula for the nth term of these sequences:

(a) 1, 4, 9, 16, 25...

(b) 3, 12, 27, 48, 75...

(c) 2, 5, 8, 11, 14...

(d) 25, 21, 17, 13...

Example

Write a formula for the perimeter of a semicircle.

Let r = the radius in cm and P = the perimeter in cm.

Half the circumference $= \frac{1}{2} \times 2\pi r = \pi r$,

so $P = 2r + \pi r$.

Remember to define your letters.

Rearranging formulae

To change the subject of a formula use the equation rule of doing the same operation to both sides to get the new subject on its own on one side of the formula.

Now try these:

Make the letter in square brackets the subject of these formulae.

6 $y = mx + c$ [c]

7 $y = mx + c$ [m]

8 $x = ab - cd$ [b]

9 $x = ab - cd$ [c]

10 $P = 2(\ell + w)$ [w]

11 $V = \frac{1}{3}\ell wh$ [h]

Remember: always do the same operation to both sides.

Example

Make u the subject of $s = \frac{(u + v)}{2} \times t$.

$2s = (u + v) \times t$ — Multiply both sides by 2.

$2s = ut + vt$ — Multiply out brackets.

$2s - vt = ut$ — Take vt from both sides.

$\frac{2s - vt}{t} = u$ — Divide both sides by t.

$u = \frac{2s - vt}{t}$ — Rewrite with u on the left.

Powers of the subject

- If the required subject is raised to a power, e.g. v^2, first make v^2 the subject and then find the square root of both sides.
- For cubes find the cube root, and so on

Example

Make u the subject of $v^2 = u^2 + 2as$.

$v^2 - 2as = u^2$ — Take $2as$ from both sides.

$u^2 = v^2 - 2as$ — Change the sides.

$u = \sqrt{v^2 - 2as}$ — Find the square root of both sides.

Subject in twice

If the required subject is in the formula twice:

- first get all the terms involving the subject on one side of the formula and all the other terms on the other side
- then take the subject out as a common factor
- then divide both sides by the bracket.

Example

Make x the subject of $ax - by = cx + d$.

$ax = cx + d + by$ — Add by to both sides.

$ax - cx = d + by$ — Take cx from both sides.

$x(a - c) = d + by$ — Factorise.

$x = \dfrac{d + by}{a - c}$ — Divide both sides by $(a - c)$.

Now try these:

Make the letter in square brackets the subject of these formulae.

Question 14 could also be written as 'Find a formula for x in terms of a and y.'

12 $A = 4\pi r^2$ [r]

13 $V = \frac{4}{3}\pi r^3$ [r]

14 $y = x^2 + a$ [x]

15 $y = ax + by$ [y]

16 $y = a(x + y)$ [y]

17 $ab + cd = ac - bd$ [c]

Here is an exam question …and its solution

The price of a handtool of size S cm is P pence.
The formula connecting P and S is $P = 20 + 12S^2$.

(a) Calculate the price of a handtool of size 3 cm.
(b) Calculate the size of a handtool whose price is 95p.
(c) Rearrange the formula $P = 20 + 12S^2$ to express S in terms of P.

(a) £1·28

$$P = 20 + 12 \times 3^2$$
$$= 20 + 12 \times 9$$
$$= 20 + 108$$
$$= 128\text{p}$$

(b) 2·5 cm

$$20 + 12S^2 = 95$$
$$12S^2 = 75$$
$$S^2 = 75 \div 12$$
$$= 6{\cdot}25$$
$$S = \sqrt{6{\cdot}25} = 2{\cdot}5$$

(c) $S = \sqrt{\dfrac{P - 20}{12}}$

$$P = 20 + 12S^2$$
$$P - 20 = 12S^2$$
$$\frac{P - 20}{12} = S^2$$
$$S = \sqrt{\frac{P - 20}{12}}$$

Now try these exam questions:

1 The cost, C pence, of printing n party invitations is given by $C = 120 + 4n$.
Find a formula for n in terms of C.

2 Using $u = 9$, $t = 48$ and $a = \frac{^{-}1}{4}$, work out the value of s from the formula $s = ut + \frac{1}{2}at^2$.

3 Make y the subject of the formula $5x + 6y = 30$.

4 The formula $f = \dfrac{uv}{u + v}$ is used in the study of light. Calculate f when $u = 14{\cdot}9$ and $v = {}^{-}10{\cdot}2$.
Give your answer to 3 s.f.

5 The time, T minutes, for cooking a piece of meat weighing P pounds is found using the instruction 'cook for 20 minutes and then add 30 minutes for each pound'. Write down a formula for T in terms of P.

6 Use the formula $F = 2(C + 15)$ to find an expression for C in terms of F.

7 Write down the nth term of this sequence
1, 4, 7, 10, 13...

8 **(a)** The volume, V cm^3, of material inside a tube is given by $V = 25\pi(R^2 - r^2)$.
Calculate the value of V when $\pi = 3{\cdot}1$, $R = 7{\cdot}3$ cm and $r = 5{\cdot}9$ cm.
(b) Make y the subject of the formula $x = 4y^2 - 3$.

9 Rearrange each of the following to give d in terms of e.
(a) $e = 5d + 3$ **(b)** $\dfrac{3d - 7}{4 + 5d} = e$

10 Given that $f = \dfrac{uv}{u + v}$, express v in terms of u and f.

Simultaneous equations and inequalities

Simultaneous equations

Here is one method of solving a pair of simultaneous equations

Step 1: Make the coefficients of x or y equal by multiplying one or both of the equations. Don't forget to multiply **every** term.

Step 2: Eliminate the term with equal coefficients:
- if the signs are the **s**ame, **s**ubtract
- if the signs are **d**ifferent, a**dd**.

Step 3: Substitute the value back into (1) or (2) to find the value of the other letter.

Step 4: Write down **both** values as your answer.

Step 5: Check your answer by substituting both values back into the equation not used in Step 3.

Example

$2x + 3y = 6$ (1)
$x + y = 4$ (2)

Multiply (2) by 2 to make the x terms the same.

$2x + 3y = 6$ (1)
$2x + 2y = 8$ (2) × 2

$2x$ in both, so subtract the equations.

$y = {}^{-}2$

(2) is easier so use this.

$x + {}^{-}2 = 4$
$x = 6.$

So $x = 6$, $y = {}^{-}2$.

Check in (1).

$2 \times 6 + 3 \times {}^{-}2 = 6$
$12 - 6 = 6$ ✓

Example

$3x - 5y = 1$ (1)
$2x + 3y = 7$ (2)

This time both equations need to be multiplied. Make the y terms the same by (1) × 3 and (2) × 5.

$9x - 15y = 3$
$10x + 15y = 35$

The signs are different so add.

$19x = 38$
$x = 2$

Substitute in (2).

$2 \times 2 + 3y = 7$
$3y = 3$
$y = 1$

$x = 2$, $y = 1$

Check in (1).

$3 \times 2 - 5 \times 1 = 1$
$6 - 5 = 1$ ✓

Now try these:

1 Solve these simultaneous equations:

(a) $3x + 2y = 13$
$4x + y = 14$

(b) $2x + y = 7$
$3x - 2y = 28$

(c) $3x - 2y = 8$
$4x + 3y = 5$

Inequalities

- The symbols used are:
  $>$ means greater than
  $<$ means less than
  $\geqslant$ means greater than or equal to
  $\leqslant$ means less than or equal to.
- Inequalities are solved using the same rules as when solving equations **except** when dividing or multiplying by a negative number. Then the inequality sign is reversed.

Example

Solve the inequality $3x - 1 \geqslant 11$.

$3x \geqslant 12$
$x \geqslant 4$

Example

Find the largest integer that satisfies $4x + 10 < 2x + 14$.

$4x - 2x < 14 - 10$
$2x < 4$
$x < 2$

The largest integer value less than 2 is 1.

Example

Solve the inequality $4x < 6x + 2$.

$^-2x < 2$
$x > {}^-1$

Turn the inequality round when dividing by a negative number.

Example

Solve $x^2 \leqslant 16$.

$x \leqslant 4$
$x \geqslant {}^-4$ or $^-4 \leqslant x \leqslant 4$

Example

Solve $^-10 < 2x + 1 \leqslant 15$.

$^-11 < 2x \leqslant 14$
$^-5{\cdot}5 < x \leqslant 7$

Now try these:

2 Solve these inequalities:
(a) $3x < x + 4$
(b) $3 - 4x > 6 + x$
(c) $2(3x - 4) \leqslant 3(4x - 3)$

3 Find the smallest integer value which satisfies $3(9 - 4x) < 9 + 6x$.

4 Solve $x^2 \geqslant 25$.

5 Solve $5 < 3 - x < 9$.

Here is an exam question ...and its solution

A gardener finds that two apple trees and five pear trees cost £90 and that three apple trees and six pear trees cost £123.
If the cost of one apple tree is £x and the cost of one pear tree is £y, write down two equations in x and y and solve them to find x and y.

Equations $2x + 5y = 90$ (1)
$3x + 6y = 123$ (2)
$x = 25$, $y = 8$

$6x + 15y = 270$ (1) × 3
$6x + 12y = 246$ (2) × 2
$3y = 24$ — Subtract.
$y = 8$
$2x + 5 \times 8 = 90$ — Substitute into (1).
$2x = 50$
$x = 25$
$3 \times 25 + 6 \times 8 = 123$ — Check in (2).
$75 + 48 = 123$ ✓

Now try these exam questions:

1 Solve these simultaneous equations.
$5x + 4y = 13$ $3x + 8y = 5$

2 Solve these simultaneous equations.
$4x + 3y = 5$ $2x + y = 1$

3 The equation of the straight line passing through the points (3, 2) and (9, 11) is $px + qy = 5$.
(a) Explain why $3p + 2q = 5$.
(b) Write down another equation in terms of p and q.
(c) Solve the two equations to find the value of p and the value of q.

4 Solve the inequality $8x + 5 > 25$.

5 Solve the inequality $2x + 17 > 4x + 6$.

6 Find all the integers that satisfy $5 < 2x + 1 \leqslant 15$.

7 Solve $x^2 < 36$.

Quadratic equations

Multiplying out brackets

When multiplying out two brackets, such as $(x + 2)(x - 3)$, every term in one bracket must be multiplied by every term in the second bracket.

Example

Expand $(x + 2)(x - 3)$.

$$(x + 2)(x - 3) = x(x - 3) + 2(x - 3) = x^2 - 3x + 2x - 6 = x^2 - x - 6$$

Now try these:

1 $(x + 4)(x + 5)$
2 $(x + 2)(x - 5)$
3 $(y - 1)(y - 3)$
4 $(x - 2)(x + 2)$
5 $(z + 1)(z + 10)$
6 $(y - 3)(y + 3)$

Don't forget that $^-1 \times {}^-3 = 3$.

Factorising quadratic expressions

These are three cases:

- when all the signs are +

Example

Factorise $x^2 + 5x + 6$.

Find two numbers with sum 5 and product 6.
These are 2 and 3.
Factors are $(x + 2)(x + 3)$.

- when the last sign is + but the x term sign is –, as in $-8x$

Example

Factorise $x^2 - 8x + 15$.

Find two negative numbers with sum $^-8$ and product 15.
These are $^-3$ and $^-5$.
Factors are $(x - 3)(x - 5)$.

- when the last sign is – as in –24.

Example

Factorise $x^2 + 2x - 24$.

Find two numbers, one positive and one negative, with sum 2 and product $^-24$.
These are 6 and $^-4$.
Factors are $(x + 6)(x - 4)$.

Now try these

7 $x^2 + 6x + 5$
8 $x^2 - 25$
9 $x^2 - 7x + 10$
10 $x^2 - 9x + 18$
11 $x^2 + 3x - 28$
12 $x^2 - x - 30$
13 $y^2 - 64$
14 $z^2 + 7z + 6$
15 $x^2 - 7x + 12$
16 $y^2 + y - 42$
17 $x^2 - x - 42$
18 $z^2 + 6z + 9$

The difference is negative in question 12.

Solving quadratic equations by factorising

- If the product of two numbers is 0 then one of the numbers is 0.
- If a quadratic expression equals 0 then one or other of its factors equals 0.

Example

$(x - 2)(x + 3) = 0$

Then either $x - 2 = 0$ or $x + 3 = 0$.
So $x = 2$ or $x = {}^{-}3$.

Example

$x^2 - 3x = 0$
$x(x - 3) = 0$

Don't forget the $x = 0$ solution.

Then either $x = 0$ or $x - 3 = 0$.
So $x = 0$ or $x = 3$.

Last sign + means the signs in the brackets are the same.
Last sign – means the signs in the brackets are different.

Now try these:

19 $(x - 3)(x - 6) = 0$

20 $(x + 4)(x - 1) = 0$

21 $(x + 3)(x + 7) = 0$

22 $(x - 1)(x + 1) = 0$

23 $x^2 + 5x + 4 = 0$

24 $x^2 - 7x + 12 = 0$

25 $x^2 + 3x - 10 = 0$

26 $x^2 - x - 30 = 0$

27 $x^2 - 9 = 0$

28 $x^2 - 4x = 0$

29 $x^2 + 9x + 14 = 0$

30 $x^2 - 2x - 48 = 0$

Here is an exam question ...and its solution

Very often an exam question will contain several parts covering different aspects of the topic.

(a) Expand and simplify $x(2x - 1) - 2(x - 3)$.

(b) Factorise this expression: $x^2 - 3x - 10$.

(a) $x(2x - 1) - 2(x - 3)$
$= 2x^2 - x - 2x + 6$
$= 2x^2 - 3x + 6$

${}^{-}2 \times {}^{-}3 = 6$

(b) $x^2 - 3x - 10$
$= (x + 2)(x - 5)$

$2 - 5 = {}^{-}3$
$2 \times {}^{-}5 = {}^{-}10$

Now try these exam questions:

1 Solve the equation $x^2 - 6x + 8 = 0$.

2 Expand and simplify these expressions:
(a) $5(2x - 1) + 3(4x - 3)$
(b) $(x - 5)(x - 4)$

3 **(a)** Factorise completely $5x^2 - 10xy$.
(b) **(i)** Factorise $x^2 - 9x + 8$.
(ii) Hence solve $x^2 - 9x + 8 = 0$.

4 **(a)** Expand and simplify $(x - 7)(x - 5)$.
(b) Factorise:
(i) $x^2 + 3x - 10$
(ii) $x^2 - 9$.

5 **(a)** Multiply out and simplify the expression $(2x + 7)(3x - 6)$.
(b) Solve the equation $x^2 - 36 = 0$.

6 Bill is making a rectangular chicken pen against a wall. The other three sides will be made from wire netting. Here is the plan:

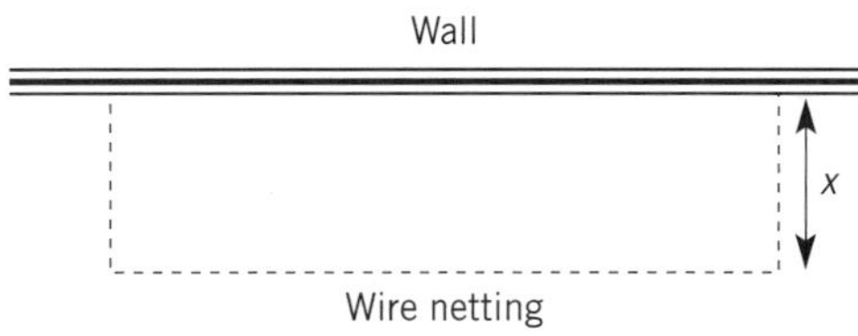

The total length of wire netting is 22 m.
The area inside the pen must be 60 m^2.
(a) Show that $x^2 - 11x + 30 = 0$.
(b) Solve the equation.
(c) Describe the size of the pen.

Numerical methods

Trial and improvement

- An approximate solution of a cubic equation can be found by graphical methods. In order to find it more accurately the method of trial and improvement needs to be used.
- Start with the given values. One will give a result which is too big and the other a result which is too small.
- Now try halfway between.
- Continue the process, working out for values between one which is too big and one which is too small.

Don't forget to write down the outcome of each trial. There is no need to keep more than four decimal places.

Example

A solution of the equation $x^3 + 4x - 8 = 0$ lies between 1 and 2. Find the solution correct to 1 d.p.

$x = 1$
$x^3 + 4x - 8 = {}^{-}3$ Too small

$x = 2$
$x^3 + 4x - 8 = 8$ Too big

Try between 1 and 2

$x = 1{\cdot}5$
$x^3 + 4x - 8 + 1{\cdot}375$ Too big

Remember that it is the solution (for x) that is required to 1 decimal place, not the outcome of the trial.

Try between 1 and 1·5

$x = 1{\cdot}2$
$x^3 + 4x - 8 = {}^{-}1{\cdot}472$ Too small

Try between 1·2 and 1·5

$x = 1{\cdot}3$
$x^3 + 4x - 8 = {}^{-}0{\cdot}603$ Too small

Try between 1· 3 and 1·5

$x = 1{\cdot}4$
$x^3 + 4x - 8 = 0{\cdot}344$ Too big

The actual answer lies between 1·3 and 1·4 so to 1 d.p. the answer is either 1·3 or 1·4. To check which is the correct one try halfway between.

$x = 1{\cdot}35$
$x^3 + 4x - 8 = {}^{-}0{\cdot}139625$ Too small

So the answer is between 1·35 and 1·4 and to 1 d.p. $x = 1{\cdot}4$.

Now try these:

Find solutions for the following equations in the region given correct to 1 d.p.

1 $x^3 + 6x - 9 = 0$ between 1 and 2

2 $x^3 - 12x + 4 = 0$ between 3 and 4

3 $x^3 - 2x + 8 = 0$ between $^{-}3$ and $^{-}2$

4 $x^3 + 4x^2 - 5 = 0$ between $^{-}4$ and $^{-}3$

5 Find the solution of the equation $x^3 - 2x - 1 = 0$ that lies between 1 and 2, correct to 2 d.p.

Here is an exam question ...and its solution

A solution of the equation $x^3 + 4x^2 = 8$ lies between $^{-}3$ and $^{-}3{\cdot}5$.

Find this solution by trial and improvement.
Give your answer correct to 2 d.p.

$x = {}^{-}3$
$x^3 + 4x^2 = {}^{-}27 + 36 = 9$ Too big

$x = {}^{-}3{\cdot}5$
$x^3 + 4x^2 = 6{\cdot}125$ Too small

$x\ {}^{-}3{\cdot}3$
$x^3 + 4x^2 = 7{\cdot}623$ Too small

Answer lies between $^{-}3{\cdot}3$ and $^{-}3$

$x = {}^{-}3{\cdot}2$
$x^3 + 4x^2 = 8{\cdot}192$ Too big

Answer lies between $^{-}3{\cdot}3$ and $^{-}3{\cdot}2$

$x = {}^{-}3{\cdot}25$
$x^3 + 4x^2 = 7{\cdot}921\,875$ Too small

Answer lies between $^{-}3{\cdot}25$ and $^{-}3{\cdot}2$

$x = {}^{-}3{\cdot}23$
$x^3 + 4x^2 = 8{\cdot}033\,333$ Too big

Answer lies between $^{-}3{\cdot}23$ and $^{-}3{\cdot}25$

$x = {}^{-}3{\cdot}24$
$x^3 + 4x^2 = 7{\cdot}978\,176$ Too small

So to 2 d.p. $x = {}^{-}3{\cdot}23$ or $^{-}3{\cdot}24$

Try half way between to check

$x = {}^{-}3{\cdot}235$
$x^3 + 4x^2 = 8{\cdot}005\,89$ Too big

So the answer is between $^{-}3{\cdot}235$ and $^{-}3{\cdot}24$ and to 2 d.p. the answer is $x = {}^{-}3{\cdot}24$.

> This solution keeps several decimal places as a check for you. There is no need to write them all down. e.g. for $x = -3{\cdot}23$, $x^3 + 4x^2 = 8{\cdot}03$ is enough.

Now try these exam questions:

1 The volume of this cuboid is 200 cm^3.

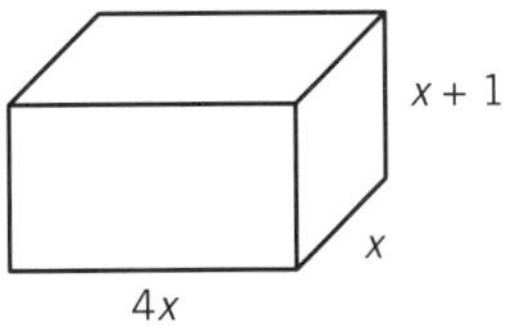

(a) Explain why $x^3 + x^2 = 50$.

(b) Find the solution of $x^3 + x^2 = 50$ that lies between 3 and 4.
Give the answer correct to 3 s.f. You must show your trials.

2 The equation $x^3 - 15x + 3 = 0$ has a solution between 3 and 4.
Use trial and improvement to find this solution.
Give your answer to 1 d.p.
Show clearly the outcomes of your trials.

3 Use trial and improvement to find the solution of $x^3 - 3x = 15$, between 2 and 3.
Give your answer to 2 d.p.
Show clearly the outcomes of your trials.

4 Use trial and improvement to calculate, correct to 2 d.p., the solution of the equation $x^3 - 5x - 2 = 0$ which lies between $x = 2$ and $x = 3$.
Show all your trials and their outcomes.

5 (a) Show that the equation $x^3 - 8x + 5 = 0$ has a root between $x = 2$ and $x = 3$.

(b) Use trial and improvement to find this root correct to 1 d.p.
Show all your trials and their outcomes.

6 The volume, $V\,cm^3$, of this cuboid is given by $V = x^3 + 6x^2$.

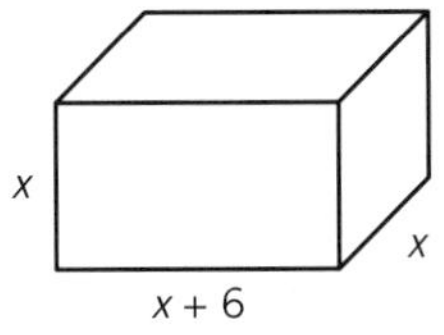

(a) Complete this table for values of x from 1 to 6.

x	1	2	3	4	5	6
V						

(b) Use trial and improvement to find the dimensions of the cuboid if its volume is 200 cm^3.
Give the answer correct to 1 d.p. Show all your trials.

Sequences

Term-to-term rules

- Every number in a sequence is called a term of the sequence. There is often a simple rule for going from one term to the next.
- Use the term-to-term rule to find the formula for a sequence.

Example

Here are the first four terms of a sequence: 3, 7, 11, 15.

(a) Find the term-to-term rule.
(b) Find the 20th term.
(c) Find a formula for the nth term of the sequence.

(a) Add 4.
(b) To get the 20th term, add four 19 times.
$3 + 19 \times 4 = 3 + 76 = 79$.
(c) The formula is $3 + (n - 1) \times 4$
$= 3 + 4n - 4 = 4n - 1$.

Now try these:

1 Find the first four terms for the sequence given by $3n + 3$.

2 Find the term-to-term rule for this sequence: 2, 7, 12, 17...

3 Find the 15th term and the formula for the nth term for this sequence: 5, 11, 17, 23...

4 Find the formula for the nth term for this sequence: 40, 36, 32...

In question 4 the n term is negative.

Common sequences

You should know and recognise common sequences.

Examples

The powers of 2: 1, 2, 4, 8, 16, 32, ... 2^n
The powers of 10: 1, 10, 100, 1000, ... 10^n
The square numbers: 1, 4, 9, 16, ... n^2
The triangle numbers: 1, 3, 6, 10 ... $\frac{n(n+1)}{2}$

Position-to-term rules

- Every number in a sequence can be expressed in terms of its position.
- Use the position-to-term rule to find the formula for the nth term of a sequence:
  - look at the difference between successive terms
  - multiply this difference by n
  - add or subtract a constant to give the required results.

Example

Find the rule for this sequence:
7, 11, 15, 19, ...

It is sometimes useful to write the sequence out in columns:

Position	Term	Difference between terms
1	7	
		4
2	11	
		4
3	15	
		4

This shows that you multiply by 4. The term $4n$ will be in the formula.

Look at position 1. The term is 7.
$4 \times n = 4 \times 1 = 4$

You need to add 3 to give the required result of 7.

Check for position 2.
$4 \times 2 + 3 = 11$ ✓

So the nth term $= 4n + 3$.

Now try these:

Find a formula for the nth term of each of these sequences.

5 3, 5, 7, 9, ...

6 10, 20, 30, 40, ...

7 $^-4$, 1, 6, 11, ...

8 32, 29, 26, 23, ...

Here is an exam question ...and its solution

(a) Write down the 10th term for the sequence:
3, 7, 11, 15, ...
(b) Write down an expression for the nth term.

(a) 39

10th term = $3 + 9 \times 4 = 39$

(b) $4n - 1$

Either:
the difference between terms is 4
so the expression will start $4n$.
If $n = 1$ then $4n = 4$
therefore subtract 1 to get 3
therefore the expression is $4n - 1$.
Or:
1st term is 3, add 4 $(n - 1)$ times
therefore nth term is $3 + 4(n - 1)$
$= 3 + 4n - 4 = 4n - 1$.

(c) Show that 137 cannot be a term in this sequence.

(c) If 137 is in the sequence then
$4n - 1 = 137$
therefore $4n = 138$
therefore $n = 138 \div 4 = 34{\cdot}5$
ie not a whole number.
Therefore 137 cannot be in the sequence.

Now try these exam questions:

1 The first four terms of a sequence are: 3, 8, 13, 18.
Find the 50th term and the rule for this sequence.

2 The first five terms of a sequence are: 1, 6, 11, 16, 21.
Find the formula for the nth term.

3 The first four terms of a sequence are 2, 9, 16, 23.
(a) Find the rule for this sequence. **(b)** Show that 300 is not in this sequence.

4 Here is a pattern of shaded and white tiles.

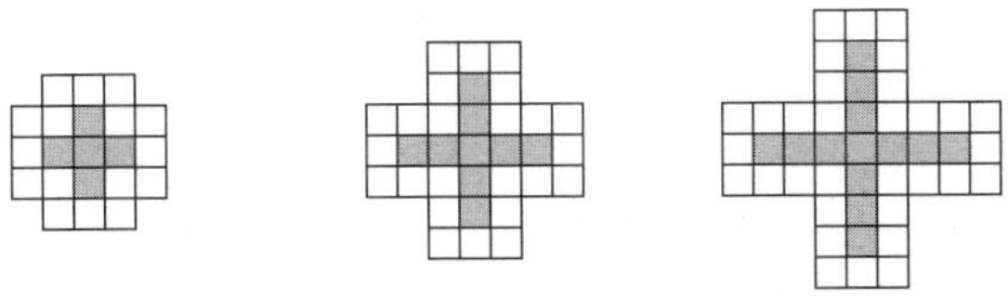

(a) Write down the rule for the shaded tiles **(b)** Write down the rule for the white tiles.

5 These classroom tables seat four children:

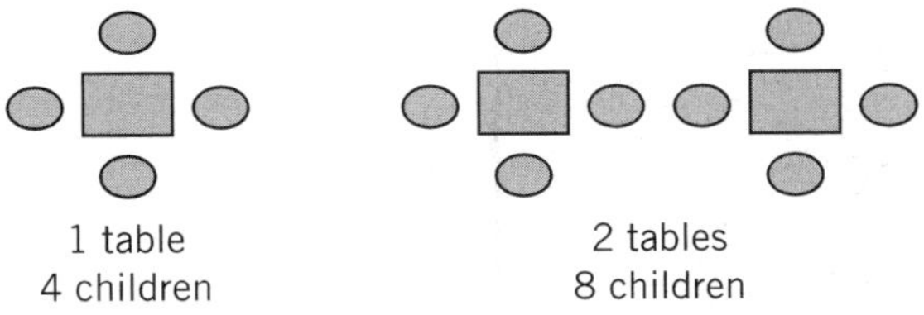

(a) For this arrangement write down a formula linking the number of children, c, to the number of tables, t.
(b) Sometimes the tables are arranged like this:

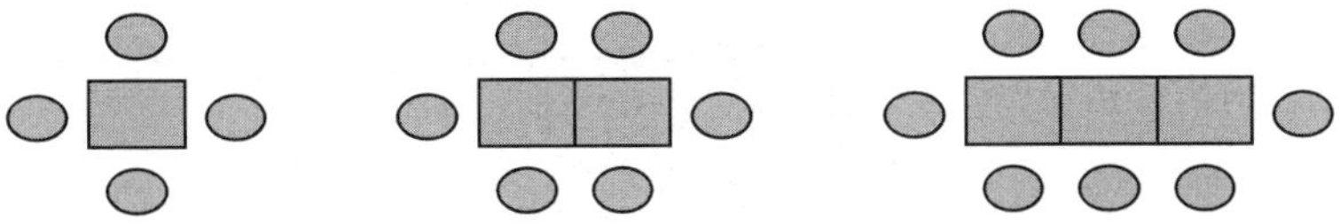

For this arrangement, write down a formula linking the number of tables, t, and the number of children, c.

Graphs of linear functions

Drawing straight-line graphs

There are two main ways of writing equations of straight-lined graphs: the type $y = 2x + 1$, and the type $3x + 2y = 6$.

To draw the first type:

Step 1: Draw up a table of values using three x numbers.
Step 2: Substitute these into the formula to find the corresponding y values.
Step 3: Plot the coordinate pairs. They should lie in a straight line.

Example

Draw the line $y = 2x + 1$.

$x = 2, y = 2 \times 2 + 1 = 5$

x	0	1	2
y	1	3	5

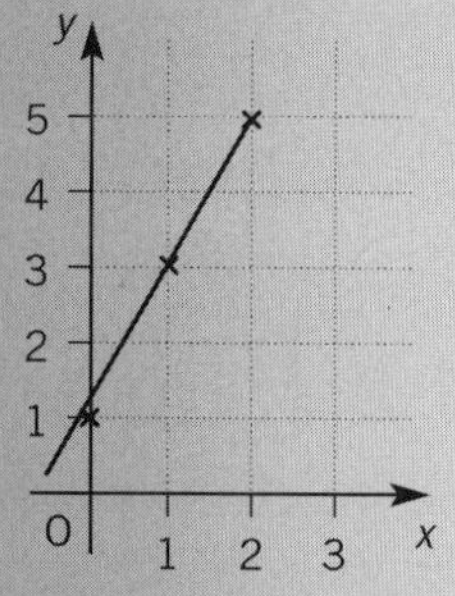

To draw the second type:

Step 1: Draw up a table of values. Use $x = 0$, $y = 0$ and one other x value.
Step 2: Substitute these into the formula to find the other values.
Step 3: Plot the coordinate pairs.

Example

Draw the line $3x + 2y = 6$.

For $x = 0$, $2y = 6$ so $y = 3$

x	0	2	1
y	3	0	$1\frac{1}{2}$

For $x = 1$, $3 + 2y = 6$ so $y = 1\frac{1}{2}$

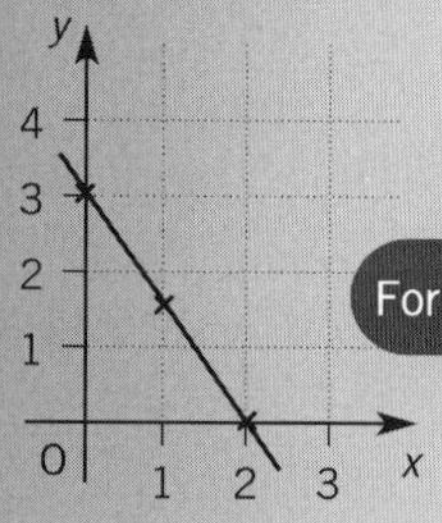

Now try these:

1 Draw the following straight-line graphs.
   (a) $y = 3x - 2$
   (b) $2x + 5y = 10$
   (c) $y = 6 - 2x$

Gradient and y-intercept

- The gradient of a line is a number indicating how steep it is. The larger the number, the steeper the line.
- Lines with positive gradient slope forwards / , lines with negative gradient slope backwards \ .
- Gradient = $\dfrac{\text{increase in } y}{\text{increase in } x}$
- The y-intercept is the value where the line crosses the y-axis.

Example

Find the gradient and intercept of these lines.

(a)

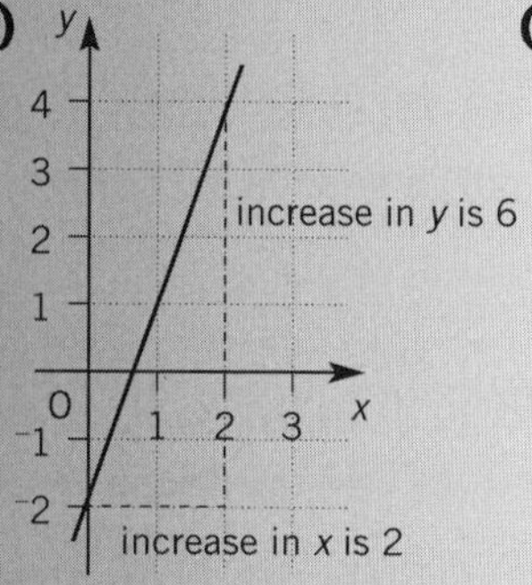

(b)

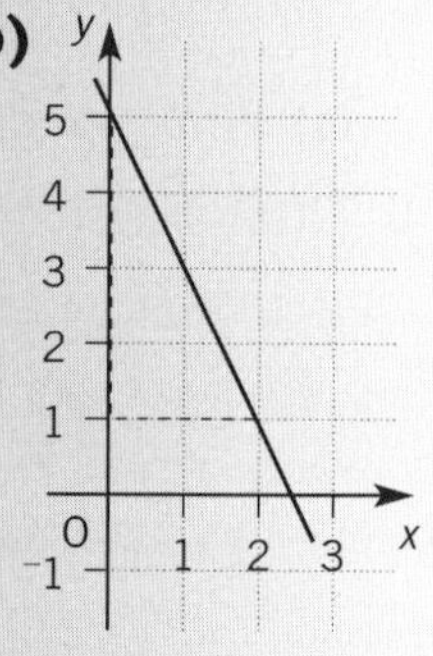

(a) Gradient = $\frac{6}{2} = 3$ y-intercept = $^{-}2$

(b) Gradient = $\frac{^{-}4}{2} = {^{-}2}$ y-intercept = 5

Now try these:

2 Find the gradient and y-intercept of each of these lines.

(a)

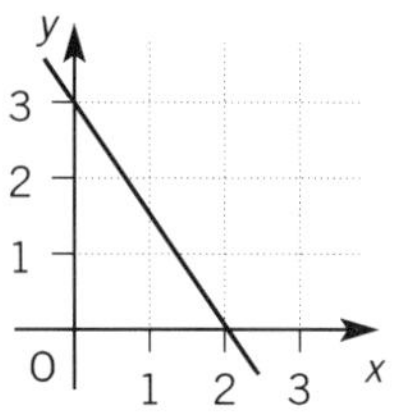

(b)

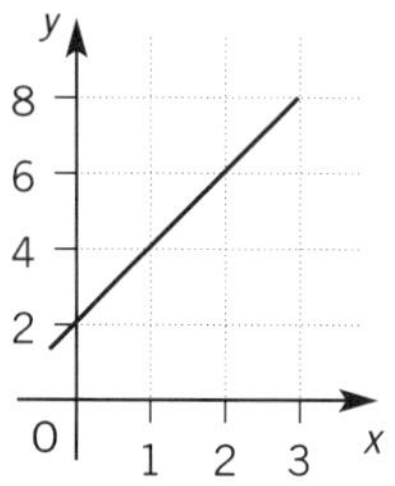

The general equation of a straight line $y = mx + c$

- In the equation, m stands for the gradient of the line and c is the y-intercept.
- The equation of a line **must** be written in the form $y = mx + c$ for the two numbers to represent the gradient and y-intercept.

Example

(a) Write down the equation of each of the lines in the previous two examples.
(b) Find the gradient and y-intercept of these lines.
(i) $y = x + 4$
(ii) $2y = 6x - 3$
(iii) $5x - 2y = 12$

(a) $y = 3x - 2 \quad y = {}^-2x + 5$

(b) (i) $y = 1x + 4 \qquad m = 1 \qquad c = 4$

÷2

(ii) $y = 3x - 1\frac{1}{2} \qquad m = 3 \qquad c = {}^-1\frac{1}{2}$

^-5x

(iii) ${}^-2y = {}^-5x + 12$

÷$^-2$

$y = 2\frac{1}{2}x - 6 \qquad m = 2\frac{1}{2} \qquad c = {}^-6$

Now try these:

3 Write down the equation of each of the lines in question 2.

4 Work out the gradient, m, and y-intercept, c, for each of the following straight lines.

(a) $y = 4x - 1$ **(d)** $y + x = 4$
(b) $y = 3 + 2x$ **(e)** $2y - 3x = 4$
(c) $y = x$ **(f)** $x - 4y = 10$

Parallel lines

Lines which are parallel have the same gradient.

Example

Find the equation of the line parallel to $y = 2x - 5$ and passing through (0, 4).

From $y = 2x - 5 \qquad m = 2$
From (0, 4) $\qquad c = 4$
The equation is $\qquad y = 2x + 4$

Now try these:

5 Which of these lines are parallel?

(a) $y = 6x - 2$ **(d)** $6y = 36x - 24$
(b) $y = 2x - 6$ **(e)** $y = 6 + x$
(c) $6y = 6x - 2$ **(f)** $6x - y = 2$

Here is an exam question ...and its solution

Find the gradient and the equation of the straight line in the diagram.

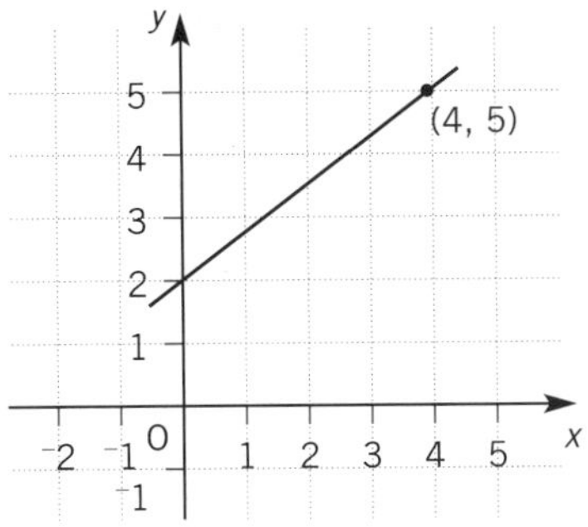

Gradient = $\frac{3}{4}$

Equation is $y = \frac{3}{4}x + 2$

Now try these exam questions:

1 Draw the graph of $y = 3x - 1$.

2 (a) Write down the gradient and y-intercept of the line with equation $y = 4 - 2x$.
(b) Write down the equation of the line parallel to $y = 4 - 2x$ and passing through the point (0, $^-1$).

3 Work out the gradient of this line.

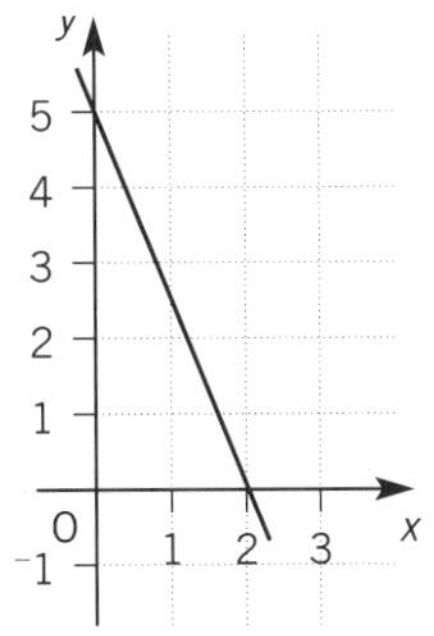

Graphical solution of simultaneous equations and linear inequalities

Graphical solution of simultaneous equations

Simultaneous equations can also be solved by graphical methods. The solution is found where the graphs intersect.

Step 1: Draw up a table of values for each equation.

Step 2: Draw the two straight-line graphs on the same grid.

Step 3: Find where the two lines cross.
Write down the x and y values of the point of intersection.

Example

Solve graphically $y = 4x - 1$
and $x + y = 4$

$y = 4x - 1$

x	0	1	2
y	$^{-}1$	3	7

$x + y = 4$

x	0	4	1
y	4	0	3

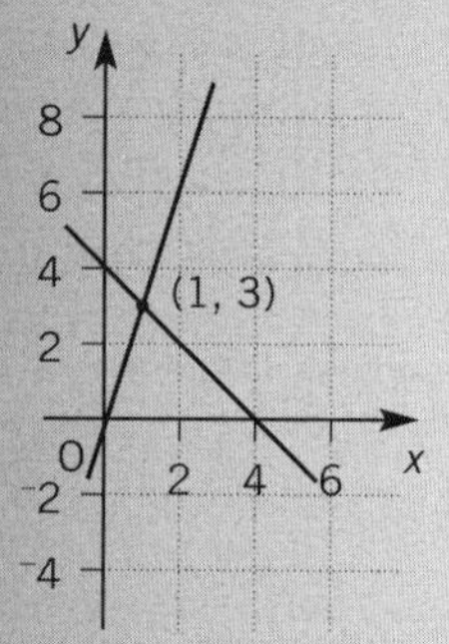

$x = 1$, $y = 3$

Now try these:

1 Solve these simultaneous equations graphically.

(a) $y = 2x - 1$
$y = x + 2$

(b) $y = 2x - 5$
$2x + y = 3$

Graphical solution of a set of inequalities

The solution will be represented by a region of the graph.

Step 1: Change the inequality sign to an equals sign and make a table of values for each line.

Step 2: Draw the lines on the same grid. Use a continuous line if there is an equals sign in the inequality and a dotted line if there is no equals sign.

Example

Find the region satisfied by
$x \geqslant 1$
$x + y < 5$
$y \geqslant 2x - 6$

$x = 1$ is a vertical line through (1, 0)

$x + y = 5$

x	0	5	1
y	5	0	4

$y = 2x - 6$

x	0	1	2
y	$^{-}6$	$^{-}4$	$^{-}2$

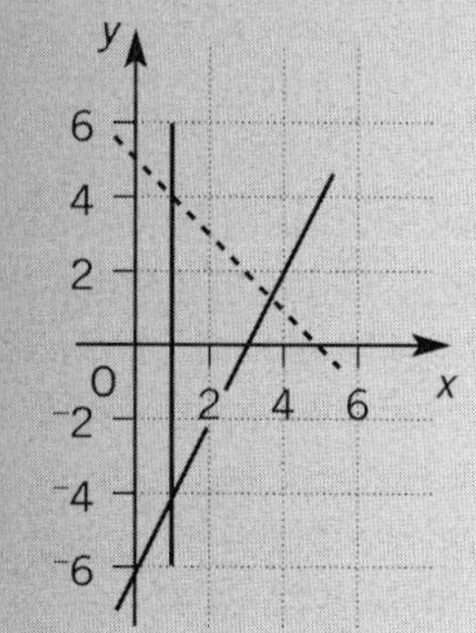

Step 3: Substitute the coordinates of the origin (0, 0) to test each inequality.
If the result is true, shade the opposite side of the line to the origin.
If the result is false, shade the same side of the line as the origin.

Step 4: The remaining unshaded area is the region of points satisfying the set of inequalities.

Shade the unwanted region unless the question says otherwise.

Example continued

$x \geqslant 1 \Rightarrow 0 \geqslant 1$	**False, shade origin side**
$x + y < 5 \Rightarrow 0 < 5$	**True, shade opposite side**
$y \geqslant 2x - 6 \Rightarrow 0 \geqslant {}^-6$	**True, shade opposite side**

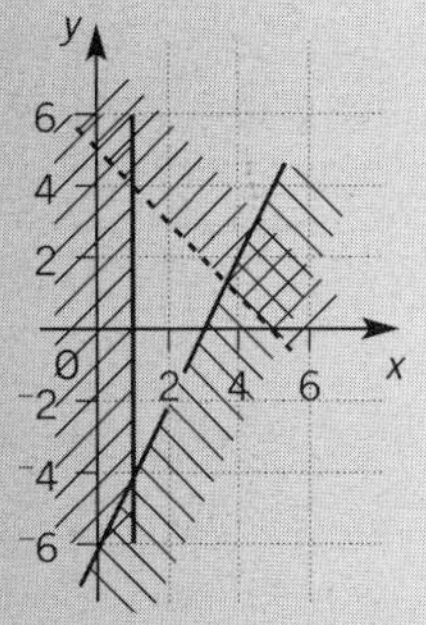

Now try these:

2 Find the region satisfied by each set of inequalities.

(a) $y \leqslant 4$
$x + y \geqslant 4$
$y \geqslant 3x - 1$

(b) $x \leqslant 2$
$2x + 3y \leqslant 12$
$5x + 2y \geqslant 10$

Here is an exam question ...and its solution

(a) Solve these simultaneous equations graphically.
$y = 3x - 1$
$y = 3 - 2x$

(a)

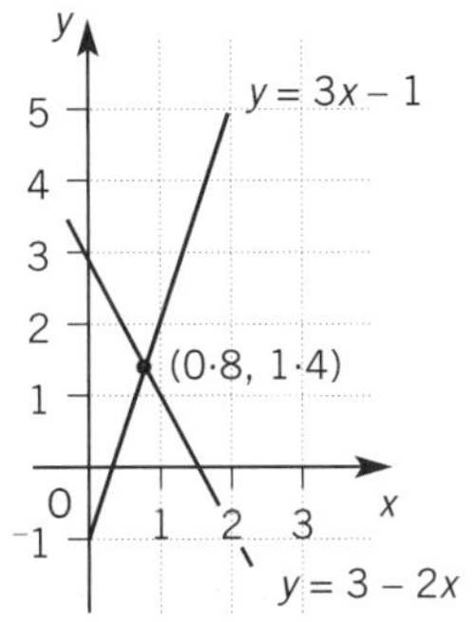

$x = 0{\cdot}8,\ y = 1{\cdot}4$

(b) Write down the three inequalities that are satisfied in the shaded region.

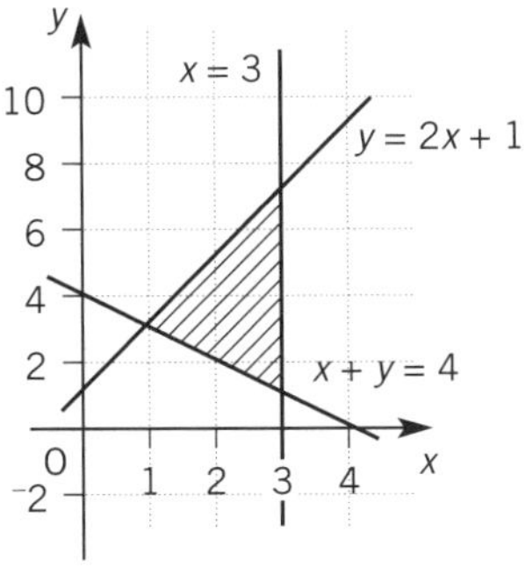

Choose a point in the region, e.g. $x = 2$, $y = 3$

(b)		
$y \leqslant 2x + 1$	$y = 2x + 1$	$3 \leqslant 2 \times 2 + 1$ so $y \leqslant 2x + 1$
$x \leqslant 3$	$x = 3$	$2 \leqslant 3$ so $x \leqslant 3$
$x + y \geqslant 4$	$x + y = 4$	$2 + 3 \geqslant 4$ so $x + y \geqslant 4$

Now try these exam questions:

1 Solve these simultaneous equations graphically.
$y = 3 - x \qquad y = 3x - 2$

2 Solve these simultaneous equations graphically.
$y = 3x + 4 \qquad x + y = 2$

3 Find the region satisfied by the inequalities:
$x + y \leqslant 5 \qquad y \leqslant 2x - 1 \qquad y \geqslant 0$

4 Look at the graph on the right.
Write down the three inequalities which are satisfied in the shaded region.

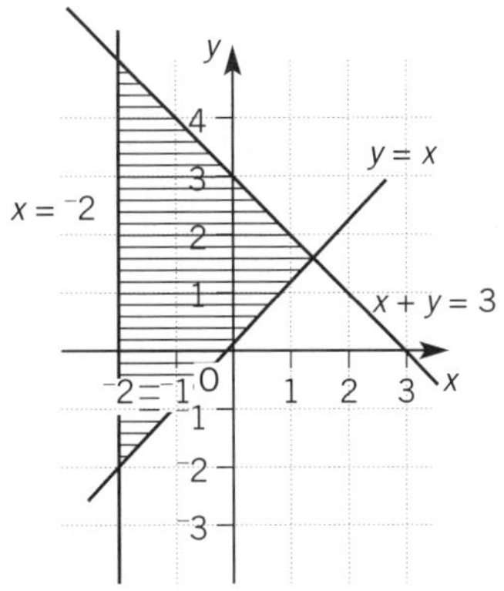

Interpreting graphs

Graphs in real situations

To interpret real life graphs:

- look at the labels on the axes – they tell you what the graph is about
- look whether the graph is a straight line or a curve
- the slope of the graph gives you the rate of change
- for distance–time graphs the rate of change is the velocity
- for speed–time graphs the rate of change is the acceleration
- the area under a velocity–time graph = distance.

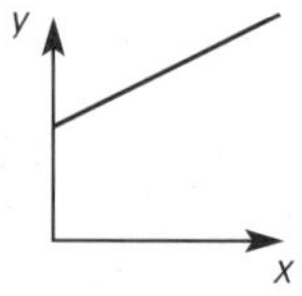

Constant rate of change

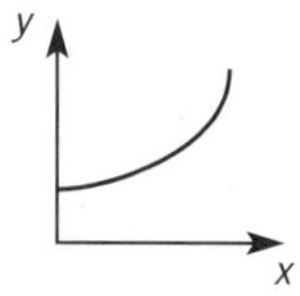

Rate of change increasing

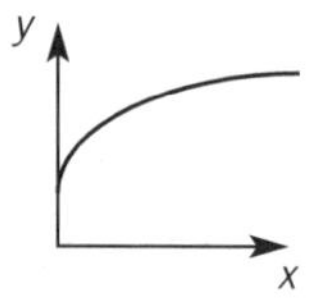

Rate of change decreasing

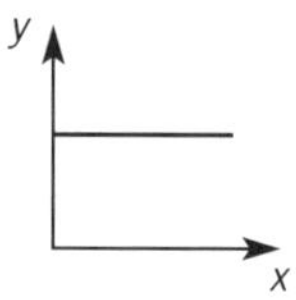

No change for the variable on the *y*-axis

Remember to find the rate of change for each part of the graph. If it is zero, say how long this lasts.

Example

Asif walked to the bus stop, waited for the bus, and then travelled on the bus to school.

The graph is a distance–time graph for Asif's journey.

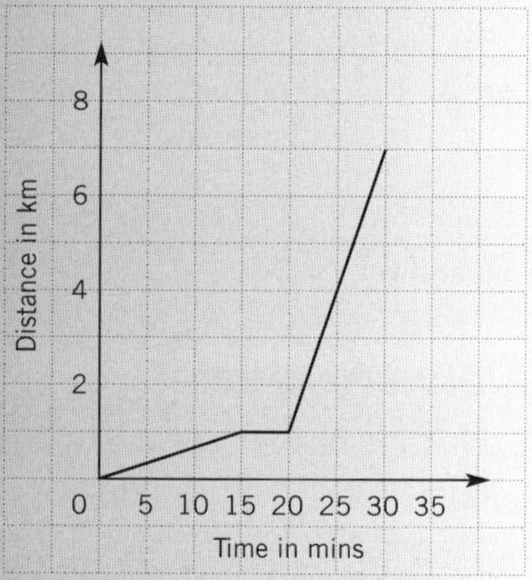

(a) How long did Asif wait at the bus stop?
(b) How far did Asif travel
(i) on foot **(ii)** by bus?
(c) How fast did Asif walk?
(d) What was the average speed of the bus?
(e) Why are the sections of the graph unlikely, in reality, to be totally straight?

(a) 5 mins
(b) **(i)** 1 km **(ii)** 6 km
(c) $\frac{1}{15}$ km/min or 4 km/h
(d) $\frac{6}{10}$ km/min or 36 km/h
(e) Stops and starts are likely to be gradual not sudden.

Now try these:

Describe what is really happening for these graphs.

1 (a)

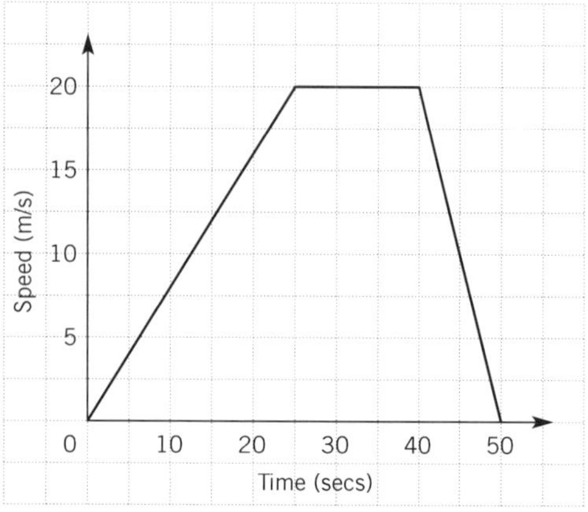

(b)

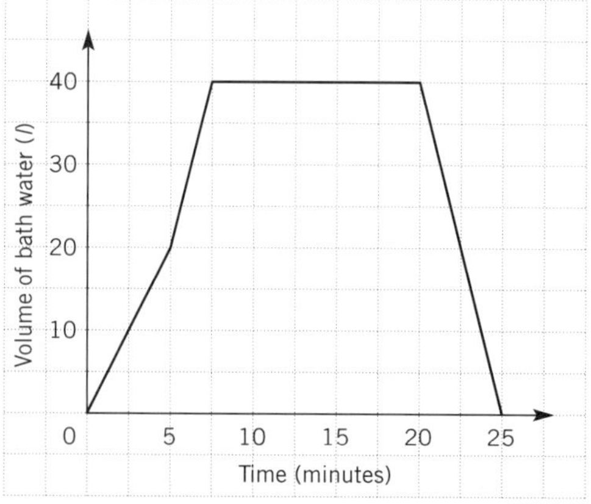

Drawing graphs

- Always label your axes with the quantity and the unit.
- Sometimes only a sketch is asked for, not an accurate plot. Always check whether the rate of change is constant, increasing or decreasing.

Example

Water is poured into this vessel at a constant rate. Sketch a graph of depth of water (*d* cm) against time (*t* secs).

Now try these:

2 A car is travelling at 70 m.p.h. on a motorway, when it approaches some roadworks where the speed limit is 50 m.p.h. It slows down from 70 m.p.h. to 50 m.p.h. in 2 mins. It goes through the roadworks at 50 m.p.h. in 5 mins and then accelerates back to 70 m.p.h. in 30 secs. Draw a velocity–time graph to show this.

3 Find the distance travelled in the first 40 secs in question 1(a).

4 Water is poured into this vessel at a constant rate. Sketch a graph of depth of water (d cm) against time (t secs).

Example continued

Since the radius is decreasing at first the rate of change will increase and then become constant.

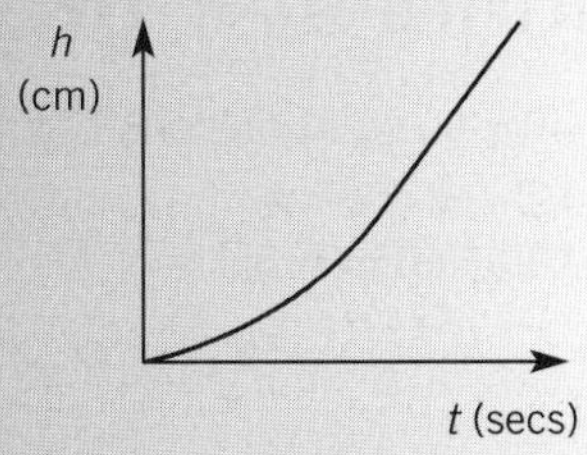

Here is an exam question ...and its solution

Tom leaves home at 8.20 a.m. and goes to school on a moped. The graph shows his distance from the school in kilometres.

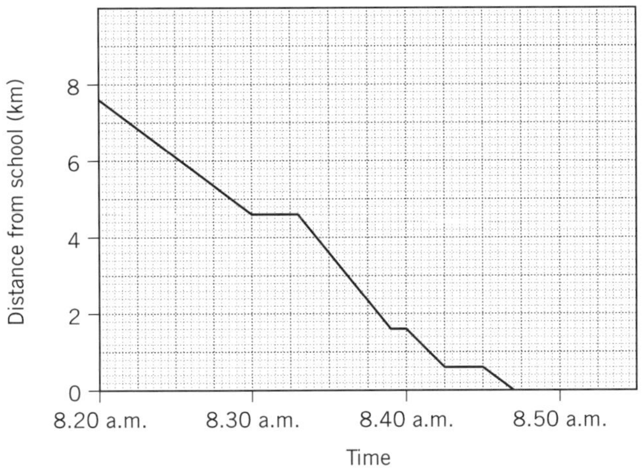

(a) How far does Tom live from school?
(b) Write down the time that Tom arrives at the school.
(c) Tom stopped three times on the journey. For how many minutes was he at the last stop?
(d) Calculate his speed in km/h between 8.20 a.m. and 8.30 a.m.

(a) 7·6 km
(b) 8.47 a.m.
(c) 2·5 minutes
(d) Distance = 7·6 – 4·6 = 3 km
Time = 10 mins
Speed = $\frac{3}{10} \times 60 = 18$ km/h

Now try these exam questions:

1 Steve travelled from home to school by walking to a bus stop and then catching a school bus.
(a) Use the information below to construct a distance–time graph for Steve's journey.
Steve left home at 8.00 a.m.
He walked at 6 km/h for 10 minutes.
He then waited for 5 minutes before catching the bus.
The bus took him a further 8 km to school at a steady speed of 32 km/h.
(b) How far was Steve from home at 8.20 a.m?

2 The graph below describes a real-life situation. Describe a possible situation that is occurring.

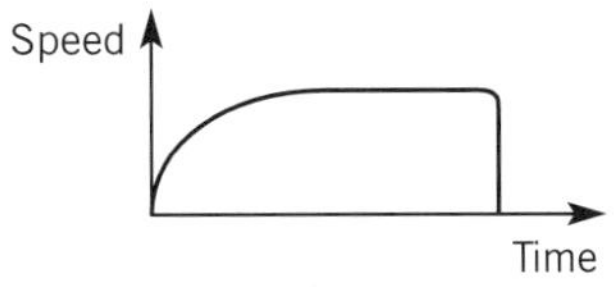

3 The diagrams show the cross-sections of three swimming pools. Water is pumped into all three at a constant rate. Sketch graphs of depth against time for each.

(a) **(b)** **(c)**

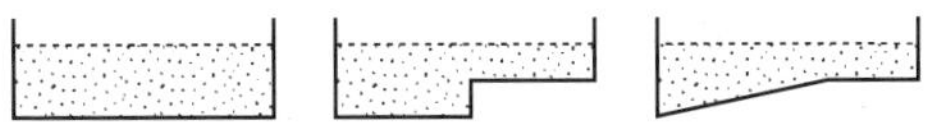

Quadratic and other functions

Quadratic graphs

- Graphs of equations of the form $y = ax^2 + bx + c$ are parabolas.
  Their shape is

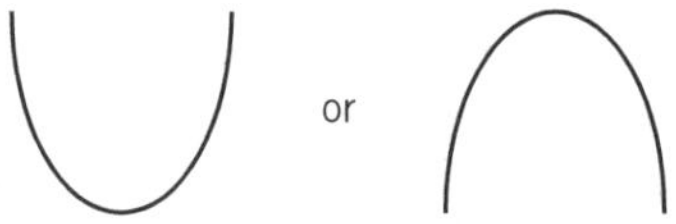

for $a > 0$ for $n < 0$

When drawing an accurate graph, use a table to work out the points, even if you are not asked to do so.

As well as doing it by hand, can you also use a spreadsheet to work out the values and draw these graphs?

- All parabolas are symmetrical.
  This symmetry can be seen on the graph and can often be seen in the table as well, as in this example.

Example

Complete this table for $y = x^2 - 4x + 3$ and draw the graph for $-1 \leqslant x \leqslant 5$.

x	$^-1$	0	1	2	3	4	5
x^2	1	0	1	4	9	16	25
^-4x	4	0	$^-4$	$^-8$	$^-12$	$^-16$	$^-20$
3	3	3	3	3	3	3	3
y	8	3	0	$^-1$	0	3	8

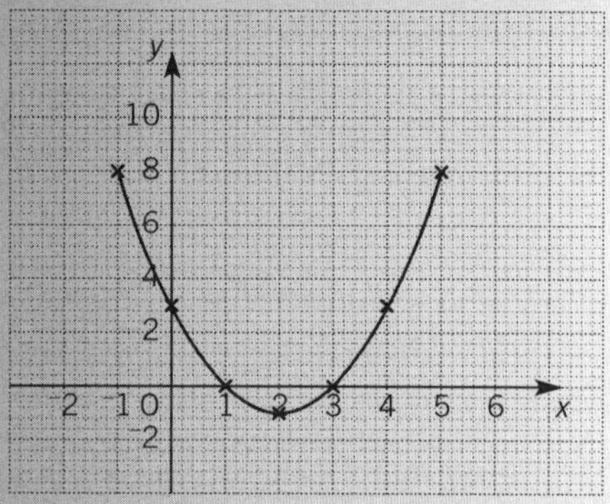

Now try these:

1 (a) Complete this table for $y = x^2 - 3x + 4$.

x	$^-1$	0	1	2	3	4
x^2						
^-3x						
4						
y						

(b) Explain why it is a good idea to add an extra column to the table and work out the value of y when $x = 1{\cdot}5$.
Then draw the graph.

2 Complete this table and draw the graph for $y = 2x^2 - 5x$ for $^-2 \leqslant x \leqslant 5$.

x	$^-2$	$^-1$	0	1	2	3	4	5
$2x^2$								
^-5x								
y								

Using graphs to solve quadratic equations

The solution of $ax^2 + bx + c = k$ is the values of x where the graph of $y = ax^2 + bx + c$ crosses the line $y = k$.

Example

Use the graph of $y = x^2 - 4x + 3$ (drawn above) to solve these equations.

(a) $x^2 - 4x + 3 = 0$
(b) $x^2 - 4x + 3 = 6$

(a) Look where the graph crosses $y = 0$, the x-axis: the solution is $x = 1$ or 3.
(b) Look where the graph crosses the line $y = 6$: the solution is $x = {}^-0{\cdot}6$ or $4{\cdot}6$, to 1 d.p.

Now try these:

3 Use the graph you drew in question 1 to solve the equations
(a) $x^2 - 3x + 4 = 4$
(b) $x^2 - 3x + 4 = 7$

4 Use the graph you drew in question 2 to solve the equations
(a) $2x^2 - 5x = 0$
(b) $2x^2 - 5x = {}^-1$

Cubic and reciprocal graphs

- You also need to be able to recognise the shape of cubic and reciprocal graphs, and to draw these graphs.
- The cubic graph $y = ax^3$ has the following shape when $a > 0$, and is reflected in the x-axis when $a < 0$.

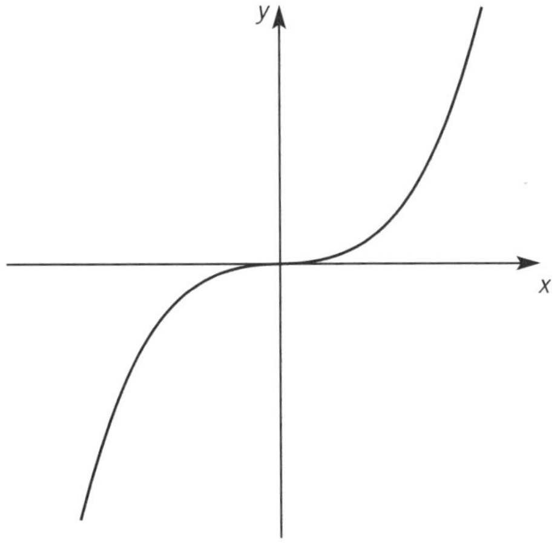

- The reciprocal graph $y = \frac{a}{x}$ has the following shape when $a > 0$, and is reflected in the x-axis when $a < 0$.

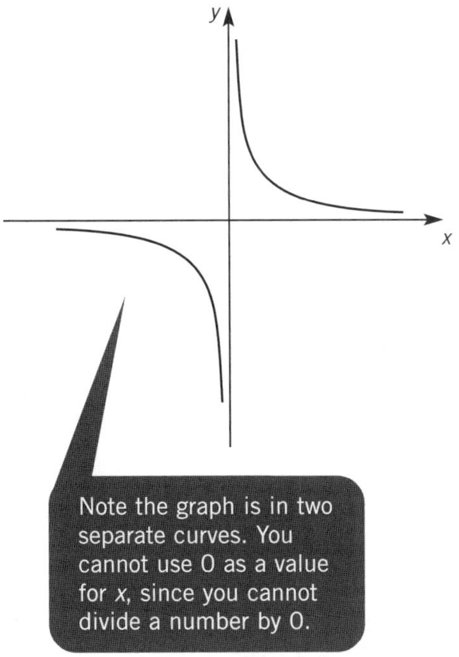

Note the graph is in two separate curves. You cannot use 0 as a value for x, since you cannot divide a number by 0.

Example

Draw the graph of $y = x^3 - 3x^2$ for values of x from $^{-}1$ to 4.

Use your graph to solve the equation $x^3 - 3x^2 = {^{-}1}$.

Make a table for the values you get:

x	$^{-}2$	$^{-}1$	0	1	2	3	4
x^3	$^{-}8$	$^{-}1$	0	1	8	27	64
$^{-}3x^2$	$^{-}12$	$^{-}3$	0	$^{-}3$	$^{-}12$	$^{-}27$	$^{-}48$
y	$^{-}20$	$^{-}4$	0	$^{-}2$	$^{-}4$	0	16

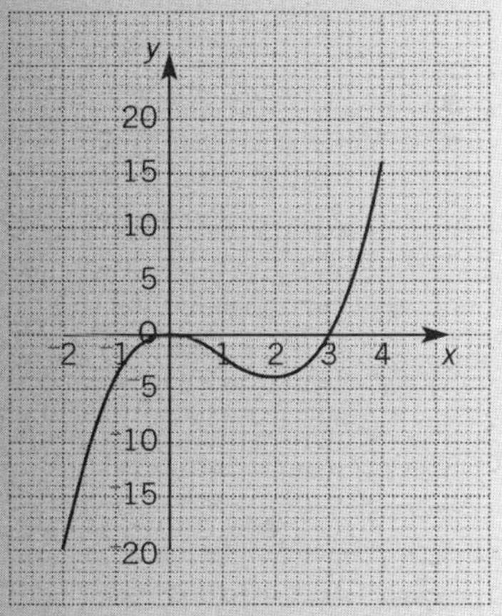

The solution of the equation is where the curve crosses the line $y = {^{-}1}$.
The solution is $x = {^{-}0{\cdot}5}$, $0{\cdot}7$ or $2{\cdot}9$.

In this example the shape of the 'double bend' is more pronounced than in the graph of $y = ax^3$. This is due to the extra term $^{-}3x^2$ in the equation.

Now try these:

5 Draw the graph of $y = \frac{12}{x}$ for values of x from $^{-}12$ to 12. Use the same scale on both axes.

6 Draw the graph of $y = x^3 - 2x$ for values of x from $^{-}2$ to 2. Use your graph to find the roots of the equation $x^3 - 2x = 0$ to 1 d.p. Then use trial and improvement to find the positive root correct to 2 d.p.

Here is an exam question ...and its solution

In this question, part of the graph was drawn. This helped not only with drawing the graph but also with some of the answers for part (c).

(a) Complete the table below for $y = x^3 - 2x^2 + 1$

x	$^-1$	$^-0{\cdot}5$	0
y		$0{\cdot}375$	

(b) Part of the graph is drawn on the grid. Add the three points from the table and complete the curve.

(c) Use the graph to solve the equation $x^3 - 2x^2 + 1 = 0$.

Solution

(a)

x	$^-1$	$^-0{\cdot}5$	0
y	$^-2$	$0{\cdot}375$	1

(b)

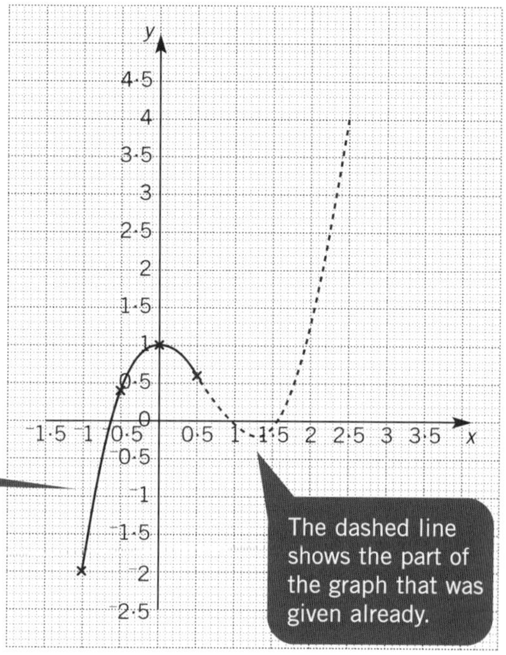

You need to draw a smooth curve. Use a pencil and turn the page so that your hand is inside the curve.

The dashed line shows the part of the graph that was given already.

(c) So $x = {}^-0{\cdot}6$, 1 or $1{\cdot}6$.

The solution is where the graph crosses the line $y = 0$.

Now try these exam questions:

1 (a) Complete the table of values and draw the graph of $y = x^2 - 2x + 1$ for values of x from $^-1$ to 3.

x	1	0	1	2	3
y		1			4

(b) Use your graph to find the values of x when $y = 3$.

2 (a) Complete the table for $y = 4x - x^2$ and draw the graph.

x	$^-1$	0	1	2	3	4	5
y			3			0	

(b) Use your graph to find:

(i) the value of x when $4x - x^2$ is as large as possible

(ii) between which values of x the value of $4x - x^2 - 2$ is larger than 0.

3 This table shows some values of x and y for the equation $y = x^3 + 5$.

x	$^{-}3$	$^{-}2$	$^{-}1$	0	1	2	3
y	$^{-}22$		4	5	6		32

(a) Complete the table and draw the graph of $y = x^3 + 5$ from $^{-}3$ to 3.
(b) Use your graph to solve the equation $x^3 + 5 = 10$.

4 The diagram shows the graphs P, Q, R, S, T and U.
State which of these graphs could correspond to each of the following equations.
(a) $y = x^3 - 1$
(b) $y = x^2 - 1$
(c) $y = x - 1$

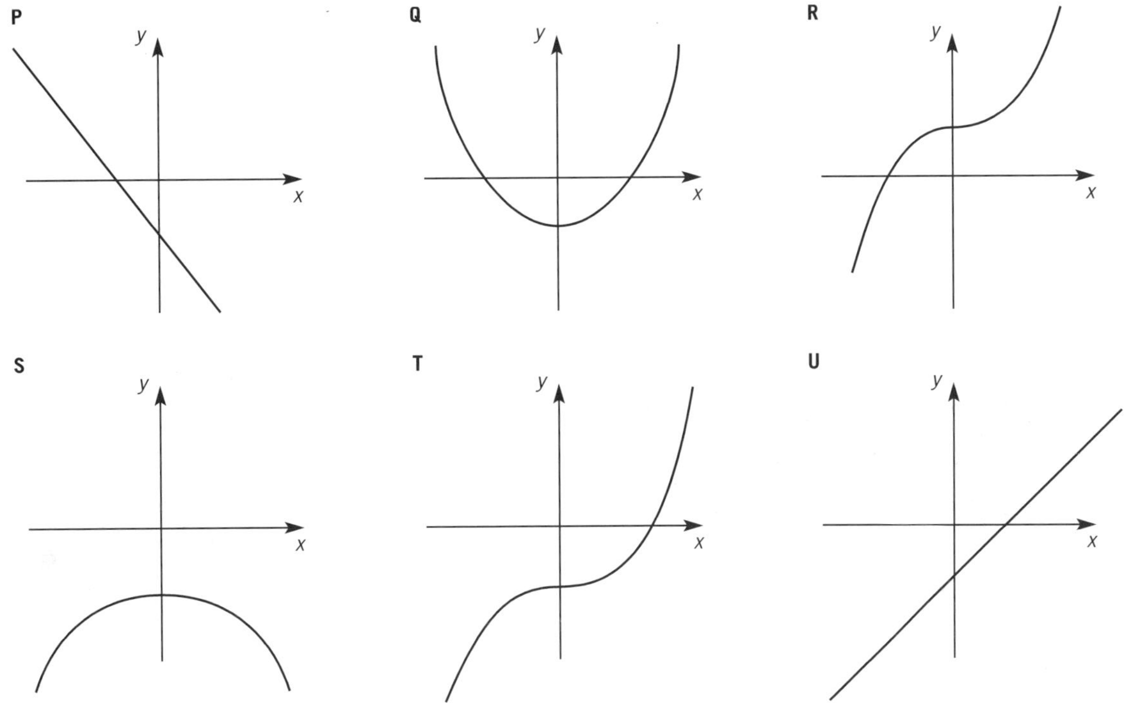

5 A cuboid has dimensions in centimetres as shown in the diagram.

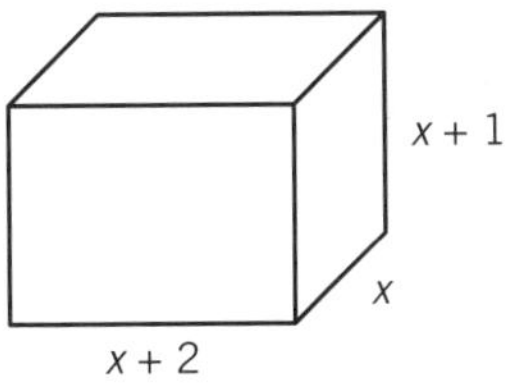

(a) Explain why the volume $V\text{cm}^3$ is given by $V = x^3 + 3x^2 + 2x$.
(b) Draw the graph of $V = x^3 + 3x^2 + 2x$ for values of x from 0 to 4.
(c) Use your graph to find the dimensions of the cuboid with volume $50\,\text{cm}^3$.

6 **(a)** Draw the graph of $y = \frac{2}{x}$ for values of x from $^{-}5$ to 5.
(b) Use your graph to solve the equation $\frac{2}{x} = 0{\cdot}8$.

Properties of triangles and other shapes

Basic angle facts

You need to know and be able to use these angle facts.

Sometimes you will be asked to give reasons for your answer. If you fail to do so you will lose marks.

- Angles on a straight line add up to 180°.
- Angles around a point add up to 360°.
- Angles of a triangle add up to 180°.
- Vertically opposite angles are equal.

Example

Work out the angles marked with letters in these diagrams.

Give reasons for your answers.

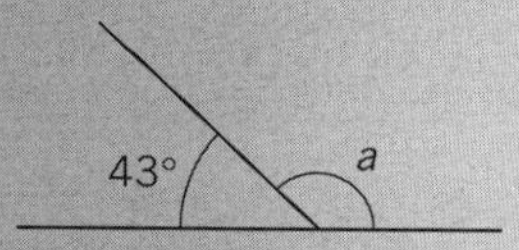

a = 137° (angles on a straight line add to 180°)

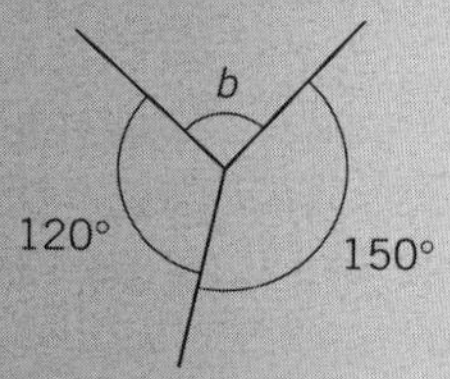

b = 90° (angles around a point add up to 360°)

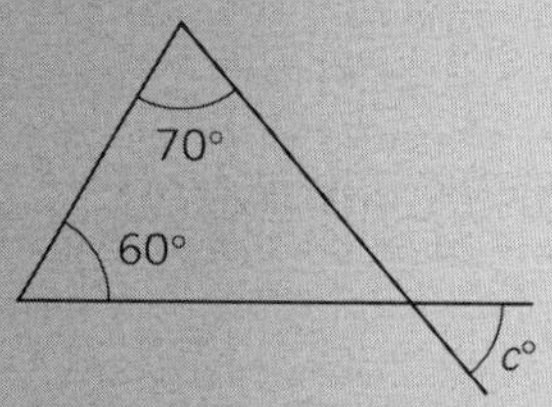

c = 50° (angles of a triangle add up to 180°, vertically opposite angles)

Angles with parallel lines

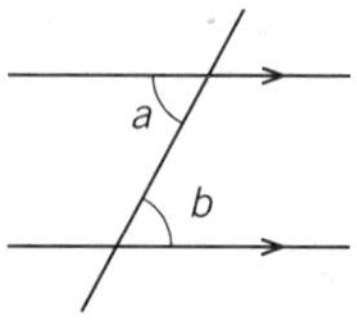

$a = b$

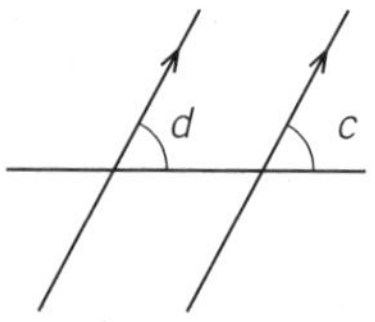

$c = d$

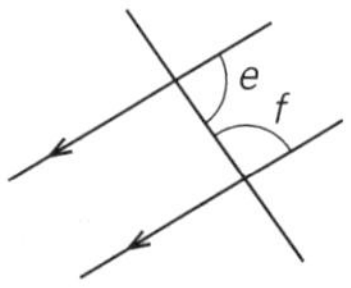

$e + f = 180°$

- *a* and *b* are called alternate angles. They are on opposite sides of the transversal.
- *c* and *d* are called corresponding angles. They are in the same position between the transversal and the parallel lines.
- *e* and *f* are called allied angles. They are the same side of the transversal between the parallel lines.

Example

Work out the angles marked with letters in these diagrams.

Give reasons for your answers.

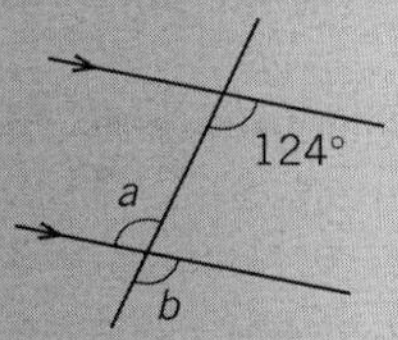

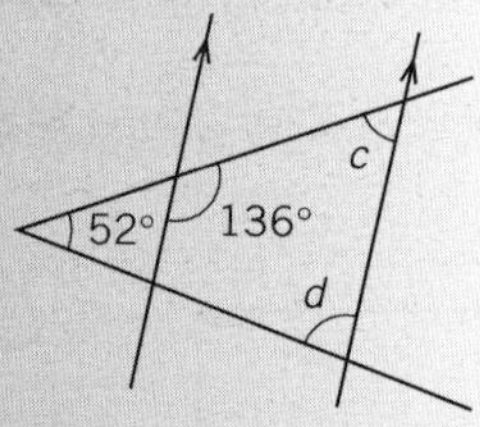

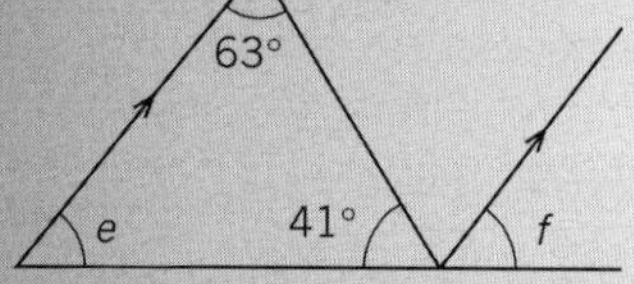

a = 124°	**Alternate angles are equal**
b = 124°	**Corresponding angles are equal *or* vertically opposite angles are equal**
c = 44°	**Allied angles add up to 180°**
d = 84°	**Angles in a triangle add up to 180°**
e = 76°	**Angles in a triangle add up to 180°**
f = 76°	**Corresponding angles are equal**

Now try these:

1 Calculate the angles marked with letters. Give reasons for your answers.

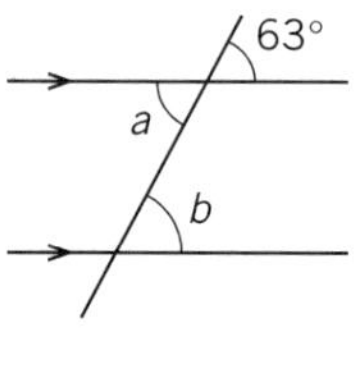

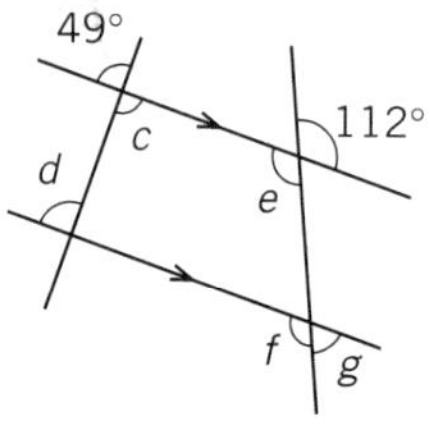

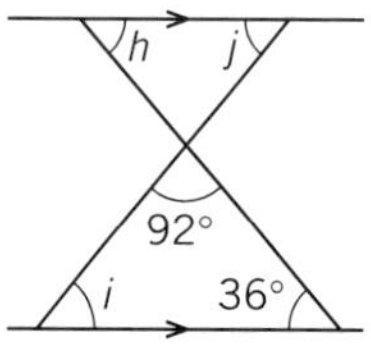

Congruent and similar shapes

Congruent shapes have:

- corresponding sides equal
- corresponding angles equal.

Similar shapes have:

- corresponding sides in proportion
- corresponding angles equal.

Example

Explain why these triangles are similar.

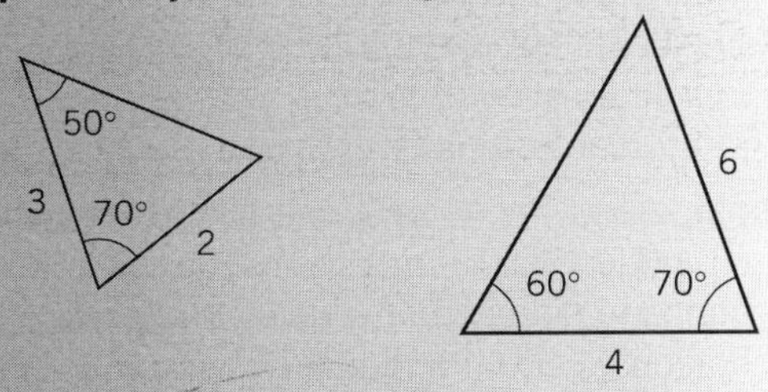

Triangles are similar as all the angles are equal (50°, 60°, 70°).

Example

These triangles are similar.

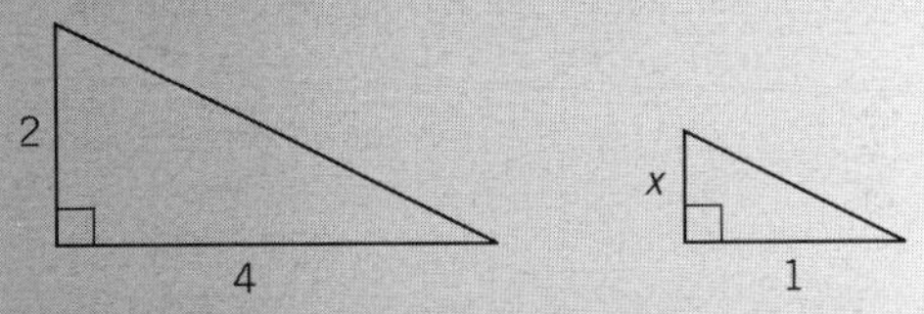

Find the length x.

Sides are in proportion, so $\frac{x}{2} = \frac{1}{4}$ and $x = \frac{1}{2}$.

Now try these:

2

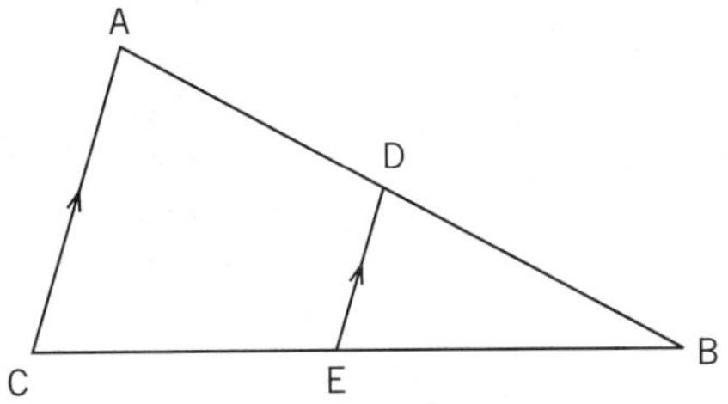

(a) Explain why triangle ABC is similar to triangle DBW.

DE = 1 cm, BE = 2 cm and EC = 4 cm.

(b) Find the length of AC.

Polygons

- The sum of the exterior angles of any polygon is 360°.
- If the interior angles are required it is easiest to work with the exterior angles and then use the fact that, at any vertex, the sum of the interior and the exterior angles is 180°.

Example

A regular polygon has 12 sides. Work out:
(a) the size of each interior angle
(b) the sum of the interior angles.

Each exterior angle = $\frac{360°}{12}$ = 30°

(a) Each interior angle = 180° – 30° = 150°.

(b) The sum of the interior angles = 150° × 12 = 1800°.

A non-regular polygon with 12 sides will have the same interior angle sum as a regular 12-sided polygon. This needs to be used when finding one of the angles when the rest are given.

Now try these:

3 Find the interior angle of a regular octagon.

4 Three interior angles of a quadrilateral are 112°, 65° and 79°. Find the size of the fourth angle.

5 A regular polygon has an interior angle of 156°. How many sides has the polygon?

6 A pentagon has 4 interior angles of 75°, 96°, 125° and 142°. Find the size of the fifth interior angle.

Different types of quadrilaterals

These are the different quadrilaterals and the facts you need to know.

- Square:
  - all angles 90°
  - all sides equal
  - opposite sides parallel
  - diagonals equal and bisect at 90°
  - four lines of symmetry
  - rotational symmetry order 4.
- Rectangle:
  - all angles 90°
  - opposite sides equal and parallel
  - diagonals equal and bisect but not at 90°
  - two lines of symmetry
  - rotational symmetry order 2.
- Parallelogram:
  - opposite angles equal
  - opposite sides equal and parallel
  - diagonals not equal but bisect though not at 90°
  - no line symmetry
  - rotational symmetry order 2.
- Rhombus:
  - opposite angles equal
  - all four sides equal
  - opposite sides parallel
  - diagonals not equal length but bisect at 90°
  - two lines of symmetry
  - rotational symmetry order 2.
- Trapezium:
  - one pair of opposite sides parallel.
- Isosceles trapezium:
  - two pairs of adjacent angles equal
  - one pair of opposite sides equal
  - other pair of sides parallel
  - diagonals equal but do not bisect or cross at 90°
  - one line of symmetry
  - no rotational symmetry.
- Kite:
  - one pair of opposite angles equal
  - two pairs of adjacent sides equal but none parallel
  - one diagonal bisected, cross at 90°
  - one line of symmetry
  - no rotational symmetry.

Example

A quadrilateral has both pairs of opposite sides parallel.
What type of quadrilateral can it be?

It can be a square, a rectangle, a parallelogram or a rhombus.

Example

Draw two quadrilaterals which have only one line of symmetry.

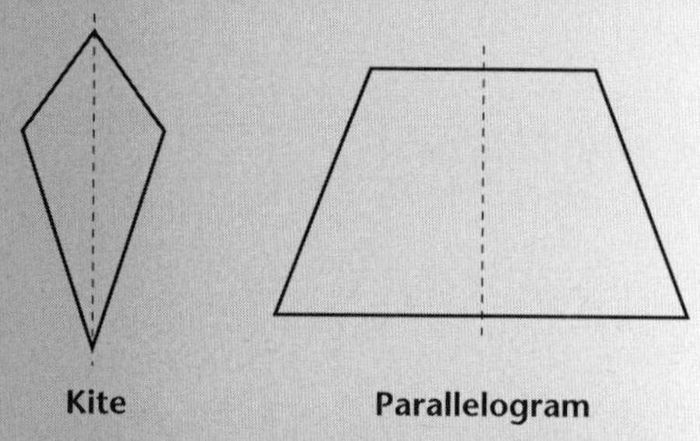

You could have drawn an arrowhead

Now try these:

7 A quadrilateral has rotational symmetry of order 2. What type of quadrilateral can it be?

8 Sketch these quadrilaterals, marking any equal angles, equal or parallel sides, and draw in all lines of symmetry:

(a) a rectangle
(b) a parallelogram
(c) an isosceles trapezium
(d) a kite.

Here is an exam question ...and its solution

The sketch shows a regular pentagon and a regular hexagon with equal length sides.

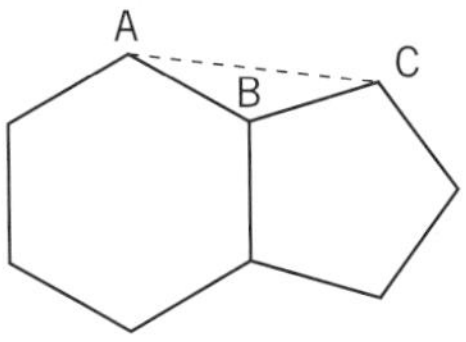

(a) Work out the size of one interior angle of:

(i) the pentagon

(ii) the hexagon.

(b) Work out the sizes of the angles in triangle ABC.

(a) (i) 108°

exterior angle $= \dfrac{360°}{5}$

$= 72°$

interior angle $= 180° - 72°$

$= 108°$

(ii) 120°

exterior angle $= \dfrac{360°}{6}$

$= 60°$

interior angle $= 180° - 60°$

$= 120°$

(b) 24°, 24°, 132°

In triangle ABC, angle ABC

$= 360° - 120° - 108°$

$= 132°$

It is isosceles as AB = BC so angle BAC and angle BAC

$= \dfrac{180° - 132°}{2}$

$= \dfrac{48°}{2}$

$= 24°.$

Now try these exam questions:

1 Here is a sketch of a regular pentagon, centre O.

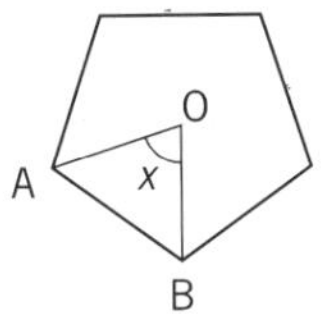

(a) Work out x.

(b) What type of triangle is OAB?

2 (a) Sketch a rhombus and mark everything that is equal.

(b) Draw in all lines of symmetry.

(c) State the order of rotational symmetry.

3 In the diagram BC is parallel to DE.

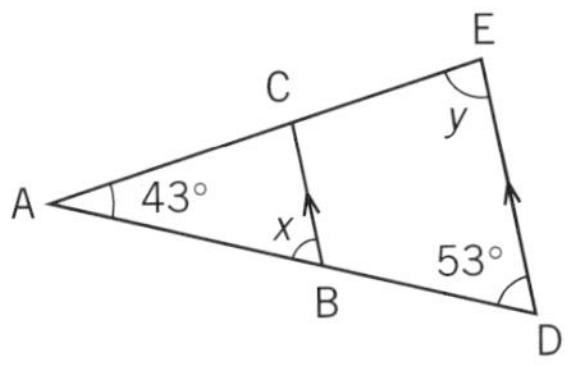

Find the size of x and y.
Give reasons for your answers.

4 The interior angle of an n-sided polygon is 48° more than the interior angle of a regular hexagon.
Find the value of n.

5 Triangles AXB and CXD are similar.

(a) Find the lengths of XC and DC.

(b) Explain why AB is parallel to DC

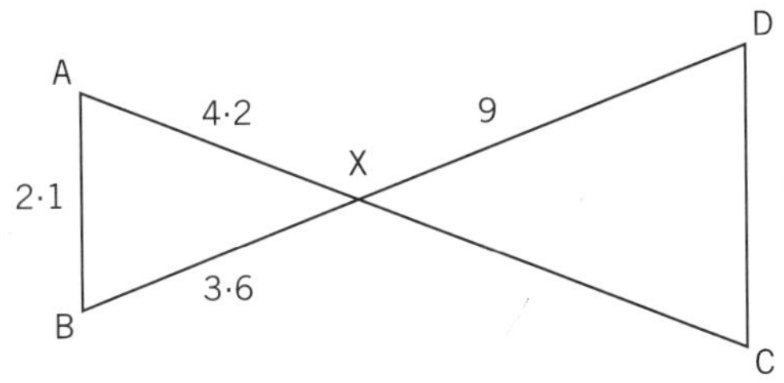

Pythagoras and trigonometry

Surds

- Expressions like $2\sqrt{3}$ or $\frac{1}{\sqrt{2}}$ which include square roots are called surds.
  They may arise in calculations using trigonometry or Pythagoras' theorem.
- Surds can often be simplified using the result $\sqrt{a \times b} = \sqrt{a} \times \sqrt{b}$.

Example

Simplify the following:

(a) $\sqrt{12}$ **(b)** $\sqrt{50}$ **(c)** $\sqrt{9} \times \sqrt{27}$

(a) $\sqrt{12} = \sqrt{4 \times 3} = \sqrt{4} \times \sqrt{3} = 2\sqrt{3}$

(b) $\sqrt{50} = \sqrt{25 \times 2} = \sqrt{25} \times \sqrt{2} = 5\sqrt{2}$

(c) $\sqrt{9} \times \sqrt{27} = 3 \times \sqrt{9 \times 3} = 3 \times \sqrt{9} \times \sqrt{3} = 3 \times 3 \times \sqrt{3} = 9\sqrt{3}$

Now try these:

Simplify the following:

1 $\sqrt{54}$

2 $\sqrt{32}$

3 $\sqrt{8} \times \sqrt{20}$

4 $\sqrt{75} \times \sqrt{30}$

Pythagoras' theorem

- In a right-angled triangle, labelled like this:

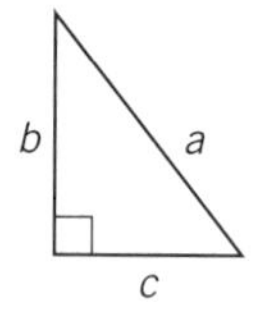

Pythagoras' theorem states that $a^2 = b^2 + c^2$.

- It is a good idea to label the triangle, using letters for the sides, and to write down the rule; then substitute the actual values for the sides before doing any rearrangement if necessary.

Example

Calculate the length of the hypotenuse in this triangle.

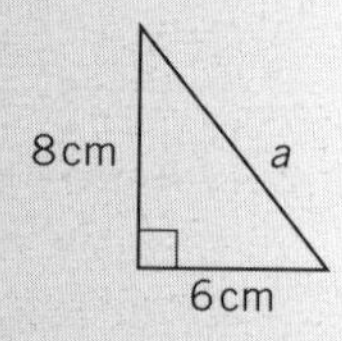

$a^2 = b^2 + c^2$
$a^2 = 8^2 + 6^2$
$a^2 = 64 + 36$
$a^2 = 100$
so $a = \sqrt{100} = 10\,\text{cm}$

Example

Calculate the length of the unknown side in this triangle.

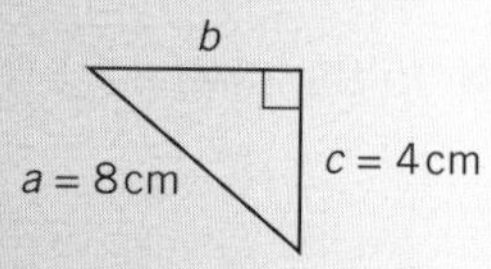

$a^2 = b^2 + c^2$
$8^2 = b^2 + 4^2$
$64 = b^2 + 16$
$b^2 = 64 - 16 = 48$
$b = \sqrt{48}$
$= 6{\cdot}9$ cm, to 1 d.p.

Example

Find the length of AB.

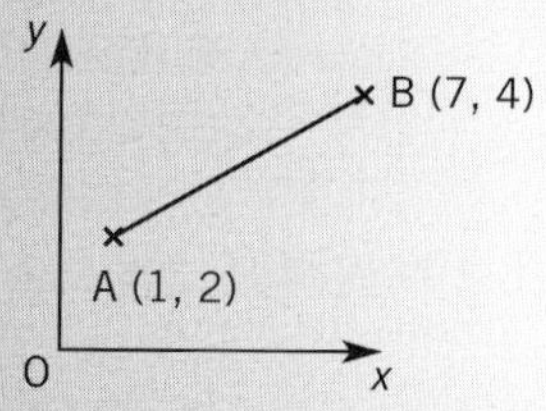

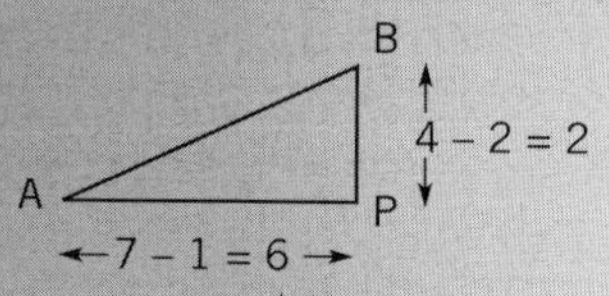

$AB^2 = AP^2 + BP^2$
$= 6^2 + 2^2 = 40$
$AB = \sqrt{40} = 6{\cdot}3$

Hint – sketch the triangle.

Now try these:

Find the length of the side marked x in each of the following. (All lengths are in cm. Give your answer correct to 1 d.p.)

5

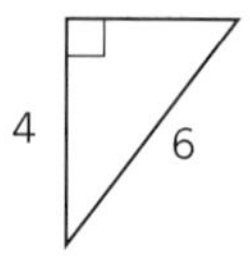

6

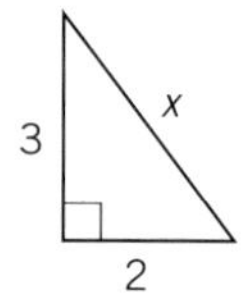

7

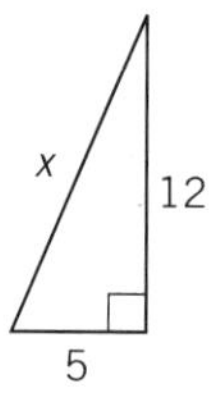

8

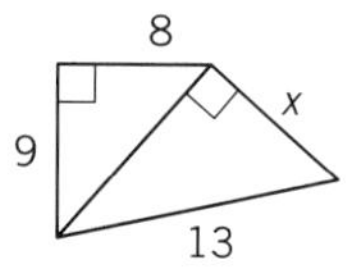

Trigonometry

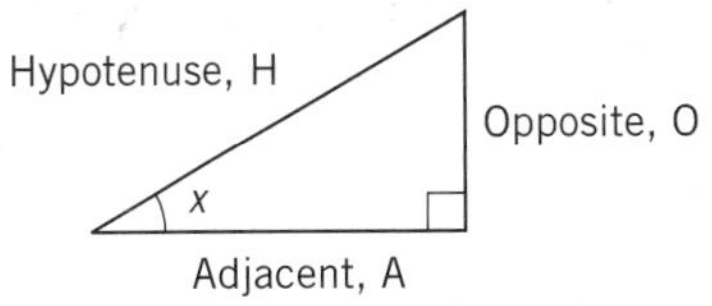

- The ratios you will need to use are sine (sin), cosine (cos) and tangent (tan).
- Using the triangle on the right, $\sin x = \frac{O}{H}$ $\cos x = \frac{A}{H}$ $\tan x = \frac{O}{A}$

- To calculate the length of a side:
  for the angle given in the triangle first label the sides 'opposite', 'adjacent' and hypotenuse', then decide on the ratio to use and substitute the value of the known side.

Example

Find the length marked x in these triangles:

(a)

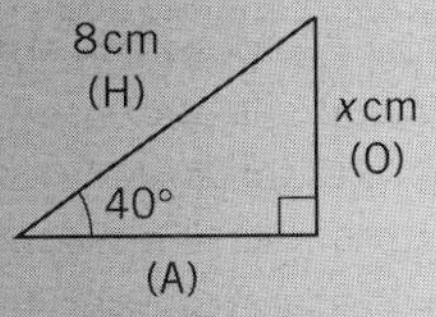

(c)

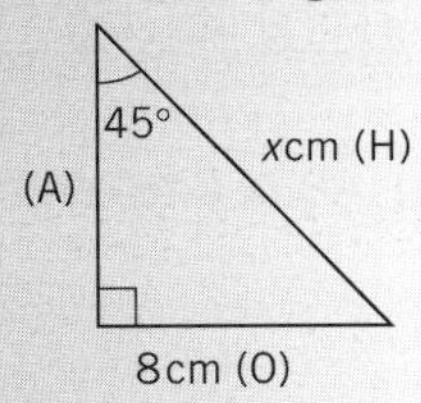

(b)

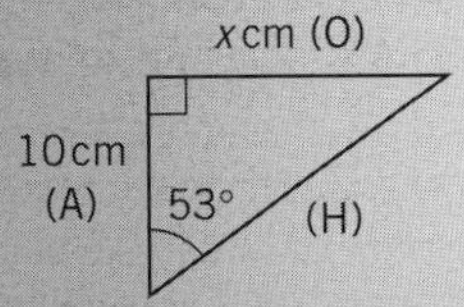

(a) $\sin = \frac{O}{H}$

$\sin 40° = \frac{x}{8}$

$x = 8\sin 40° = 8 \times 0{\cdot}6428 = 5{\cdot}14$ cm

> Make sure your calculator finds sin40°.

(b) $\tan = \frac{O}{A}$

$\frac{x}{10} = \tan 53°$

$x = 10 \times \tan 53°$

$= 10 \times 1{\cdot}327 = 13{\cdot}27$ cm

> It is important to write down the expression you are going to calculate, e.g. 10 × tan53°. It is not necessary to write 10 × 1·327 – read the result from your calculator directly.

(c) $\sin = \frac{O}{H}$

$\frac{8}{x} = \sin 45°$

$8 = x \times \sin 45°$

$x = \frac{8}{\sin 45°} = \frac{8}{0{\cdot}7071}$

$= 11{\cdot}31$ cm

- To calculate the size of an angle:
  as before, label the sides of the triangle 'opposite, 'adjacent' and 'hypotenuse' for the angle required, select the appropriate ratio and substitute the values of the sides.

Example

Calculate the size of the angle marked x in the following triangles

(a)

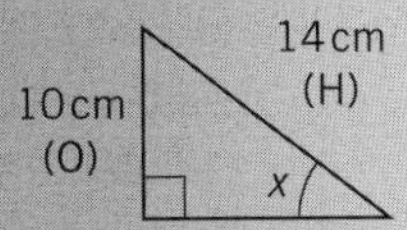

(b)

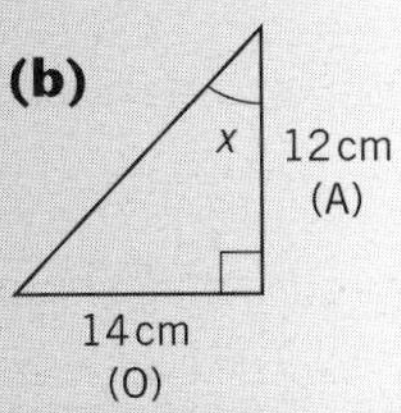

(a) $\sin x = \frac{O}{H} = \frac{10}{14} = 0{\cdot}7143$

$x = \sin^{-1} 0{\cdot}7143 = 45{\cdot}6°$

(b) $\tan x = \frac{O}{A} = \frac{14}{12} = 1{\cdot}1667$

$x = \tan^{-1} 1{\cdot}1667 = 49{\cdot}4°$

Now try these:

Find the length marked x in each of the following, giving your answer correct to 2 d.p.

9

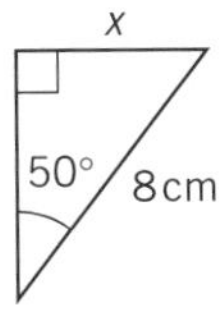

11

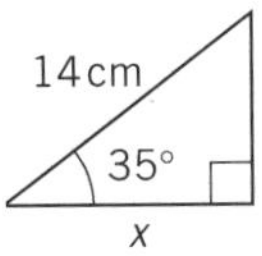

10

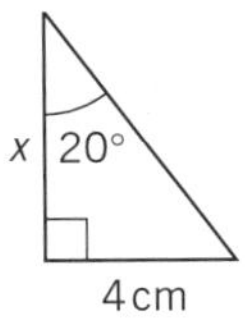

12

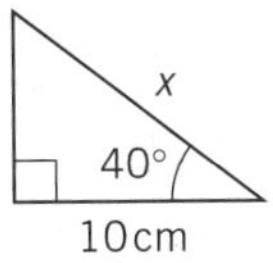

Find the size of the angle marked x in the following, giving your answer to the nearest degree.

13

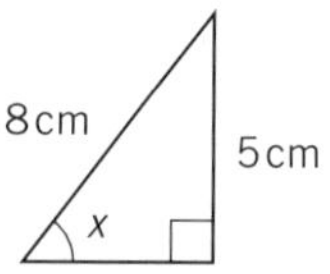

14

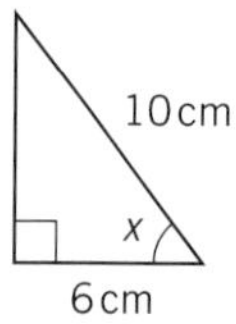

15

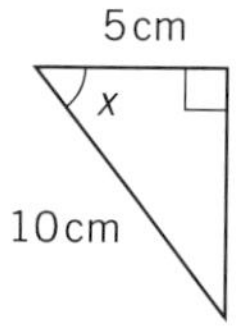

16

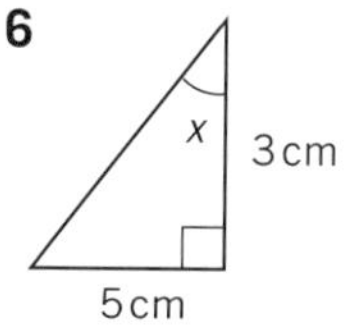

Here is an exam question ...and its solution

(a) AP is a telegraph pole.

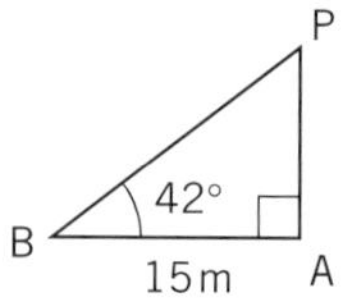

The angle of elevation of the top of the pole from a point B on the ground is 42°. Calculate the height of the pole.

(b) A slide in an open air swimming pool is built down the side of a bank. The slide is 8·5 m long and descends 2·6 m from the top to the water level.

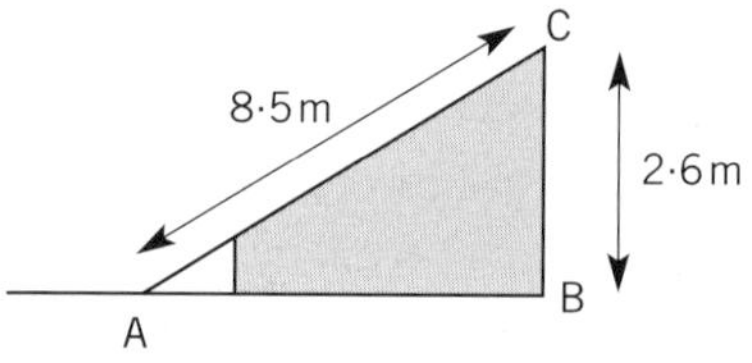

(i) Calculate the distance AB.
(ii) Calculate the angle that the slide makes with the horizontal, AB.

(a) 13·5 m

$\tan 42° = \frac{AP}{AB} = \frac{AP}{15}$

Therefore $AP = 15 \times \tan 42°$

$= 15 \times 0{\cdot}9004$

$AP = 13{\cdot}5$

(b) (i) 8.1 m

$AC^2 = AB^2 + BC^2$
$8{\cdot}5^2 = AB^2 + 2{\cdot}6^2$
$AB^2 = 8{\cdot}5^2 - 2{\cdot}6^2$
$= 65{\cdot}49$
$AB = 8{\cdot}1$

(ii) 17·8°

$\sin A = \frac{O}{H}$
$= \frac{2{\cdot}6}{8{\cdot}5}$
$= 0{\cdot}3059$

Therefore angle A = 17·8

Now try these exam questions:

1 (a) Find the length of the side marked x.

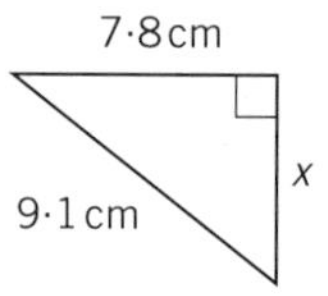

(b) Find the angle marked x.

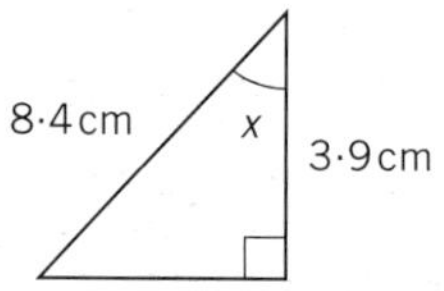

2 Calculate the lengths marked with letters.

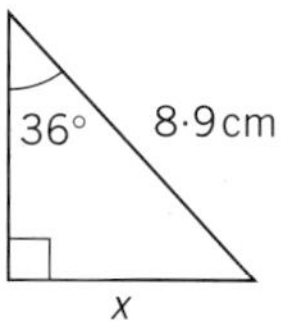

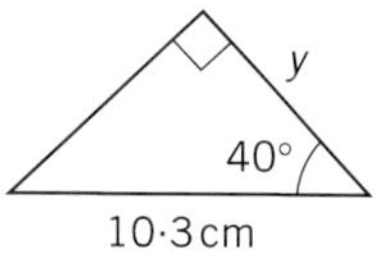

3 The drawing shows the side of a building. Calculate the length of the sloping roof.

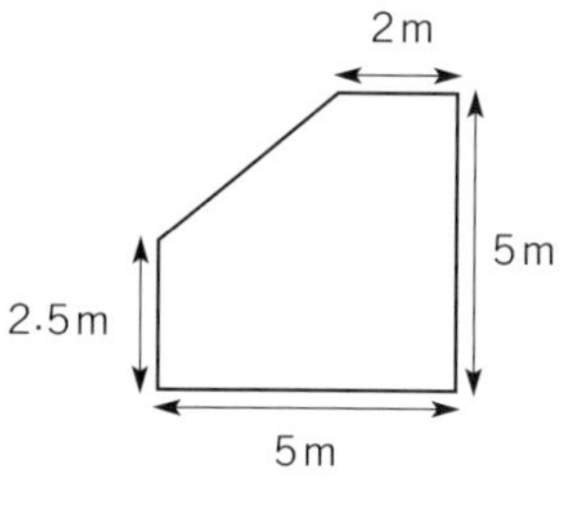

4 Calculate:
(a) the length of this ladder
(b) the angle between the ladder and the ground.

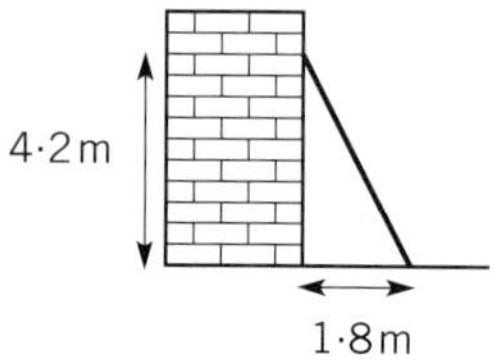

Properties of circles

Terms connected with circles

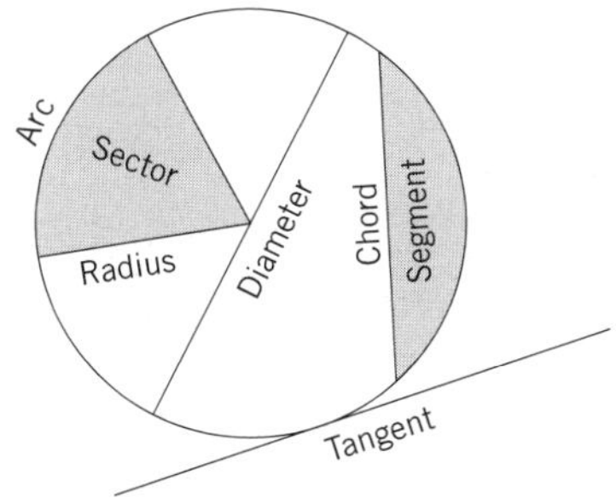

Remember to learn all these terms and what they mean.

Remember that the distance all the way round the circle is called the circumference.

Tangent properties of circles

- The tangent at any point on a circle is at right angles to the radius at that point.
- The two tangents from a point outside a circle, to the circle, are equal in length.

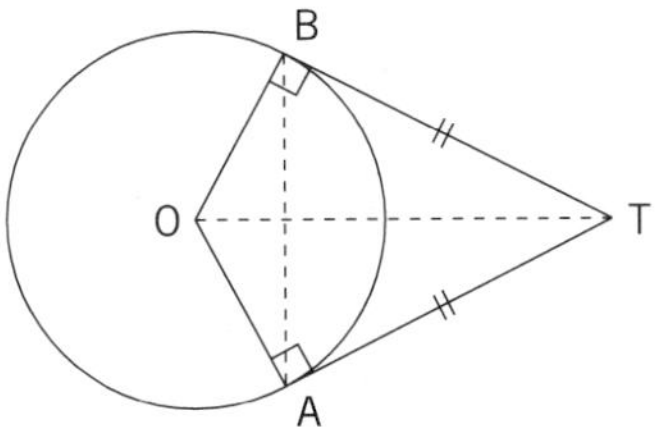

Figure A

So angle TAO = angle TBO = 90° and TA = TB

Example

In Figure A, TA = 9 cm and TO = 10 cm. Find the radius of the circle.

Since angle TOA = 90°, use Pythagoras.

$OA^2 + 9^2 = 10^2$

$OA = \sqrt{100 - 81} = 4{\cdot}36$ cm

Example

In Figure A, angle ATB = 50°. Find angle TAB.

Since TA = TB, triangle TAB is isosceles.

angle TAB $= \frac{1}{2}(180 - 50) = 65°$

Chord properties of circles

The perpendicular from the centre of a circle to a chord bisects the chord.

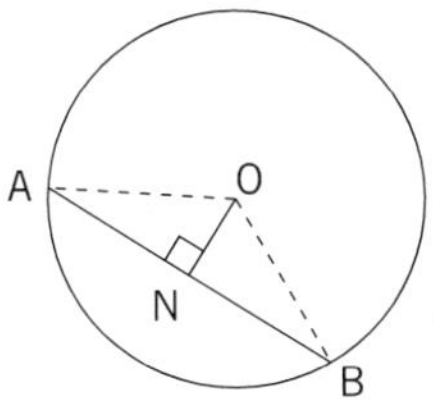

Figure B

So AN = BN.

The reason is that OA and OB are both radii, so triangle OAB is isosceles. Since ON is perpendicular to AB it is the line of symmetry for the triangle. Therefore AN = BN.

Example

In Figure B, angle AOB = 120° and the radius of the circle = 5 cm. Find AB.

angle BON $= \frac{1}{2}(120°) = 60°$

$\frac{BN}{OB} = \sin 60$. Therefore $BN = 5 \times \sin 60 = 4{\cdot}33$ cm.

Since AN = BN, $AB = 4{\cdot}33 \times 2 = 8{\cdot}66$ cm.

Now try these:

Questions 1 to 3 refer to Figure A.

1. TA = 15 cm and AO = 8 cm. Calculate the length of TO.
2. TA = 7 cm and angle ATB = 70°. Calculate the radius of the circle.
3. Angle OAB = 25°. Find angle ATB.
4. In Figure B, ON = 4 cm and OB = 6 cm. Calculate the length AB.
5. PQ and PR are tangents which touch a circle, centre O, at Q and R respectively. If angle PQR = 70°, find angle QRO.

Draw a diagram.

Angle properties of circles

- The angle subtended by an arc at the centre is twice the angle subtended at the circumference.

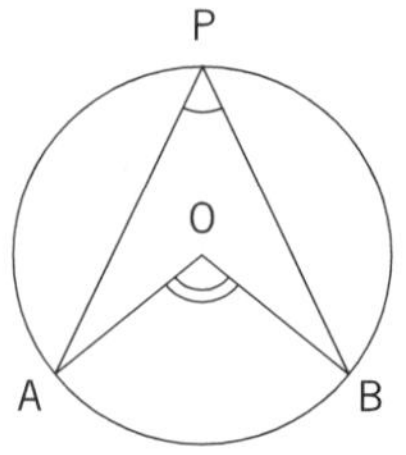

Figure C

angle AOB
= 2 × angle APB

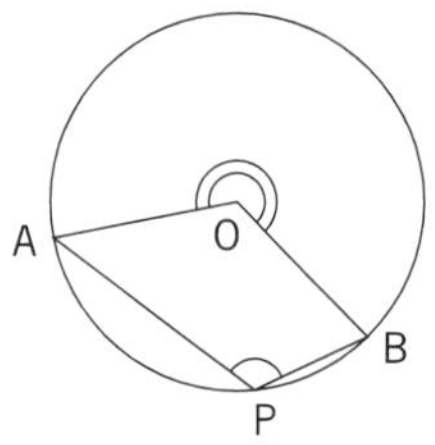

Figure D

reflex angle AOB
= 2 × angle APB

- The angle in a semi-circle is a right angle.

angle ACB = 90°

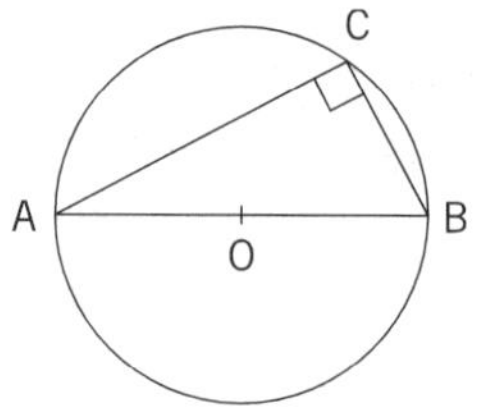

Figure E

Example

(a) In Figure C angle AOB = 68°.
Find angle APB.

(b) In Figure D angle APB = 115°.
Find **(i)** reflex angle AOB
(ii) angle AOB

(a) angle APB = $\frac{1}{2}$ angle AOB = $\frac{1}{2} \times 68 = 34°$

(b) (i) Reflex angle AOB = 2 × angle APB = 2 × 115 = 230°

(ii) angle AOB = 360 − 230 = 130°

Example

In Figure E angle CAO = 38° and O is the centre of the circle. AOBD is a straight line. Find angle CBD.

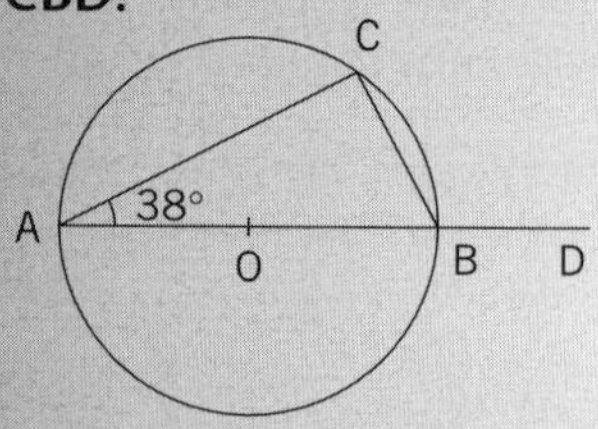

---

angle ACB = 90°.
∴ angle CBA = 180 − 38 − 90 = 52°
∴ angle CBD = 180 − 52 = 128°

- Angles in the same segment are equal.

angle ADB = angle ACB and
angle DAC = angle DBC

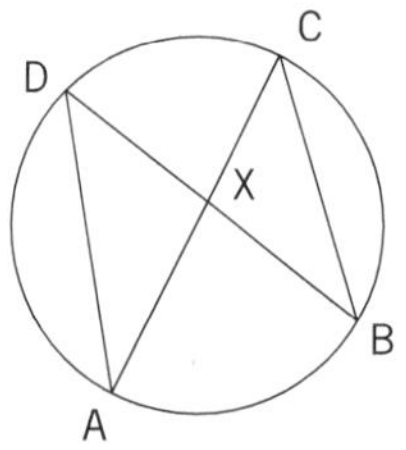

Figure F

Example

In Figure F if angle ACB = 35°, find angle ADB. Give your reasons.

---

angle ADB = 35° because angle ACB and angle ADB are angles in the same segment.

- Opposite angles of a cyclic quadrilateral add up to 180°.

angle ABC + angle CDA = 180°
angle BAD + angle BCD = 180°

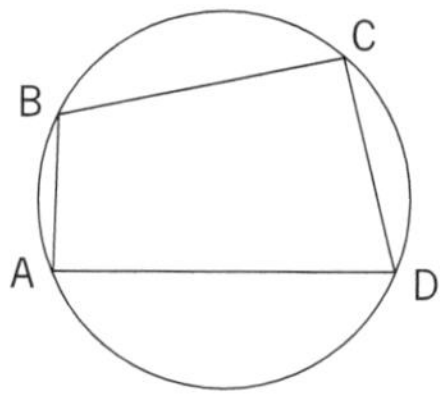

Figure G

Example

In Figure G, if angle BCD = 102°, find angle BAD. Give your reasons.

---

angle BAD = 180 − 102 = 78° because angle BCD and angle BAD are opposite angles of a cyclic quadrilateral.

Now try these:

6 Find **(a)** angle CAD **(b)** angle CBD

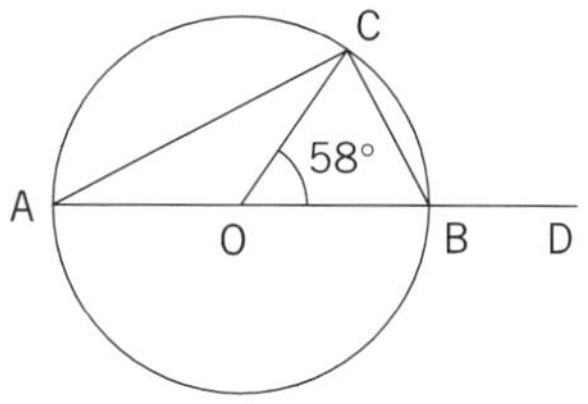

7 Find angle CDE, giving your reasons.

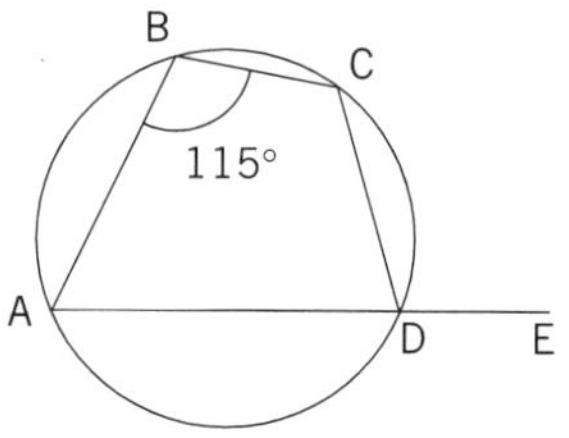

8 In Figure F, explain why triangle DXA is similar to triangle CXB. Give reasons for each of your statements.

9 Find angles a, b and c.

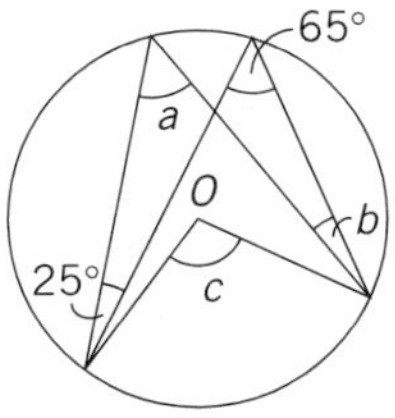

When giving reasons, use the standard phrases, e.g:
'angles in a semicircle'
'angles in the same segment'
'angles at centre = twice angle at circumference'
'opposite angles of a cyclic quadrilateral'.

Here is an exam question

In the diagram O is the centre of the circle and angle ATB is 50°. TA and TB are tangents.

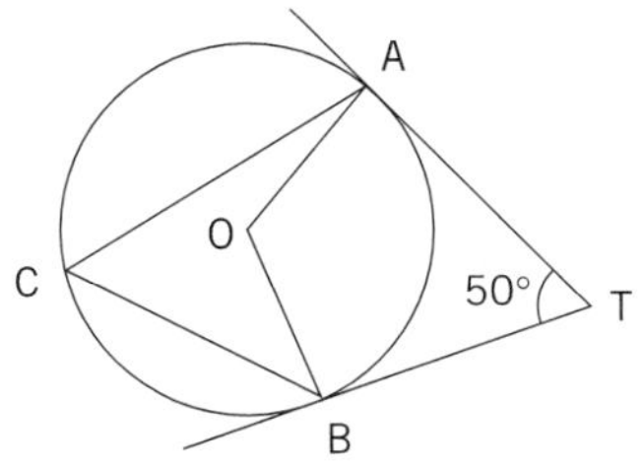

(a) Find angle AOB.
(b) Find angle ACB, giving a reason for your answer.

...and its solution

(a) 130°

angle OAT = angle OBT = 90°

angle AOB = 360 – 90 – 90 – 50 = 130°

(b) 65° (angle at centre = twice angle at circumference)

angle ACB $= \frac{1}{2}(130°)$ = 65°

Now try these exam questions:

1 The line AC is a diameter of the disc.
Angle A is 37°.

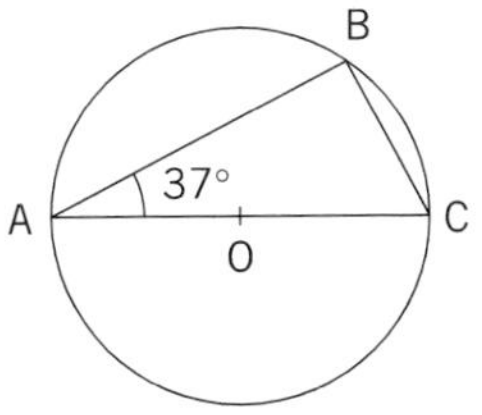

Find angle C. Give reasons for your answer.

2 A, B, C and D are points on a circle, centre O.
TA is a tangent to the circle.

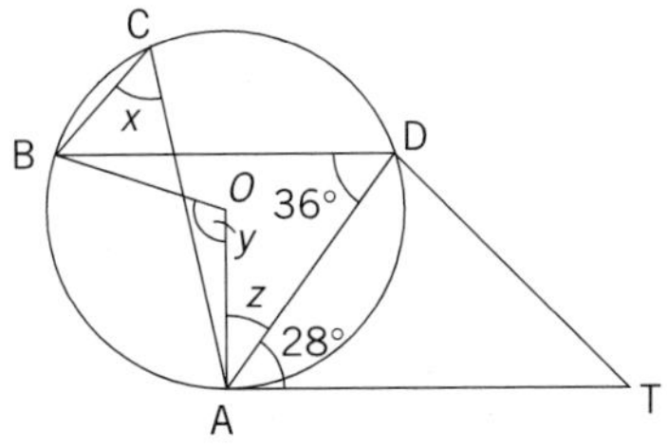

Find the size of each of the angles labelled x, y and z in the diagram. Write down the circle property you used to obtain your answer.

3 The diagram shows a circle, centre O.
The diameter AB is produced to T and TC is a tangent to the circle.

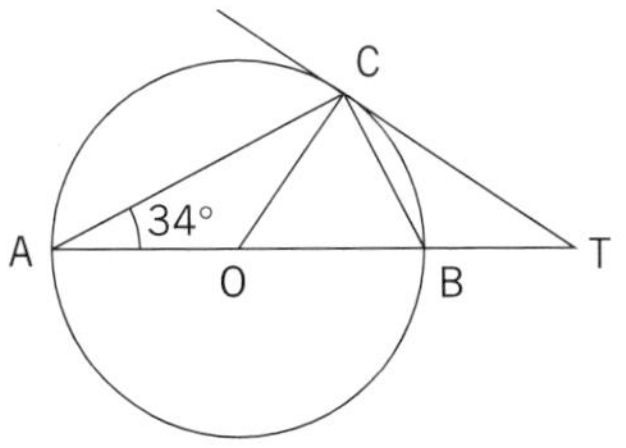

Calculate
(a) angle OCB **(b)** angle CBT **(c)** angle CTA

4 In the diagram, O is the centre of the circle, AD is a diameter and AB is a tangent.
angle ACE = $x°$

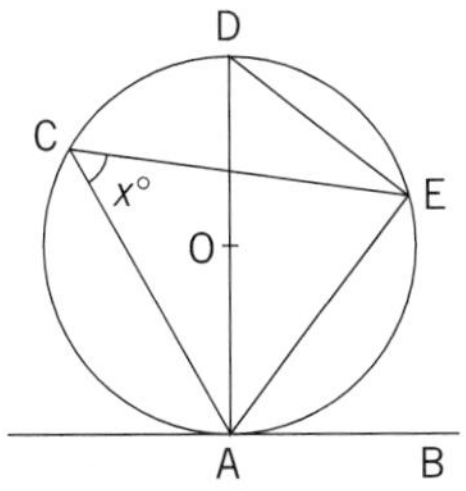

Find, in terms of x, the size of:
(a) angle ADE
(b) angle DAE
(c) angle EAB
(d) angle AOE

3D shapes

Plan and elevations

- The **plan view** is the view of a 3D object seen directly from above.
- The **front elevation** is the view seen directly from the front.
- The **side evelation** (two choices) is the view seen directly from one side.

Now try these:

1 Sketch the plan (P), front elevation (F) and side elevation (S) of each of these shapes.

(a)

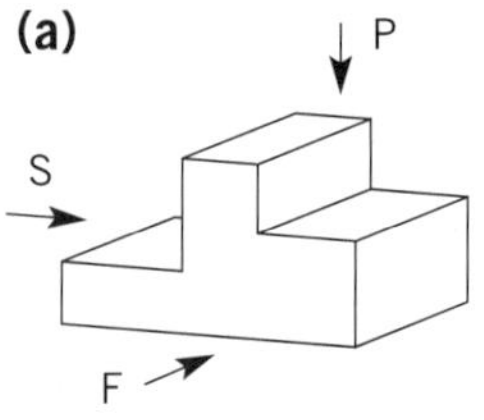

(b)

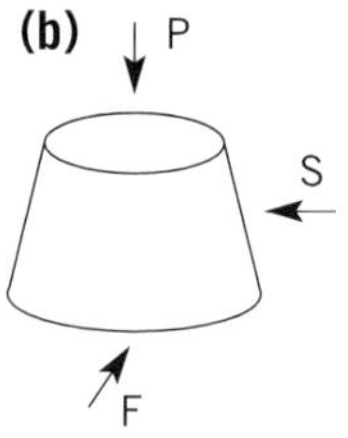

2 **(a)** Draw accurately the plan (P), the front elevation (F) and side elevation (S) of this shape.

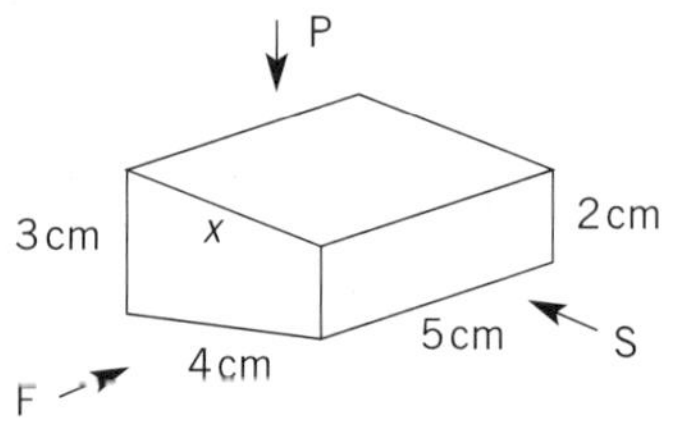

(b) Use your diagram to find the length marked x.

Example

Sketch the plan (P), the front elevation (F) and side elevations (S_1 and S_2) of this 3D shape.

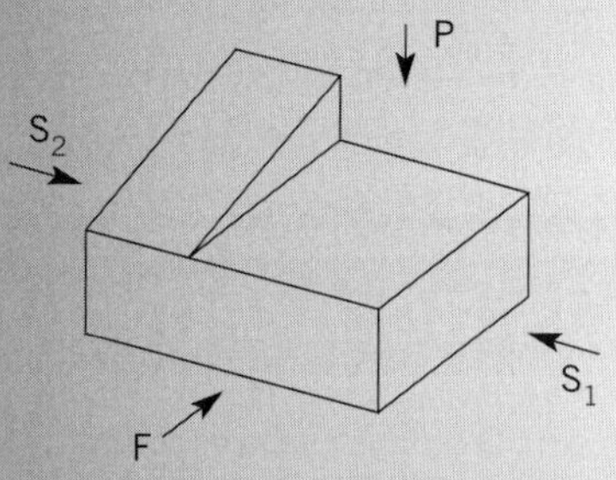

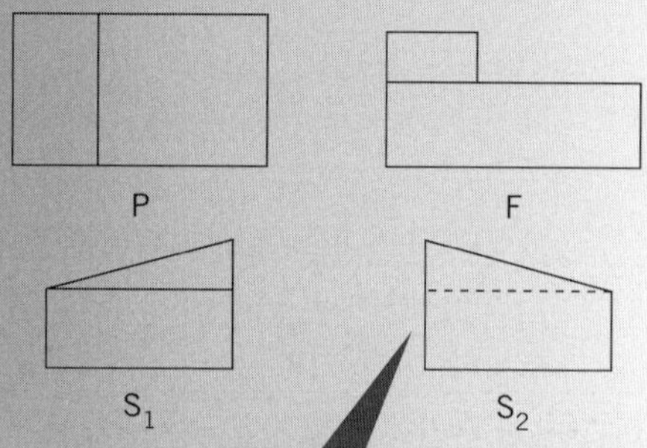

Remember that hidden edges are shown as dotted lines.

Prisms

- A **prism** is a 3D shape with a constant cross-section.
- Examples of prisms are:

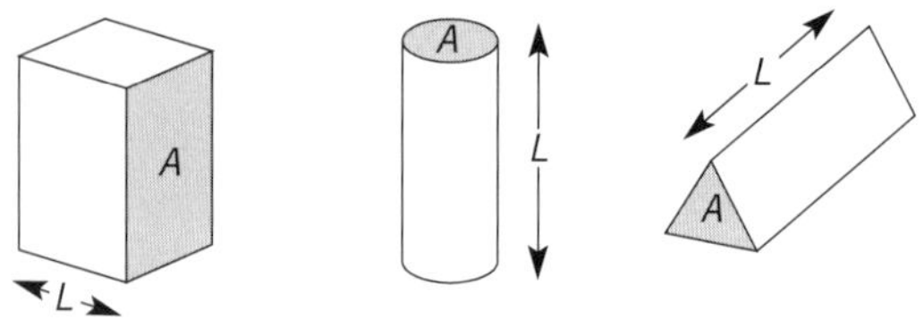

Cuboid   Cylinder   Triangular prism

- For all prisms:
  Volume = area of cross-section × length
  $V = A \times L$
- The surface area of a prism is the total area of all the surfaces of the prism.

Don't forget to include the units in your answer.

Example

Find the volume and surface area of this prism.

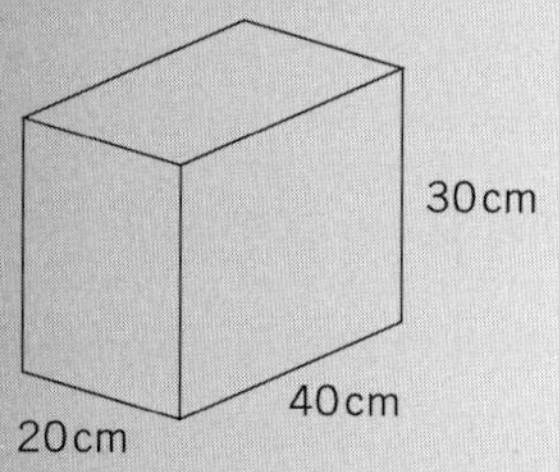

Volume = area of cross-section × length
$= (40 \times 30) \times 20$
$= 24\,000\ \text{cm}^3$

Surface area = 2 × top + 2 × side + 2 × front
$= 2(20 \times 30) + 2(30 \times 40) + 2(20 \times 40)$
$= 5200\ \text{cm}^2$

Now try these:

3 The volume of water in the tank is $2000\,cm^3$.
Find the depth of the water.

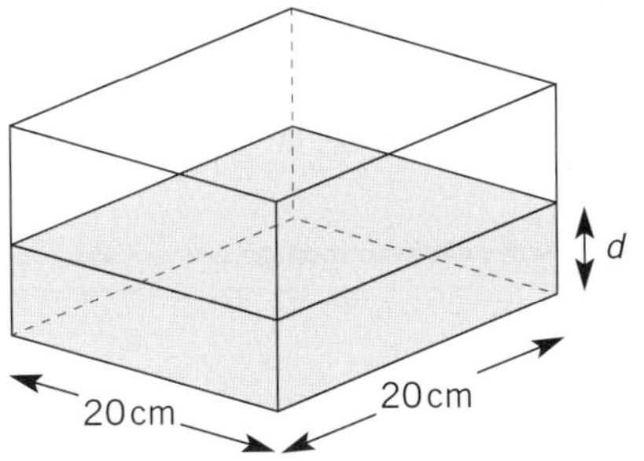

4 Find the volume of this bar of gold.

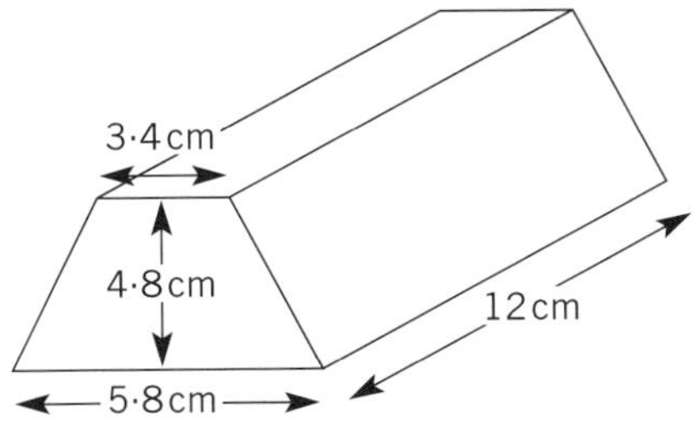

Example

The volume of this packet of sweets is $68\,cm^3$. Find its length.

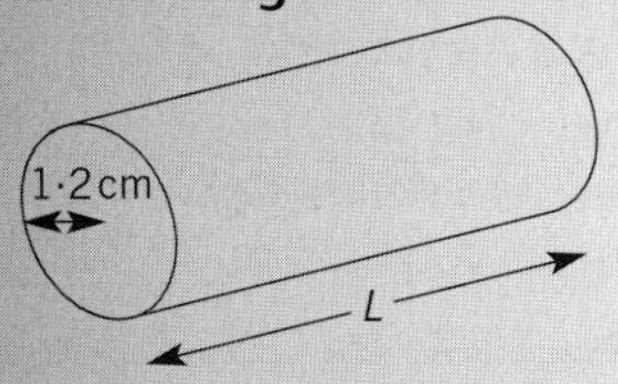

Volume = area of cross-section × length

$$68 = (\pi \times 1{\cdot}2^2) \times L$$

$$L = \frac{68}{\pi \times 1{\cdot}2^2} = 15\,cm$$

5 The volume of this cylinder is $50\,cm^3$.
Find the radius, r, of the circular end of the tube.

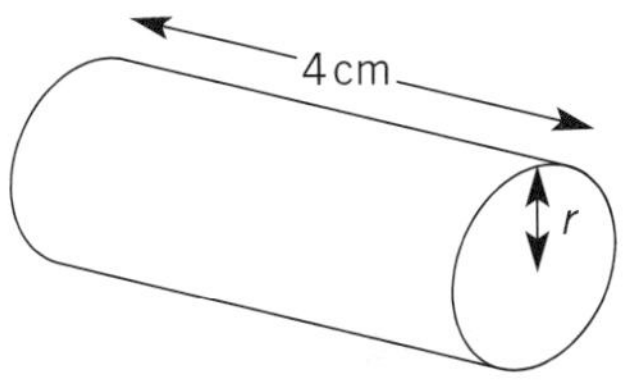

Here is an exam question ...and its solution

Find the volume of this green house.
The ends are semi-circles.

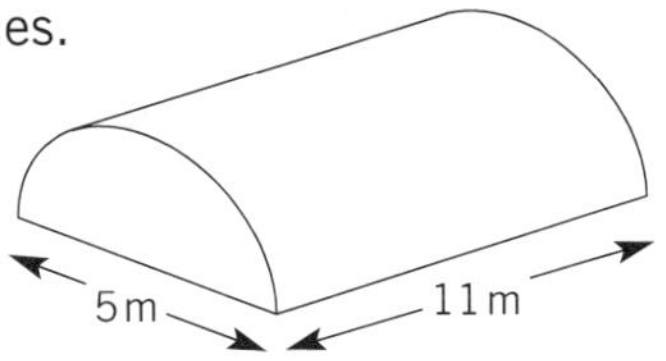

Volume = area of end × length

$$= \left(\frac{1}{2} \times \pi \times 2{\cdot}5^2\right) \times 11$$

$$= 108\,m^3$$

Now try these:

1 Sketch the plan (P) and the side elevation (S) of this shape.

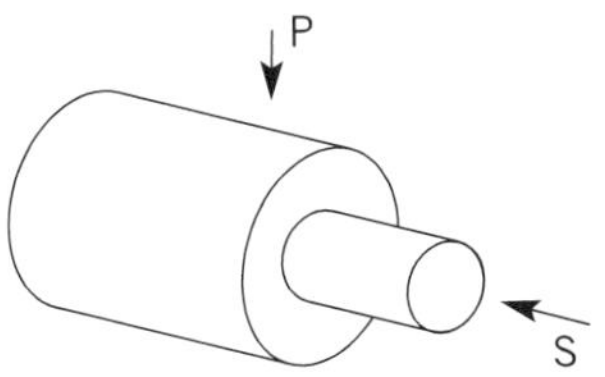

2 Find the volume of coffee in this cylindrical tin.

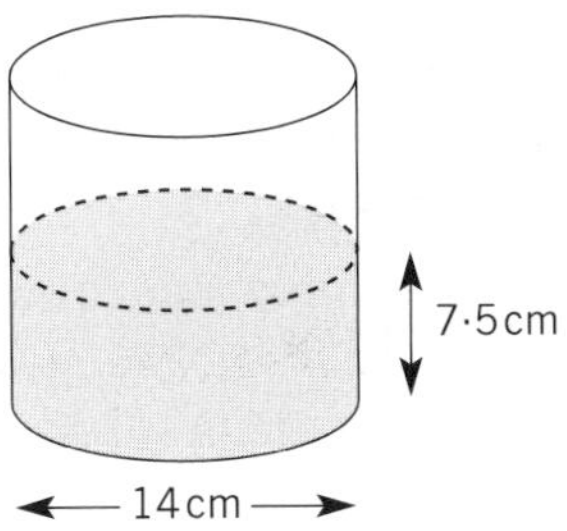

3 Find the volume of this trunk. The end face of the lid is a semi-circle.

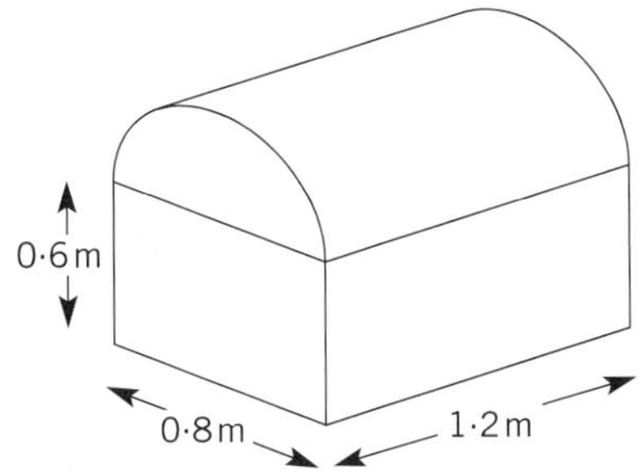

4 The volume of this triangular prism is $42\,cm^3$.
Find its surface area.

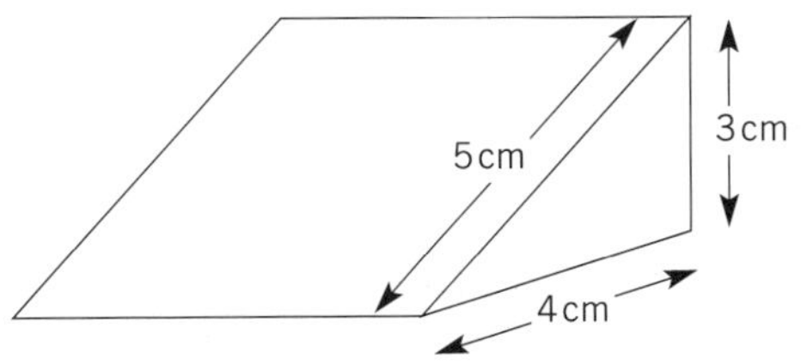

Transformations, coordinates and vectors

Transformations

- At GCSE, you meet four types of transformations: reflection, rotation, enlargement, translation.
- You may be asked to follow instructions and draw the result of a transformation or to describe a transformation which has taken place. When describing, give the type of transformation first, then the extra information required.

Reflection

- The image is the same shape and size as the object, but is reversed.
- Each point on the image is the same distance from the mirror line as the corresponding point on the object.
- When describing a reflection, state the mirror line.

Example

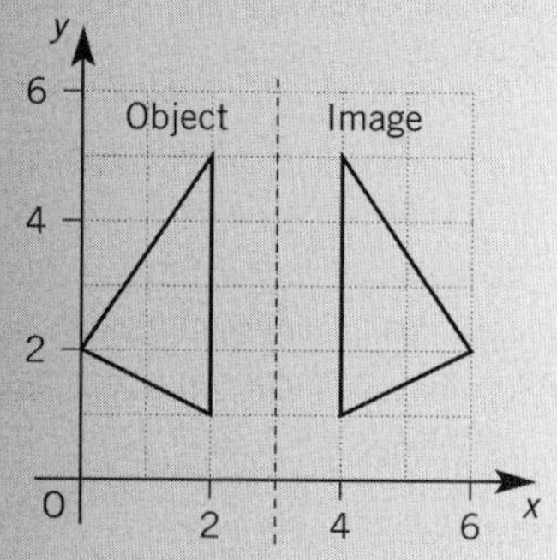

Here, the object has been reflected in the line $x = 3$.

Now try these:

1 Draw axes from $^{-}6$ to 6 for x and y. Plot and join (3, 1) (1, 1) and (1, 4) and label this triangle A.

(a) Reflect A in the x-axis and label the result B.

(b) Reflect A in the line $x = {}^{-}1$ and label the result C.

2 Triangle A has been transformed to triangle B. Describe this transformation.

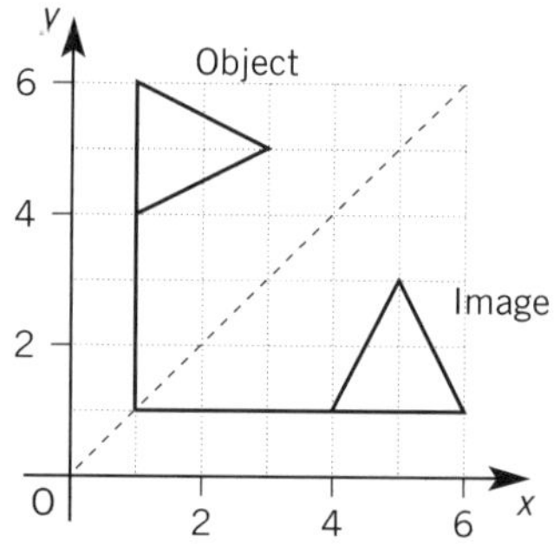

Rotation

- The image is the same shape and size as the object, but is turned round.
- Each point on the image is the same distance from the centre of rotation as the corresponding point on the object.
- To find a centre of rotation, tracing paper may often be used. If construction is required, draw the perpendicular bisectors of lines joining corresponding points. Where they meet is the centre of rotation.
- When describing a rotation, state
  - the centre of rotation
  - the angle
  - the direction – clockwise or anticlockwise.

Example

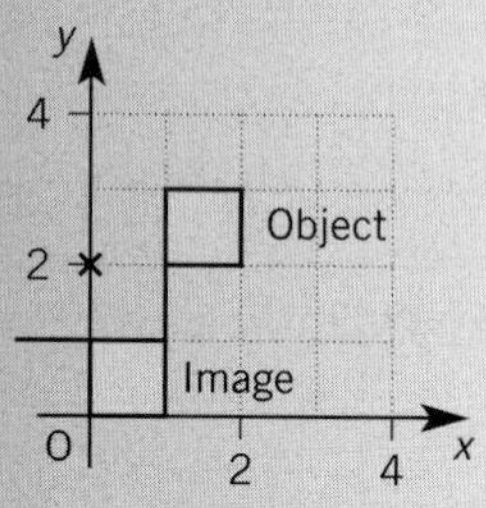

Here, the object has been rotated though 90° clockwise about centre (0, 2).

Now try these:

3 Draw axes from $^{-}6$ to 6 for x and y. Plot and join (3, 1) (1, 1) and (1, 4) and label this triangle A.

(a) Rotate A through 180° about (0, 0) and label the result B.

(b) Rotate A through 90° anticlockwise about (0, 1) and label the result C.

4 Describe this transformation.

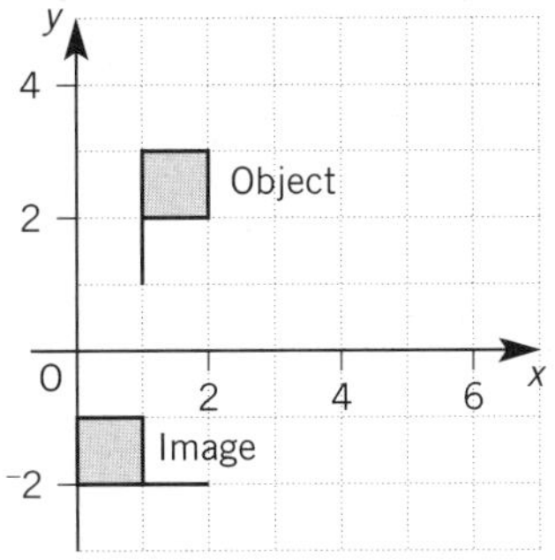

Enlargement

- The image is the same shape as the object but each length on the image is the corresponding length on the object multiplied by the scale factor. This is the only transformation you meet at GCSE where the object and image are not congruent.
- The distance of each point on the object from the centre of enlargement is multiplied by the scale factor to find the distance from the centre of the corresponding points on the image.
- To find the centre of enlargement, join corresponding points on the object and image and extend the lines until they meet.
- When describing an enlargement, state:
  - the centre of enlargement
  - the scale factor.

Example

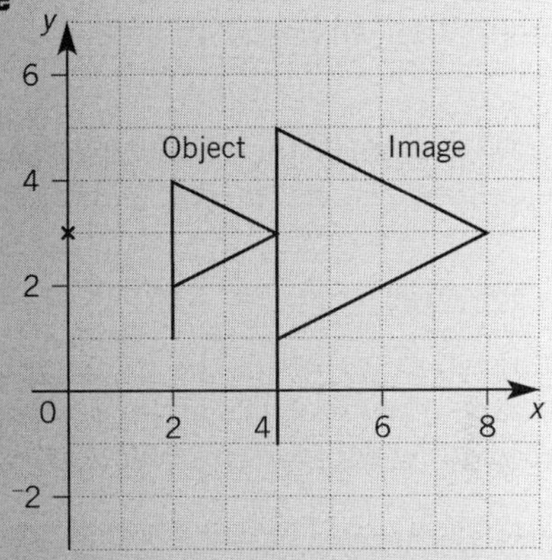

Here, the object has been enlarged with centre (0, 3) and scale factor 2.

Now try these:

5 Draw axes from 0 to 5 for x and y. Plot the points (3, 1) (3, 2) (3, 3) and (4, 2) and join them to form a flag, A.
Enlarge flag A with centre (1, 0) and scale factor $\frac{1}{2}$.
Label the image B.

6 Find the centre and scale factor of the enlargement below.

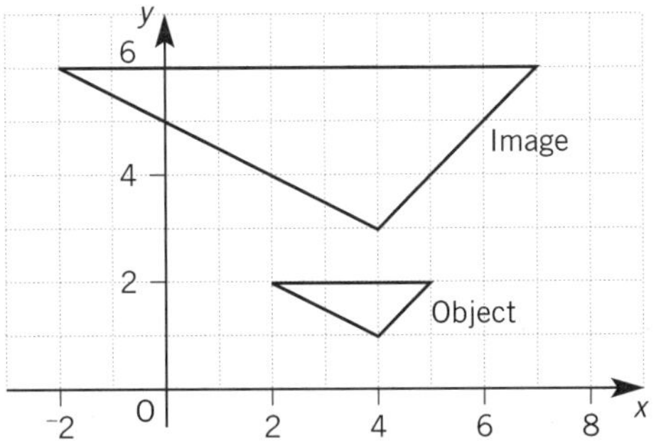

Translation

- Each point on the image has moved the same distance and direction from its corresponding point on the object.
- The image is the same shape and size as the object and is the same way up.
- When describing a translation, state the column vector, or how many units the object has moved in each direction.
  For example, translate by the column vector $\begin{pmatrix} ^{-}2 \\ 5 \end{pmatrix}$ means move 2 units across to the left and 5 units up.

Example

Here, the object has been translated by by $\begin{pmatrix} ^{-}2 \\ 5 \end{pmatrix}$

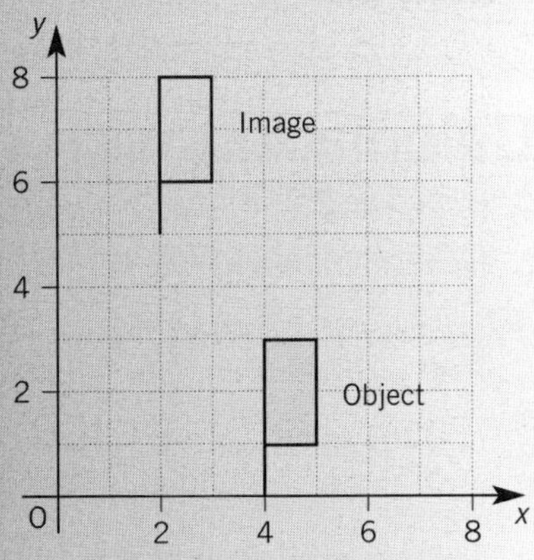

Now try these:

7 Draw axes from 0 to 5 for x and y. Plot the points (3, 1) (3, 2) (3, 3) and (4, 2) and join them to form flag A. Translate flag A by $\begin{pmatrix} 2 \\ ^-1 \end{pmatrix}$. Label the image B.

8 Look at the graph on the right. Describe the transformation that maps A onto B.

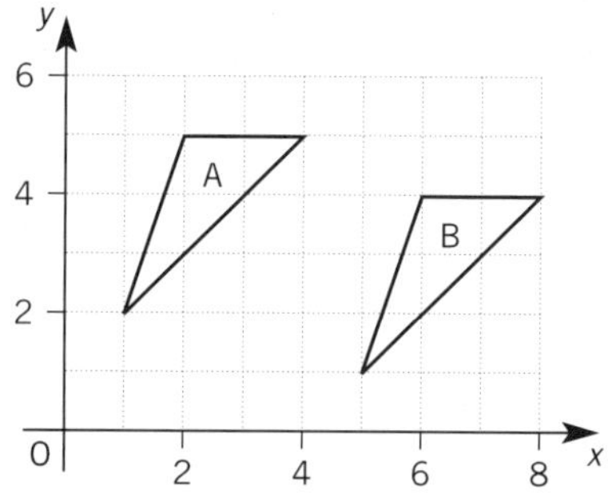

Combining transformations

- Two or more transformations may follow each other.
- You may be asked to describe a single transformation which would have the same effect as two transformations that you have done.

Take care that you label diagrams carefully and transform the shape you have been asked to and not another one!

Example

B is the image of A after reflection in the y-axis. C is the image of B after reflection in the x-axis. Describe the single transformation which maps A directly onto C.

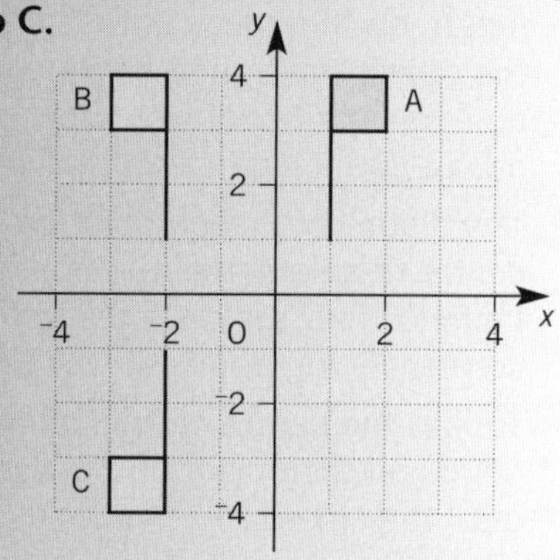

A rotation through 180° with centre (0, 0).

Now try these:

In each question, carry out the transformations on a simple shape of your choice, then describe the single transformation which is equivalent to the combination.

9 A translation of $\begin{pmatrix} 1 \\ 4 \end{pmatrix}$ followed by a translation of $\begin{pmatrix} 2 \\ ^-3 \end{pmatrix}$.

10 A reflection in the line $x = 3$ followed by a reflection in the line $y = 2$.

11 A reflection in the x-axis, followed by a rotation through 90° anticlockwise about (0, 0).

12 A rotation through 90° anticlockwise about (0, 0) followed by a reflection in the x-axis.

Coordinates

- On a flat surface (2D) we need two coordinates to describe the position of a point.
- In 2D, you may be asked to plot a point whose coordinates you are given, or to give the coordinates of a point which is plotted already.
- You may be asked to complete a diagram, for instance to complete a square and give the coordinates of the missing corner.
- To describe a position in 3D we would need to describe height too and would need three coordinates.
- On a line (1D) we would need just one coordinate.

Example

When A is (1, 5) and B is (7, 2),

the midpoint of AB is $\left(\frac{1+7}{2}, \frac{5+2}{2}\right) = (4, 3{\cdot}5)$

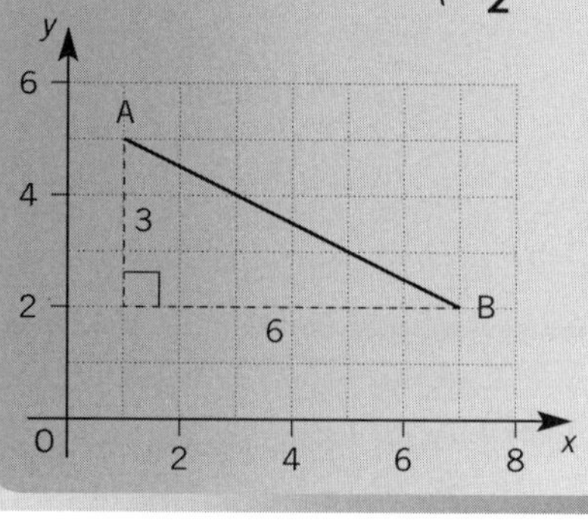

$$AB^2 = 6^2 + 3^2$$
$$= 45$$
$$AB = \sqrt{45}$$
$$= 6{\cdot}7 \text{ units to 1 d.p.}$$

Calculating with coordinates

- To find the midpoint of the line joining A and B, find the mean of their coordinates.
- To find the length AB use Pythagoras' theorem.

Now try these:

13 Find **(i)** the midpoint of AB and **(ii)** the length of AB when:
(a) A is (1, 2) and B is (8, 6)
(b) A is (⁻1, 2) and B is (8, ⁻6)
(c) A is (⁻3, ⁻4) and B is (5, 2).

14 Draw axes from ⁻5 to 5 for x and y. Plot the points A(1, 3) B(⁻4, 1) and C(⁻5, ⁻3). Join AB and BC. Mark point D so that ABCD is a parallelogram. Write down the coordinates of D.

Here is an exam question ...and its solution

Triangle T is rotated 90° clockwise about the point (0, 0). Its image is triangle S. Triangle S is reflected in the *y*-axis. Its image is triangle R.

(a) Draw triangle S and triangle R on the diagram. Label each triangle clearly.

(b) Describe a single transformation which maps R onto T.

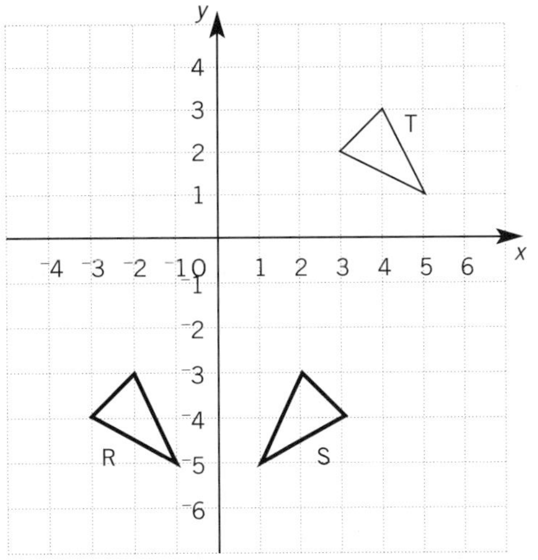

(a) Triangles S and R have been drawn on the diagram.

(b) A reflection in the line $y = {}^{-}x$.

Now try these exam questions:

1 **(a)** ABCD is a kite. Mark D on the diagram and write down its coordinates.

(b) Find the coordinates of the midpoint of AB.

(c) Calculate the length of BC, showing your working.

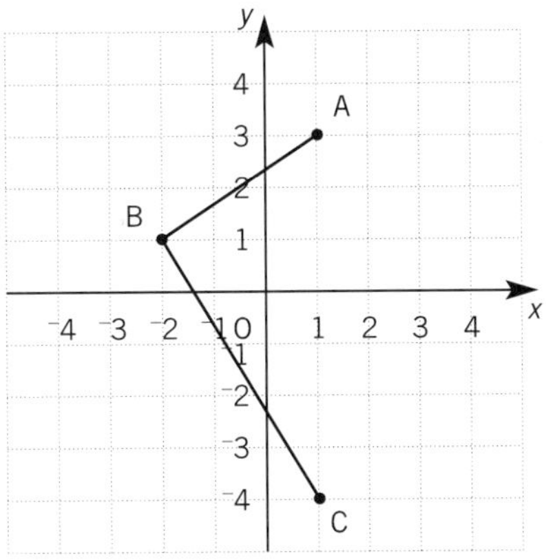

2 The diagram shows the shapes A and B and the line L.

(a) Shape B is an enlargement of shape A. For this enlargement, write down

(i) the scale factor

(ii) the coordinates of the centre of enlargement.

(b) Draw the image of shape B after a reflection in the line L. Label this shape C. Note that you will need *x* and *y*-axes from +7 to $^{-}7$.

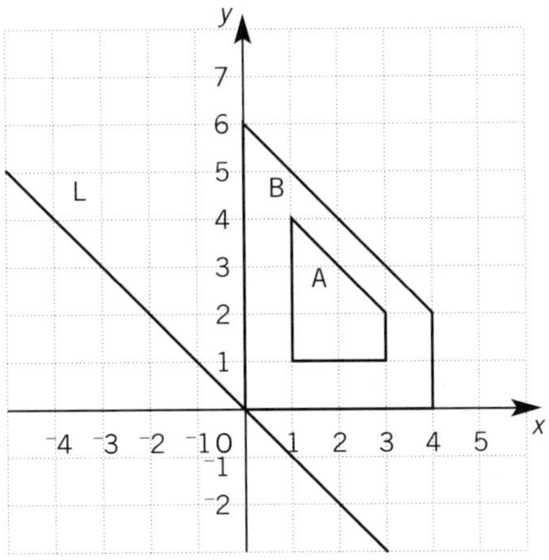

3 The diagram shows shapes A and B.

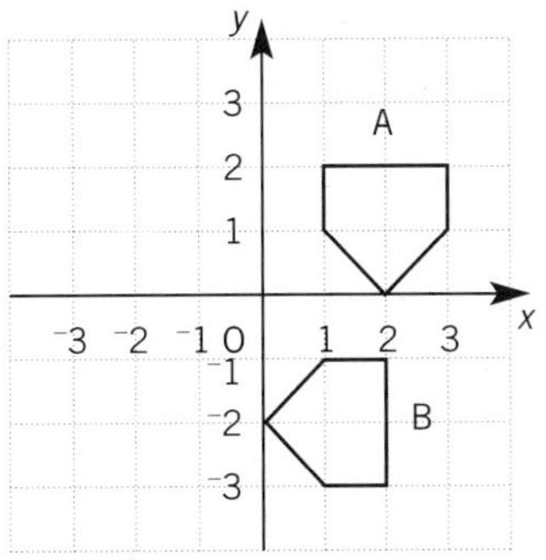

(a) Describe fully the single transformation that maps shape A onto shape B.

(b) Draw the image of shape A after a reflection in the *y*-axis. Label this shape C.

(c) Draw the shape A after an enlargement. Use (0, 0) as the centre and scale factor 3. Label this shape D. Note that you will need an *x*-axis from $^{-}5$ to 10 and a *y*-axis from $^{-}5$ to 8.

4 **(a)** For these quadrilaterals, describe fully the single transformation that maps Q onto R.

(b) Q is reflected in $x = 4$ and then in $y = 1$. Describe fully the single transformation that is equivalent to these two transformations.

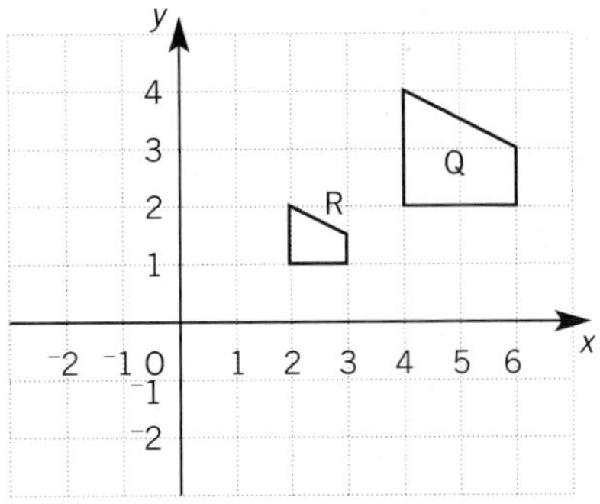

Measures

Bearings

- Three-figure bearings are measured clockwise from north and must have three figures. An angle of 27° would be written as a bearing of 027°.
- The bearing of B from A is the angle at A, clockwise from north to the line to B, the angle marked x in the diagram. The bearing of A from B is the angle marked y in the diagram.

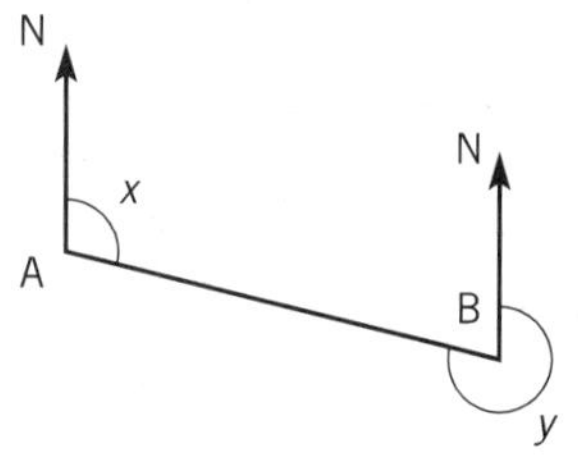

- A useful rule to remember is that the difference between the bearing of B from A and the bearing of A from B is 180°.

Example

Measure the bearings of A, B and C from O.

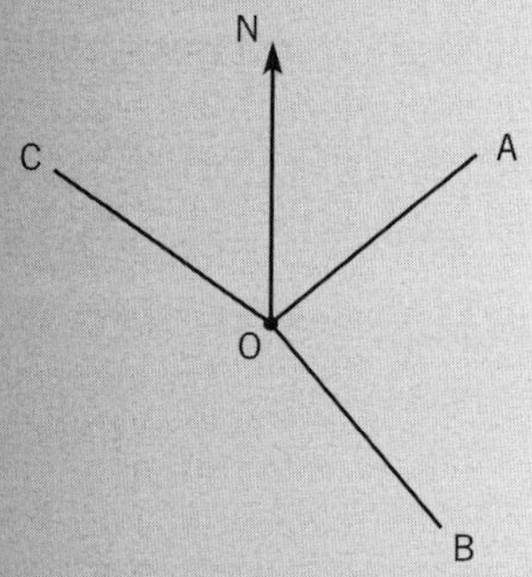

A 050° B 140° C 305°

Often questions are asked that involve drawing distances and bearings to find places. Accurate drawing is essential in these questions. It is also useful first to do a sketch.

Now try these:

1 Mark a point O. Draw a north line through O. Mark points A, B and C all 5 cm from O on these bearings from O: A 060°, B 135° C 295°.

2 The bearing of A from B is 127°. What is the bearing of B from A?

3 Anytown is 8 miles from Briston and on a bearing of 125° from Briston. Make a scale drawing showing Anytown and Briston. Use a scale of 1 cm to 1 mile.

Changing units

- You need to know how to change between the common metric units, including area and volume units.
- Here is a list.

Length	1 cm = 10 mm	1 m = 1000 mm
	1 m = 100 cm	1 km = 1000 m
Area	$1\text{ cm}^2 = 10^2\text{ mm}^2 = 100\text{ mm}^2$	
	$1\text{ m}^2 = 100^2\text{ cm}^2 = 10\,000\text{ cm}^2$	
Volume	$1\text{ cm}^3 = 10^3\text{ mm}^3 = 1000\text{ mm}^3$	
	$1\text{ m}^3 = 100^3\text{ cm}^3 = 1\,000\,000\text{ cm}^3$	
Mass	1 g = 1000 mg	1 kg = 1000 g
	1 tonne = 1000 kg	
Capacity	1 litre = 1000 ml	

Example

Change these units.

(a) **15 cm to mm**
(b) **105 m to cm**
(c) **1058 m to km**
(d) **10 500 cm^2 to m^2**
(e) **4·2 cm^3 to mm^3**
(f) **1·2 kg to g**
(g) **5 litres to ml**
(h) **6521 g to kg.**

(a) **150 mm (× by 10)**
(b) **10 500 cm (× by 100)**
(c) **1·058 km (÷ by 1000)**
(d) **1·05 m^2 (÷ by 10 000)**
(e) **4200 mm^3 (× by 1000)**
(f) **1200 g (× by 1000)**
(g) **5000 ml (× by 1000)**
(h) **6·521 kg (÷ by 1000)**

Now try these:

Change these units

4 40 mm to cm
5 150 cm to m
6 1·5 kg to g
7 500 mm^2 to cm^2
8 5 254 000 cm^3 to m^3
9 52 litres to ml
10 15·3 cm to mm
11 1465 g to kg
12 1340 ml to litres
13 75 mm to m

Bounds of measurement

- A length measured as 45 cm to the nearest centimetre lies between 44·5 and 45·5 cm. So the bounds are 44·5 and 45·5 cm.
- A mass measured as 1·38 kg correct to 3 s.f. has bounds 1·375 and 1·385 kg.
- The bounds are always a half unit down and up in the figure after the degree of accuracy.

Example

Give the bounds of these measurements. The accuracy of the measurements is given in brackets.

(a) 80 cm (10 cm)
(b) 8·6 cm (mm)
(c) 48 g (g)
(d) 10·5 seconds (tenth of a second)
(e) 5·23 litres (3 s.f.)

A very common error is to give the upper bound in (a) as 84·999 and in (b) as 8·6499 etc.

(a) 75 to 85 cm
(b) 8·55 to 8·65 cm
(c) 47·5 to 48·5 g
(d) 10·45 to 10·55 s
(e) 5·225 to 5·235 litres

Now try these:

14 Give the bounds of these measurements. The accuracy is given in brackets.
(a) 73 g (g)
(b) 140 m (10 m)
(c) 4·3 litre (0·1 litre)
(d) 47 cm (cm)

15 Jack won a race in 25·7 seconds. The time was measured to the nearest tenth of a second. Between what values must the time lie?

Here is an exam question

Simon went orienteering. This is a sketch he made of part of the course.

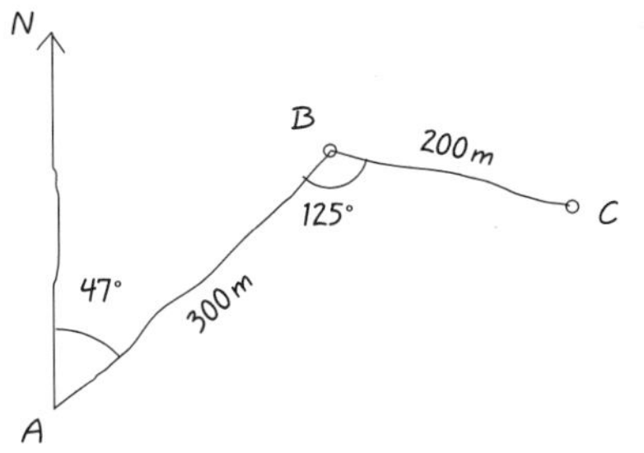

(a) Draw an accurate plan of this part of the course. Use a scale of 1 cm to 50 m.
(b) Use your drawing to find the bearing of C from A.

...and its solution

(a) Diagram shown half-size.

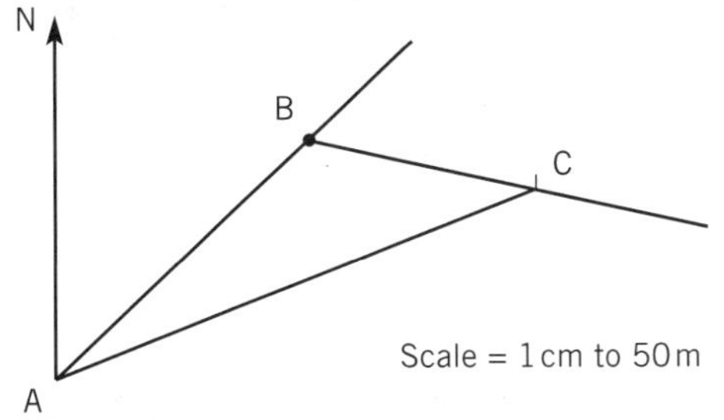

(b) 069°

Now try these exam questions:

1 A ship leaves port and travels on a bearing of 070° for 6 miles to A and then on a bearing of 120° for 4 miles to B.
(a) Make a scale drawing of the route of the ship with a scale of 1 cm to 1 mile.
(b) At B, how far and on what bearing is the ship from the port?

2 A rectangle has dimensions 3·54 m by 64 cm.
(a) Work out the area **(i)** in cm^2 **(ii)** in m^2.
(b) The dimensions were measured to the nearest cm. Write down the bounds between which the dimensions must lie.

3 P is 8 km from O on a bearing of 037° and Q is 7 km due east of O.
(a) Make a scale drawing showing O, P and Q, using a scale of 1 cm to 2 km.
(b) **(i)** Find the length of PQ
(ii) Find the bearing of P from Q.

4 A report says that 1·2 million packets of crisps are sold per hour in the UK. This figure is correct to 1 d.p. What are the bounds between which it must lie?

5 The bearing of Rugby from Coventry is 105° and the distance is 11 miles.
(a) What is the bearing of Coventry from Rugby?
(b) Draw a scale drawing of these places using a scale of 1 cm to 2 miles.

Constructions

Drawing triangles

You should be able to construct a triangle given:

- three sides

Example

Step 1: Draw line AB of given length.
Step 2: Use compasses to construct arcs AC and BC with the compasses set to the given lengths.
Step 3: Draw AC and BC.

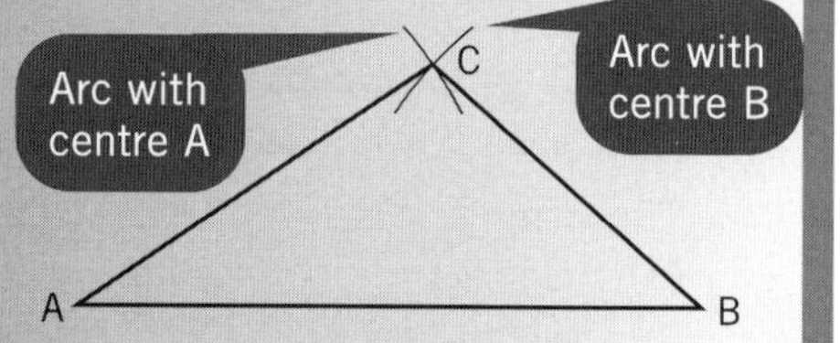

- two sides and the angle between them

Example

Step 1: Draw line AB of given length.
Step 2: Draw angle at A.
Step 3: Draw line AC of given length.
Step 4: Join C to B.

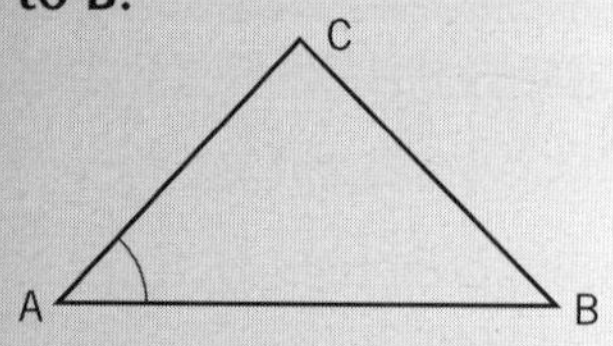

- two angles and one side

Example

Step 1: Draw line AB of given length.
Step 2: Draw angles at A and B.
Step 3: Draw lines AC and BC.

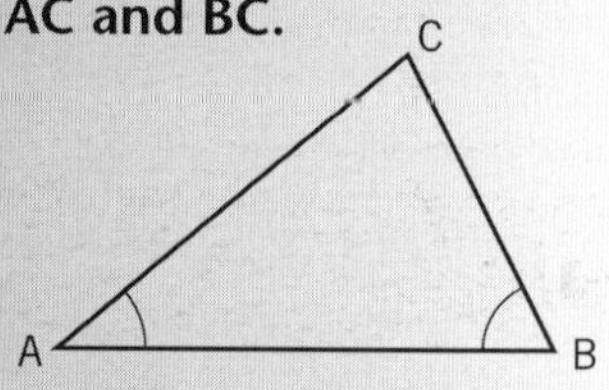

- two sides and an angle.

Example

Step 1: Draw line AB of given length.
Step 2: Draw angle at A.
Step 3: Draw line from A towards C.
Step 4: To fix C, draw an arc at B, the radius of the arc being the second given length.

This construction may give two possible triangles, ABC or ABC '.

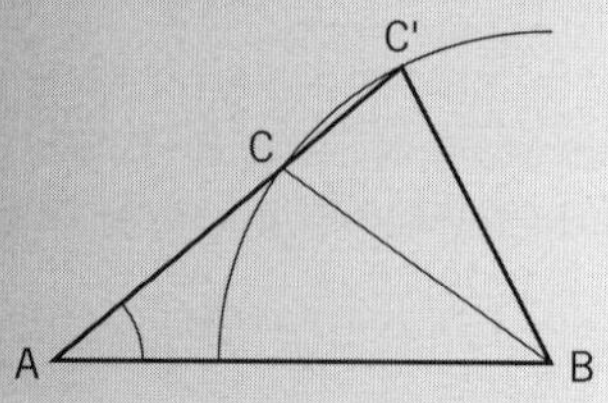

Now try these:

Draw these triangles accurately.
For each triangle measure the length of the unmarked side and the size of the unknown angles.

1

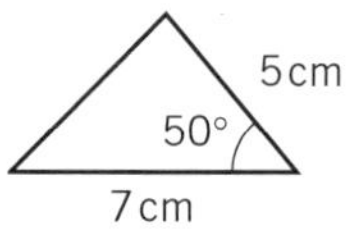

2

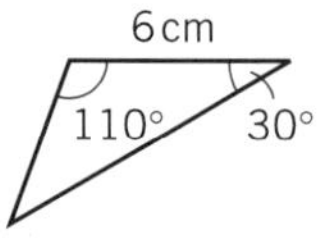

3

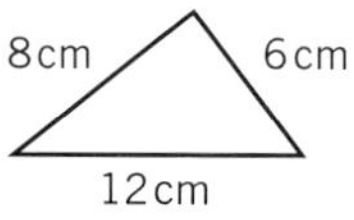

4

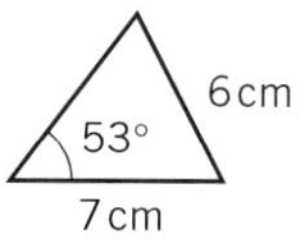

Angle constructions

You also need to construct, using ruler and compasses:

- perpendicular bisector of a line
- bisector of an angle.

Now try these:

5 Draw this triangle accurately. PX is the perpendicular bisector of line AB. AZ is the bisector of the angle at A and crosses PX at Z. Draw these lines accurately and measure the distance AZ.

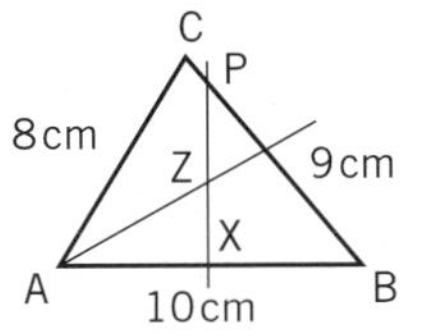

6 Draw, using ruler and compasses only, an equilateral triangle, ABC, of side 10 cm. Bisect two of the angles as shown, making an isosceles triangle, BXC. Measure the two equal sides, BX and CX, of this isosceles triangle.

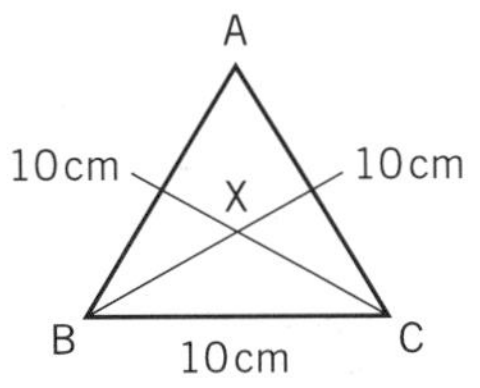

Example

AB is the given line.
At centres A and B draw arcs of the same radius, as shown.
Join the intersections of the arcs. This line is the perpendicular bisector of line *AB*.

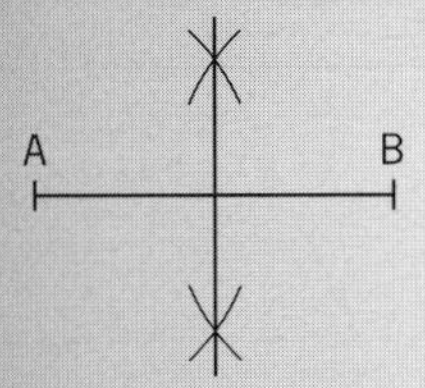

Example

AB and AC are the two lines making the given angle.
At centre A draw arcs of the same radius at B and C as shown.
At centres B and C draw two more arcs of the same radius,
Join the point where these arcs intersect to A. This line is the bisector of angle A.

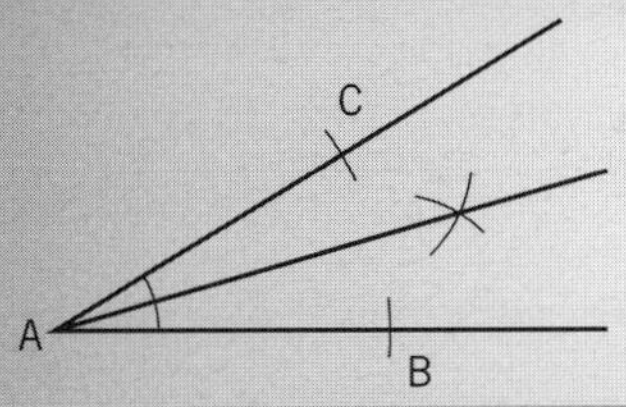

Here is an exam question

Two buoys are anchored at A and B.
A boat is anchored at C.

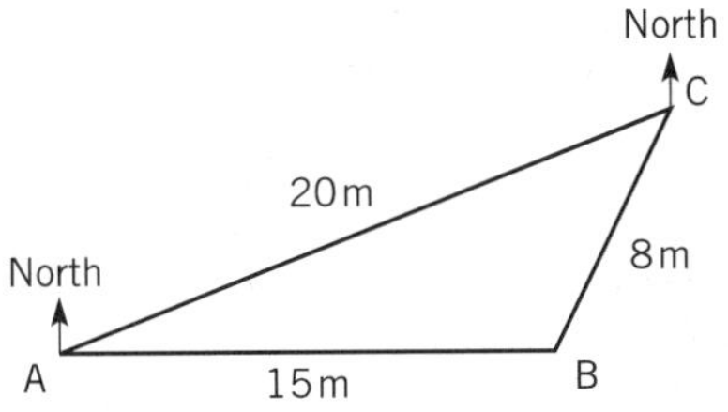

Using a scale of 1 cm to 2 m draw the triangle ABC and measure the bearing of the boat, C, from buoy A.

...and its solution

This is a standard construction as shown above:

Draw line AB, 7·5 cm long. Using compasses measure an arc 10 cm long from A and 4 cm long from B.
Mark the point C where the arcs cross.

Using a protractor measure angle CAB and subtract the measurement from 90°. The bearing should be between 69° and 70°.

Now try these exam questions:

1 The diagram shows a triangle ABC. The bisector of the angle at A meets line BC at X.
Construct the triangle and measure the distance AX.

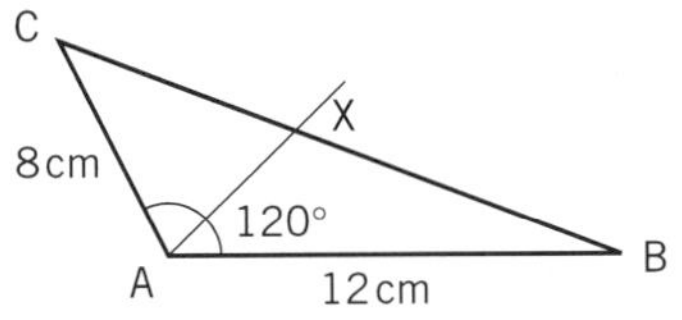

2 ABC is an equilateral triangle of side 10 cm. MX is the perpendicular bisector of side AB, MY the perpendicular bisector of side BC and MZ the perpendicular bisector of side AC.
Draw the triangle and measure the distance MZ.

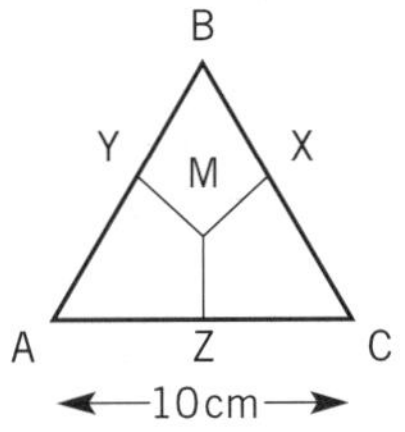

Mensuration

Area formulae and circumference of a circle

These formulae should be learned:

- Rectangle

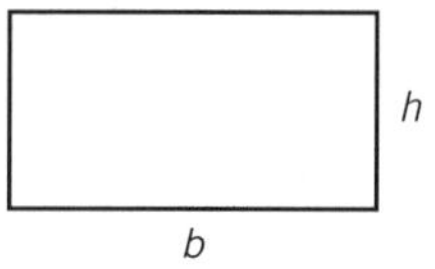

$A = b \times h$

- Triangle

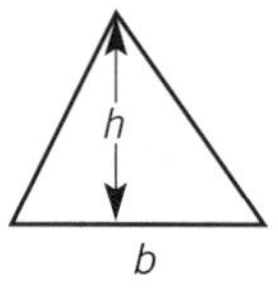

$A = \dfrac{b \times h}{2}$

- Parallelogram

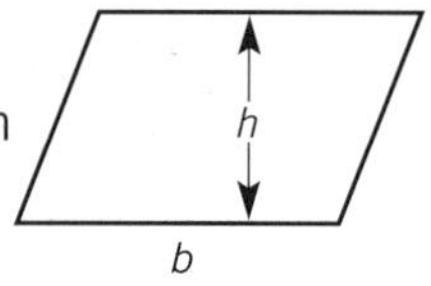

$A = b \times h$

- Trapezium

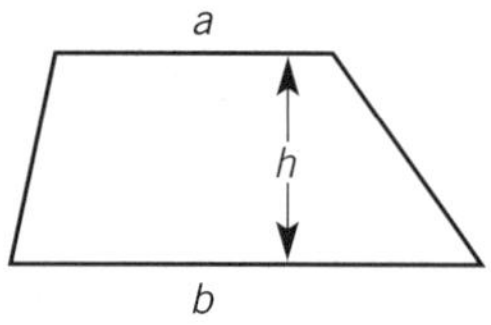

$A = \dfrac{h}{2}(a + b)$

- Circle

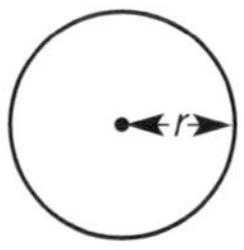

$A = \pi \times r^2$

- The circumference is just another name for the perimeter of the circle.

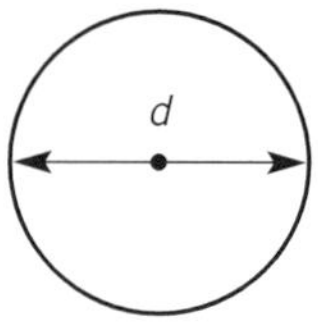

$C = \pi \times d$

Example

The corners of a triangle are (2, 1), (2, $^{-}3$) and (14, $^{-}3$). Find its area.

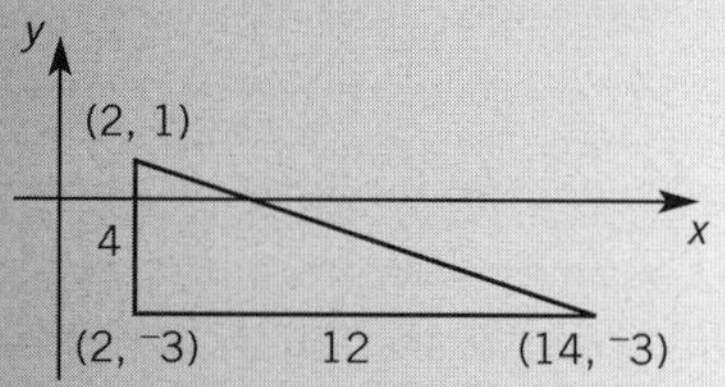

$A = \dfrac{12 \times 4}{2} = 24\,\text{cm}^2$

Example

Find the area and perimeter of this shape.

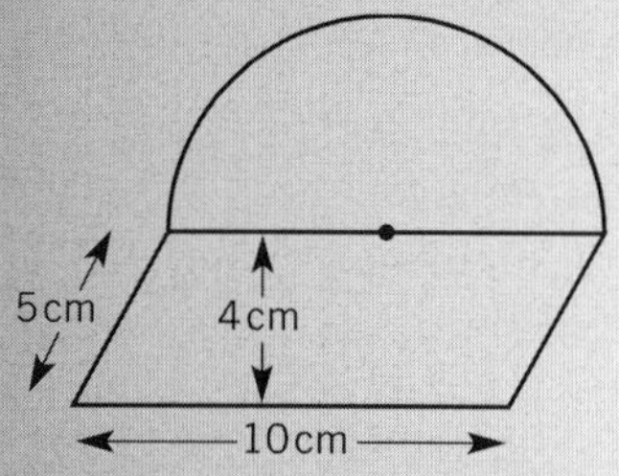

$A = \frac{1}{2} \times \pi \times 5^2 + 10 \times 4$
$= 39{\cdot}3 + 40$
$= 79{\cdot}3\ \text{cm}^2$

$P = 5 + 10 + 5 + \frac{1}{2} \times \pi \times 10$
$= 35{\cdot}7\ \text{cm}$

Example

A circular pond has an area of 40 m^2. Find the radius of the pond.

$A = \pi \times r^2$
$40 = \pi \times r^2$
$\dfrac{40}{\pi} = r^2$
$r = \sqrt{\dfrac{40}{\pi}}$
$r = 3{\cdot}57\ \text{cm}$

Now try these:

1 Find the area of this shape.

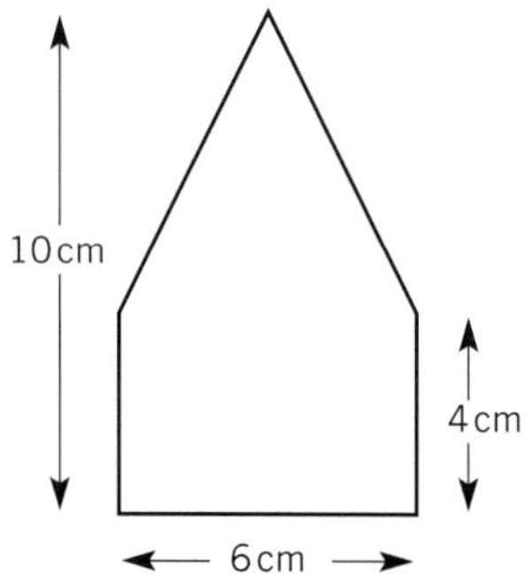

2 A semi-circular rug has a radius of 0·7 m. Calculate the area of the rug.

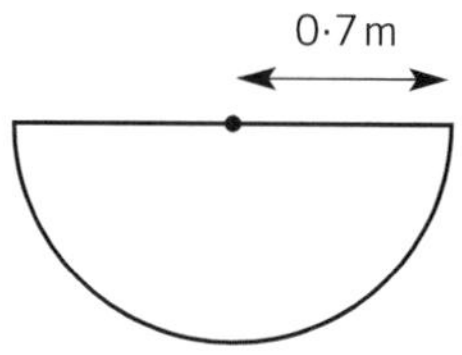

3 A circular path has an internal radius of 8 m and an external radius of 12 m. Find the area of the path.

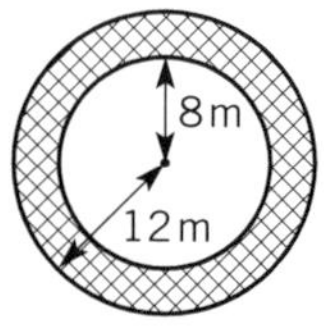

Dimensions

Length is 1 dimension.
Area (length × length) is 2 dimensions.
Volume (length × length × length) is 3 dimensions.

Now try these:

4 State whether these are lengths, areas, volumes or none of these (x, y and z are lengths).

(a) $\pi x^2 + 2\pi xz$

(b) $x^2(y^2 + z^2)$

(c) $\frac{1}{3}\pi x^2 y$

Example

***p*, *q* and *r* are lengths. Use dimensions to state whether the following represents lengths, areas or volumes.**

(a) pqr **(b)** $2\pi r^2$ **(c)** $\pi(p + q)$

(a) is a volume.
(b) is an area (π is a number).
(c) is a length (π is a number and length + length = length).

Here is an exam question ...and its solution

A heart shape is made from a square and two semi-circles. Find the area and perimeter of the heart shape.

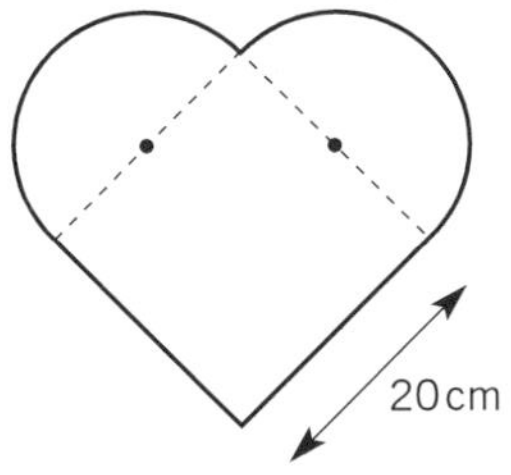

$A = 714{\cdot}2\,\text{cm}^2$	$2(\frac{1}{2} \times \pi \times 10^2) + (20 \times 20)$ $= 714{\cdot}2$
$P = 102.8\,\text{cm}$	$2(\frac{1}{2} \times \pi \times 20) + 20 + 20$ $= 102{\cdot}8$

Now try these exam questions:

1 Find the total area of this shape.

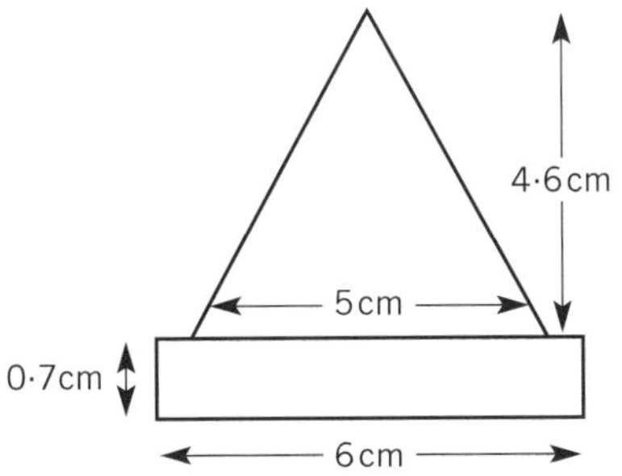

2 The Earth is a sphere. It has a circumference of 40 200 km. Work out the radius of the Earth.

3 Work out the area of the lawn in this diagram.

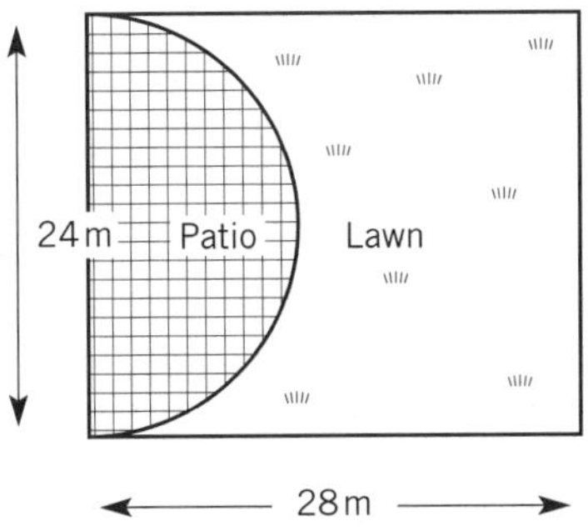

4 A rectangular garden contains eight identical triangular flower beds. The rest of the garden is paths. Work out the total area of the paths.

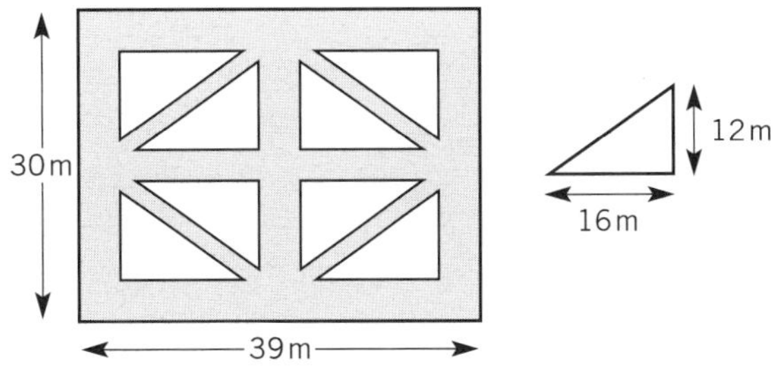

5 r, a and b are all lengths. Which of the following expressions could be a volume?

(a) $\frac{ar}{2}(4b + \pi r)$

(b) $2(ab)^2 + \pi r^2 b$

(c) $4a^2b + rb^3$

(d) $2abr + \frac{\pi ar^2}{2}$

Loci

Basic loci

- A locus is a path or region where a point can move according to a rule.
- The locus of a point which moves so it is 3 cm from a fixed point *A* is a circle, centre *A*, radius 3 cm.

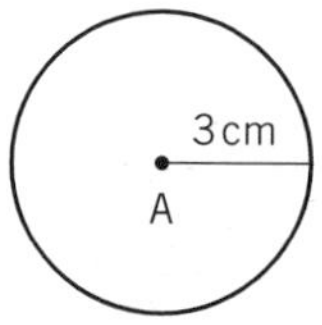

- The locus of a point which moves so it is less than 3 cm from a fixed point *A* is the region inside a circle, centre *A*, radius 3 cm.

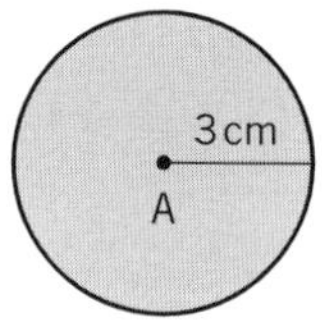

- The locus of a point which moves so it is more than 3 cm from a fixed point *A* is the region outside a circle, centre *A*, radius 3 cm.

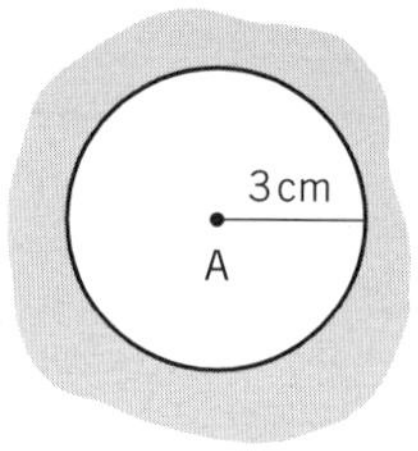

Example

A goat is tethered by a 2 m rope to a rail 3 m long fixed in a field of grass. Draw a scale diagram to show the region of grass which the goat can eat.

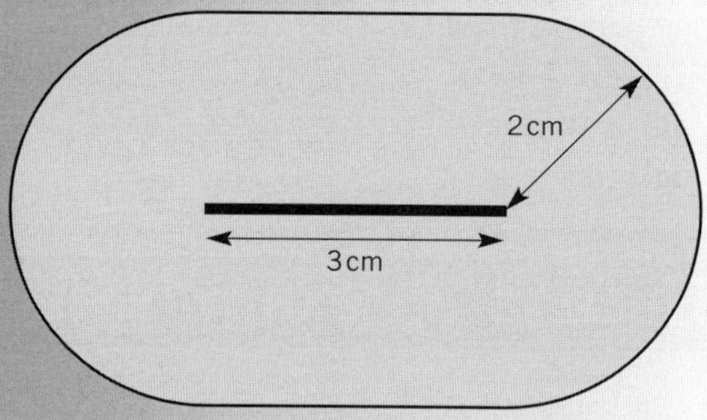

Scale: 1 cm to 1 m

- The locus of a point which stays 2 cm from a fixed straight line is one of a pair of lines parallel to that line.

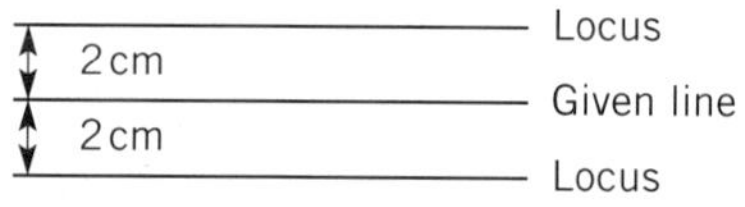

- The locus of a point which stays an equal distance from two fixed points is the perpendicular bisector of the line joining the two points.

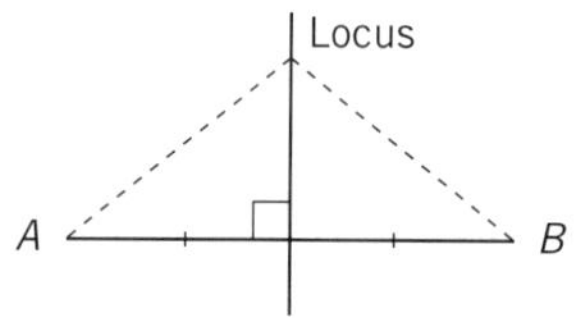

- The locus of a point which stays an equal distance from two fixed lines is one or both of the angle bisectors of the lines.

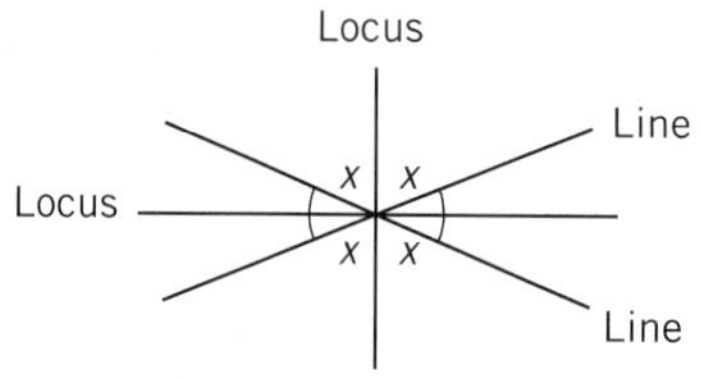

Now try these:

Draw accurately the locus for each of the following.

1 A point moves so it is 4 cm from a fixed point P.

2 A and B are fixed points 6·5 cm apart.
 (a) Draw the locus of points which are equidistant from A and B.
 (b) Shade the locus of points which are nearer A than B.

3 Two sides of a field meet at an angle of 70°. A footpath starts from this corner of the field and goes across the field keeping the same distance from each side of the field. Draw the footpath.

4 A stretch of coast has the shoreline running south-east to north-west. A boat moves keeping 500 m from this shore. Draw a scale diagram to show its path.

Problems involving intersecting loci

Often, exam questions involve more than one locus. Solve these questions in stages, drawing one locus at a time.

If the question does not tell you which to shade, you may shade the required region or those not required. Shading those not required is often easier if there are several loci. Remember to give a key or label the diagram to make it clear which you have done.

Here is an exam question

This is the plan of a garden drawn on a scale of 1 cm to 2 m. A pond is to be dug in the garden.

It must be at least 4 m from the tree. It must be at least 3 m from the house.

Shade the region where the pond could be dug.

Show all your construction lines.

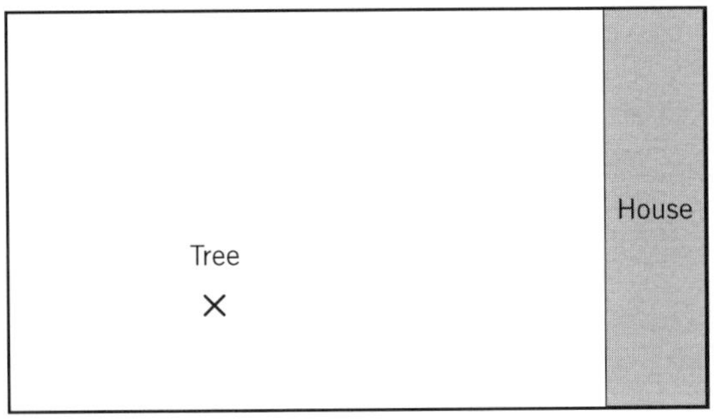

...and its solution

Scale 1 cm to 2 m

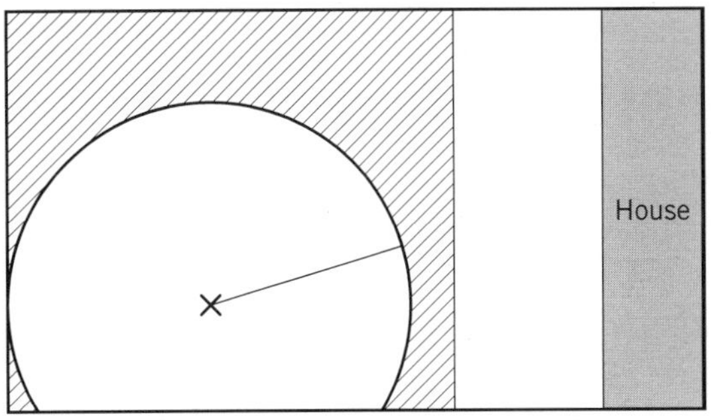

At least 4 m from the tree – so outside a circle radius 2 cm centre the tree. At least 3 m from the house, so to the left of a line parallel to the house and 1·5 cm from it.

Now try these exam questions:

1 Ashwell and Buxbourne are two towns, 50 km apart. Chris is house hunting. He has decided he would like to live closer to Buxbourne than Ashwell but no further than 30 km from Ashwell. Using a scale of 1 cm to represent 5 km, shade the area in which Chris should look for a house.

2 Ashad's garden is a rectangle. He is deciding where to plant a new apple tree. It must be nearer to the hedge AB than the house CD. It must be at least 2 m from fences AC and BD. It must be more than 6 m from corner A.
Shade the region where the tree can be planted.
Leave in all your construction lines.
Make the scale of your drawing 1 cm to 2 m.

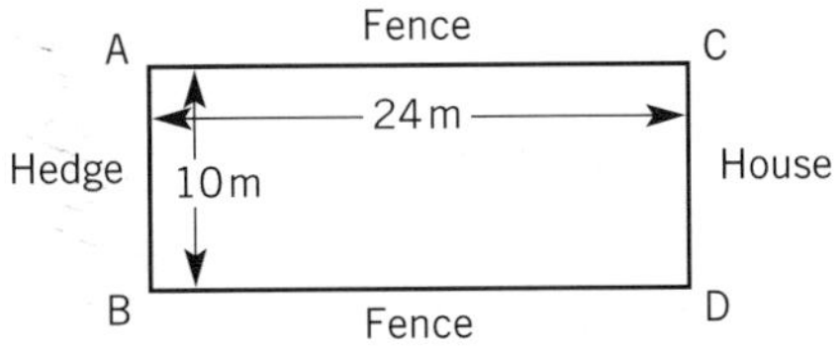

3 Sandtown council wants to build a pavilion on a playing field. They decided to site it at an equal distance from both gates and not more than 250 m from the toilet block.
On a scale drawing, make suitable constructions to locate the site. Leave in your construction lines.
Show clearly where the pavilion can be built.
Scale: 1 cm represents 50 m.

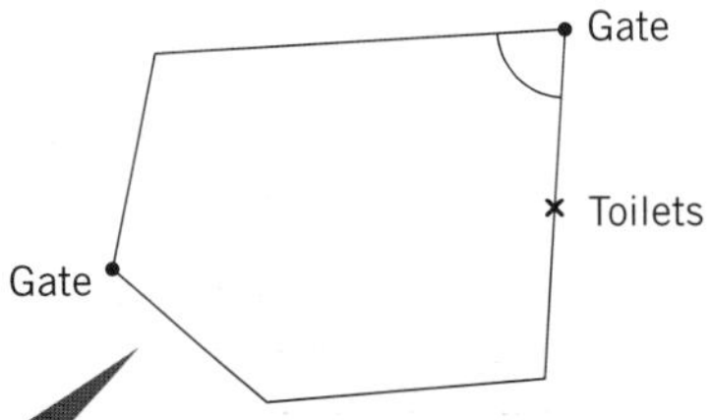

To answer this question, draw a pentagon of about this shape, with the gates 13·2 cm apart and the toilet block 4·5 cm from one gate. The angle at the top, as indicated, is 82°.

Identification and selection of data

Primary and secondary data

- Primary data is data which is collected by the person using the information.
- Secondary data is data obtained from elsewhere such as books or databases.

Now try these:

1 Which of the following are examples of primary data and which are secondary data?
  (a) Using hospital records to see how many babies of each sex were born each day over a period of a month.
  (b) Using newspapers to see how many comedy, sport, drama, etc. programmes there were on TV last week.
  (c) Using holiday brochures to find out the hours of sunshine in different resorts.
  (d) Measuring how accurate people are at measuring distance.

Grouped data and class intervals

- When handling lots of data it is useful to collect the data into groups.
- Often grouped data is put into 'equal class intervals', that is into groups of equal width.

Example

Here are the times in minutes that 30 children claim to have spent on their homework.

26	48	52	23	21	59	29	31	26	33
23	33	37	44	29	26	21	45	31	60
52	51	39	54	37	39	40	52	39	48

Grouping these times into equal intervals gives the following frequency table:

Time (min)	Tally	Frequency
21–30	~~||||~~ ||||	9
31–40	~~||||~~ ~~||||~~	10
41–50	||||	4
51–60	~~||||~~ ||	7

Bias

Questions you ask should not be biased – that is they should not be leading questions.

Now try these:

2 Which of these questions do you think is biased?
  (a) It is important to eat breakfast. Do you eat breakfast?
  (b) Normal teenagers wear clothes with designer labels. Do you wear clothes with designer labels?
  (c) How many hours of television did you watch last weekend?
  (d) It is essential to eat five portions of fruit each day. How many portions did you eat yesterday?

Example

'Normal people enjoy watching soaps like EastEnders. Do you watch EastEnders?'

This is a biased question because if you do not watch soaps, in general, or EastEnders in particular, you would think that you weren't normal.

Collecting data

Data can be collected using questionnaires. Some issues about questions are mentioned above. Other issues are:

- questions can give a choice of possible answers
- they should not cause embarrassment
- they should be short, clear, easy to understand and relevant.

Now try these:

3 Amy wants to chose a sample of 100 adults from the town where she lives. She considers these methods of choosing her sample:
Method 1 – choose people shopping in the town centre on Saturday
Method 2 – choose names at random from the electoral role
Method 3 – choose people living in streets near her home.
Which of these methods is most likely to provide an unbiased sample? Give reasons for your answer.

4 Amy wants to find out about people's TV viewing habits. Write down three questions Amy could ask.

Here is an exam question

Here are two questions that Amy wanted to include in a survey she was going to do to find out if people liked the new shopping centre in her town.

Rewrite each one to show how you would word the questions in a questionnaire and why you would change it.

(a) How old are you?

(b) This new shopping centre appears to be a success. Do you agree?

...and its solution

Possible answers would be:

(a) The question may be thought to be personal – some people may not answer.
Change to:
What is your age? tick the appropriate box.
☐ 10–19 ☐ 20–29 ☐ 30–39
☐ 40–49 ☐ 50–59 ☐ Over 60

(b) This is a leading question. Change to:
Do you think the shopping centre is a success? Tick the appropriate box.
☐ yes ☐ no ☐ don't know

Now try these exam questions:

1 Here is a list of questions.
Which of these questions do you think needs to change and why?

(a) How heavy are you?
(b) Where did you go on holiday last year?
(c) How many newspapers have you read this week?
(d) Do you enjoy sport?
(e) How much money do you earn?
(f) How many children do you have?

2 The Ayton Taxi Company attempted to estimate the number of people who used their taxis to go home in the evening.
They phoned 100 people in Ayton and asked if they had used one of their taxis in the last week. 19 people said 'yes' so the taxi company claimed that '19% of the people of Ayton use our taxis'.
Give three reasons why this was not a good method of estimating customer usage.

Processing and representing data

Frequency diagrams

For grouped information with equal intervals a frequency diagram can be drawn with the heights of the bars equal to the frequency.

Frequency polygons

A frequency polygon is formed by joining, with straight lines, the midpoints of the tops of the bars in a frequency diagram.

Example

The table shows the amount of pocket money received by the members of class 10h.

Amount (£)	0–3·99	4–7·99	8–11·99	12–15·99
Frequency	3	10	12	5

To show this information, draw

(a) a frequency diagram

(b) a frequency polygon.

(a)

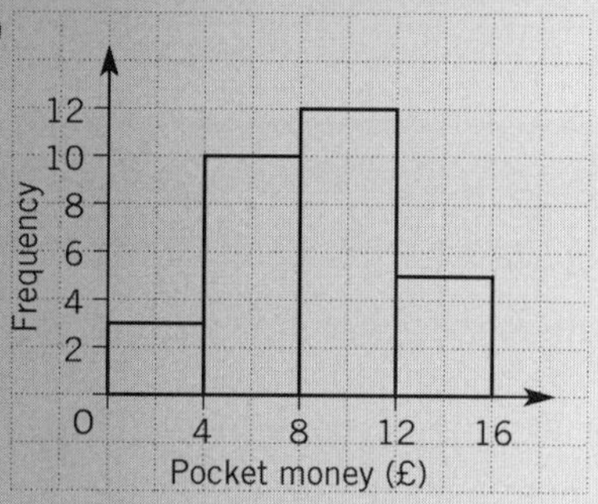

(b)

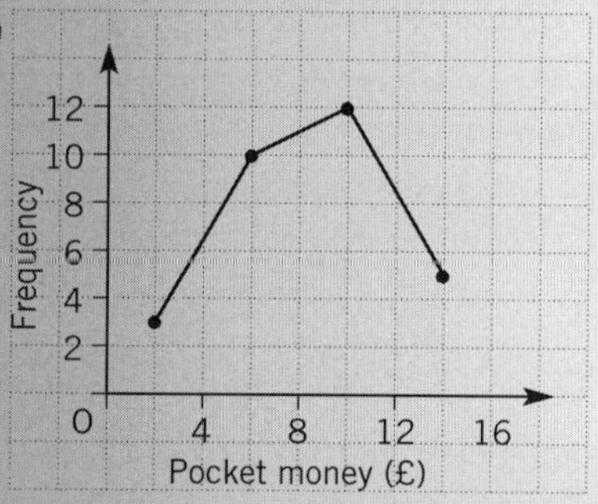

Now try these:

1 The lengths (l cm) of 100 oak tree leaves are shown in the following frequency table.

l (cm)	f
$8 \leqslant l < 9$	8
$9 \leqslant l < 10$	18
$10 \leqslant l < 11$	35
$11 \leqslant l < 12$	23
$12 \leqslant l < 13$	16

For this information:

(a) draw a frequency diagram

(b) draw a frequency polygon

Pie charts

To draw a pie chart, first find out the angle needed to represent one observation by dividing 360° by the total frequency. Then multiply this amount by the frequency for each group.

Now try these:

2 These are the results of a survey Habib carried out in his school on methods of travel to school.

Bus	Car	Cycle	Train	Walk
27	20	16	4	23

Show this information in a pie chart.

Example

Class 10h had a choice of four tasks for their course work. The number who chose each task is shown in the table.
Draw a pie chart to show this information.

Billiard tables (BT)	6	× 12 = 72°
Number trees (NT)	8	× 12 = 96°
Economical shapes (ES)	5	× 12 = 60°
Stacking cans (SC)	11	× 12 = 132°
Total		360°

360 ÷ 30 = 12, so each member of the class is represented by 12°.

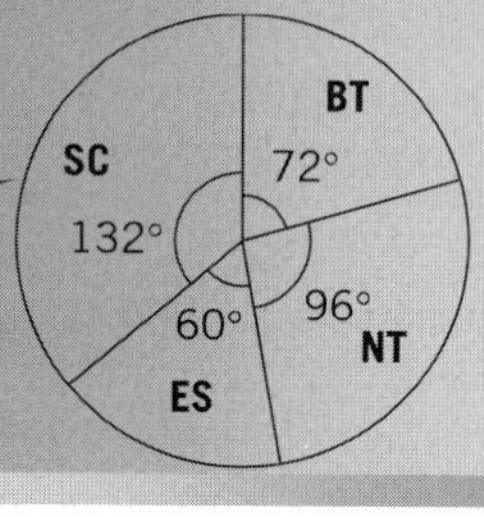

Always label the sectors.

Scatter diagrams and lines of best fit

- Scatter diagrams (or graphs) are drawn to investigate any possible link between two variables. Values of the two variables are plotted as points on a graph. If the points lie approximately in a straight line then there is a **correlation** between the two variables. The closer the points are to a straight line, the stronger the correlation.
- The correlation is **positive** if the higher the value of x, the higher the value of y.

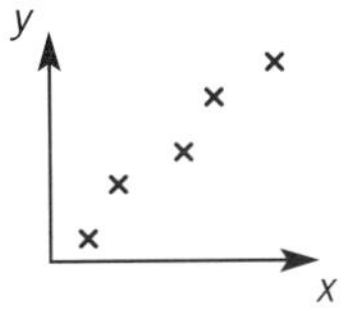

- The correlation is **negative** if the higher the value of x, the lower the value of y.

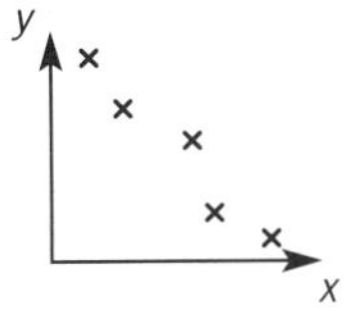

- If there is a correlation, then a **line of best fit** can be drawn. It should reflect the slope of the points and have approximately the same number of points on either side. It can be used to estimate a value of y from a given value of x. It should **not** be used to estimate too far outside the range of the data.

Example

The table below shows the time spent and marks gained for 10 students' coursework.

Time (h)	5	8	3	6	6	7	4	10	8	7
Mark	12	15	9	14	11	13	10	19	16	14

(a) Plot a scatter diagram for this information.
(b) What conclusions can be drawn?
(c) Draw a line of best fit.
(d) Use your line of best fit to estimate the mark of a student who spent nine hours on the course work.

(a) (c)

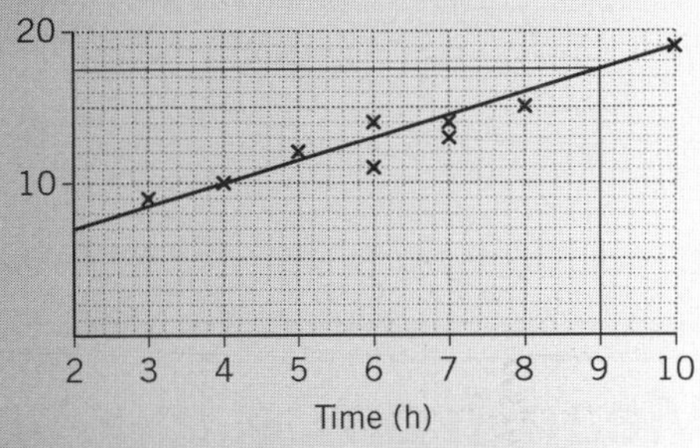

(b) Fairly strong position correlation.
(d) 17 or 18

Now try these:

3 The table shows the height and shoe size of seven students.

Height (cm)	165	152	145	161	148	158	156
Shoe size	6	5	$3\frac{1}{2}$	$5\frac{1}{2}$	4	$5\frac{1}{2}$	5

(a) Draw a scatter diagram. Describe the correlation.
(b) Draw a line of best fit.
(c) Estimate the shoe size for a student of height 151 cm.

4 Market research suggests the following sales (in thousands) would result from pricing an item at the given price.

Price (£)	35	40	45	50	55	60	65
Sales	25	24	23	20	16	14	11

(a) Draw a scatter diagram. Describe the correlation.
(b) Draw a line of best fit.
(c) Estimate the sales if the price was £52.

Time series and moving averages

- A time series is simply a graph where the x-axis is time and the y-axis is any quantity which varies with time. For example, quarterly sales of a company.
- A moving average is used where the graph shows a cyclical change. For example, higher sales always in the summer, lower sales always in the winter.
- To calculate the moving average in the example of quarterly sales:
  - **(i)** Find the mean for the four quarters in the first year.
  - **(ii)** Omit the first quarter of year one, include the first quarter of year two, and find the new mean.
  - **(iii)** Omit the second quarter of year one and include the second quarter of year two, and find the mean, and so on.

Example

The table below gives the sales figures in £millions for a company.

Quarter	1st	2nd	3rd	4th
1998	4·2	5·6	7·2	4·9
1999	3·9	5·5	6·8	4·7
2000	3·8	5·2	6·5	4·6

(a) Plot a time series graph.
(b) Calculate the four quarter moving averages and plot them on the graph.
(c) Comment on the graphs.

Now try these:

5 A company keeps records for four weeks about the daily absences from work of their employees. The results are in this table.

	Mon	Tue	Wed	Thur	Fri
Week 1	55	43	35	38	47
Week 2	58	44	32	36	45
Week 3	57	47	38	40	48
Week 4	62	48	40	42	50

(a) Plot these on a time series graph.
(b) Calculate the five-day moving averages.
(c) Plot the moving averages on your graph.
(d) Comment on the graphs.

Example continued

(a) (b)

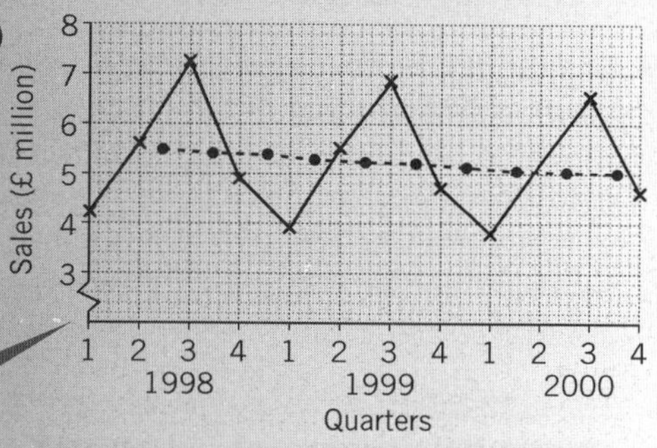

The moving average is plotted in the middle of the 4 quarters.

(b) $(4{\cdot}2 + 5{\cdot}6 + 7{\cdot}2 + 4{\cdot}9) \div 4 = 5{\cdot}475$
$(5{\cdot}6 + 7{\cdot}2 + 4{\cdot}9 + 3{\cdot}9) \div 4 = 5{\cdot}4$
$(7{\cdot}2 + 4{\cdot}9 + 3{\cdot}9 + 5{\cdot}5) \div 4 = 5{\cdot}375$
$(4{\cdot}9 + 3{\cdot}9 + 5{\cdot}5 + 6{\cdot}8) \div 4 = 5{\cdot}275$
$(3{\cdot}9 + 5{\cdot}5 + 6{\cdot}8 + 4{\cdot}7) \div 4 = 5{\cdot}225$
and so on giving 5·2, 5·125, 5·05, 5·025

(c) Third quarter always highest and first always lowest. Trend down.

Mean from a frequency distribution

- To calculate the mean from a frequency distribution:
  - **(i)** Multiply each observation (x) by its corresponding frequency.
  - **(ii)** Then add up these results.
  - **(iii)** Finally divided by the total frequency.
- For grouped data, use the middle of the interval for the value of x.

You are often told the total frequency in the question.

Example

The table below shows the number of letters delivered one morning to a street of 100 houses. Find the mean number of letters.

No. of letter (x)	0	1	2	3	4	5
Frequency	8	19	28	25	17	3

$$\text{Mean} = \frac{0\times8+1\times19+2\times28+3\times25+4\times17+5\times3}{100}$$
$$= 233 \div 100 = 2{\cdot}33$$

Example

Find the mean amount of pocket money received by the students in 10h on page 70.

Mid-interval value (x)	2	6	10	14
Frequency	3	10	12	5

$$\text{Mean} = \frac{2\times3 + 6\times10 + 10\times12 + 14\times5}{3 + 10 + 12 + 5}$$
$$= 256 \div 30 = £8{\cdot}53$$

Now try these:

6 Find the mean length of the oak tree leaves in question 1.

Stem-and-leaf diagrams and median

- Large numbers of two-digit data can be displayed in a stem-and-leaf diagram. The tens digit (the stem) is written in the left-hand column and the units digits (the leaves) are written in the right-hand column, as in the example on the next page.
- It is best to draw a stem-and-leaf diagram, initially with ‘leaves’ unordered, and then redraw it with the ‘leaves’ ordered.

- You can also use a stem-and-leaf diagram, for example, with the units as the 'stem' and the first decimal place as the 'leaves'.
- It is fairly easy to then find the median by counting up to the middle value.

Example

Here are the test marks for a group of students.

63	54	34	42	38	76	69	52	45	54
67	71	64	43	57	59	47	66	57	63

Unordered

3	4 8
4	2 5 3 7
5	4 2 4 7 9 7
6	3 9 7 4 6 3
7	6 1

Ordered

3	4 8
4	2 3 5 7
5	2 4 4 7 7 9
6	3 3 4 6 7 9
7	1 6

Key: 3 | 4 means 34

Since there are 20 in the group there are two middle ones, the 10th and 11th. They are both 57, so the median is 57.

Now try these:

7 Below are the masses in grams of 30 potatoes. Draw a stem-and-leaf diagram for this information and find the median mass.

43	65	89	46	82	79	58	97	83	54
49	62	71	58	79	82	48	63	52	57
60	57	82	95	76	68	53	72	66	71

Cumulative frequency graphs

- Cumulative frequency is the running total of the frequencies in a distribution. The last cumulative frequency is the total of the frequencies and is often given in the question.
- Cumulative frequency is plotted at the upper bound of each interval. The points can be joined by a curve or by straight lines. The graph opposite shows a fairly typical shape for a cumulative frequency graph.

Median, quartiles and interquartile range

- To find the median of a frequency distribution draw a line across the graph at $\frac{1}{2}$(total frequency) to meet the curve and then down to read off the value on the *x*-axis.
- To find the quartiles of a frequency distribution draw a line across the graph at $\frac{1}{4}$(total frequency) and $\frac{3}{4}$(total frequency) to meet the curve and then down to read off the values on the *x*-axis.
- Interquartile range (upper quartile – lower quartile) is a measure of spread.

Box plots

These are a useful way of displaying data.

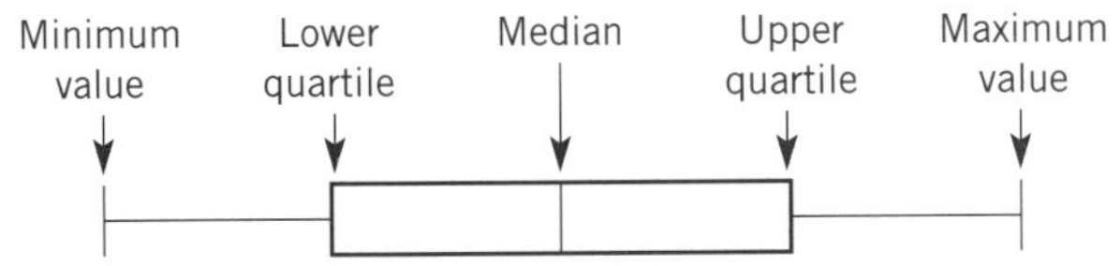

These are sometimes called box-and-whisker plots.

Example

The table below shows the distribution of the masses (*m* g) of 80 tomatoes.

(a) Complete the right-hand column to show the cumulative frequencies.

Mass (g)	Frequency	Cumulative frequency (a)
$70 < m \leq 75$	4	4
$75 < m \leq 80$	10	14
$80 < m \leq 85$	22	36
$85 < m \leq 90$	27	63
$90 < m \leq 95$	14	77
$95 < m \leq 100$	3	80

(b) Draw a cumulative frequency graph.
(c) Estimate the number of tomatoes weighing more than 93 g.
(d) Find the median and interquartile range.
(e) Draw a box and whisker plot.

(b)

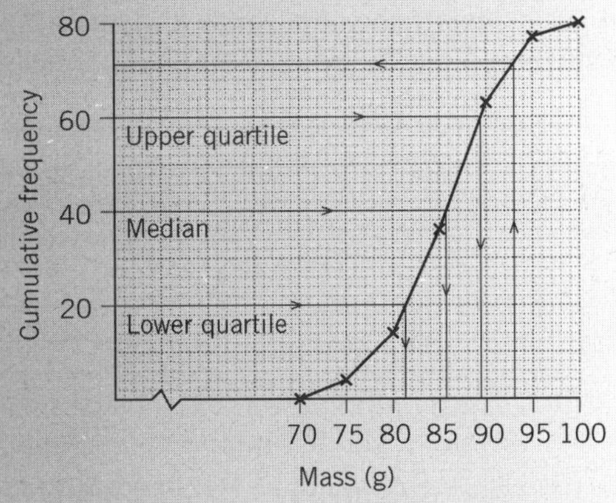

Now try these:

8 The table shows the results of a survey on the times (t minutes) taken for 100 students to get to school.

Time (t minutes)	Frequency
$0 < t \leqslant 10$	8
$10 < t \leqslant 20$	15
$20 < t \leqslant 30$	33
$30 < t \leqslant 40$	22
$40 < t \leqslant 50$	17
$50 < t \leqslant 60$	5

(a) Draw a table of cumulative frequencies.
(b) Draw a cumulative frequency graph.
(c) Use your graph to find:
  (i) the number of students who took over 45 minutes to get to school
  (ii) the median time
  (iii) the interquartile range.

9 The cumulative frequency graph on the right shows the marks obtained by 120 students in their last maths exam.
(a) The pass mark was 45. How many passed?
(b) Find the median and interquartile range.
(c) Draw a box plot for the distribution.

Example continued

(c) 80 – 71 = 9
(d) Median = 86 g
  Interquartile range = 89·5 – 81·5 = 8 g
(e)

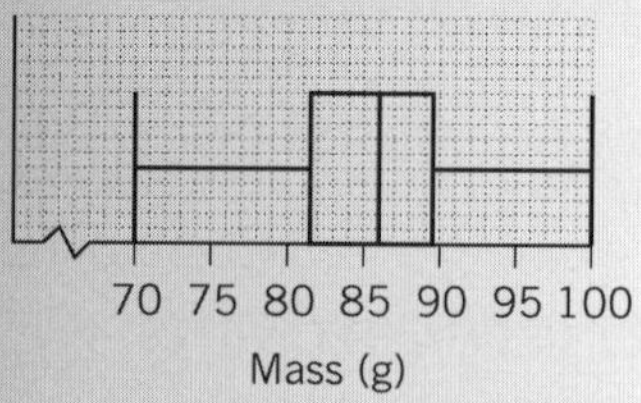

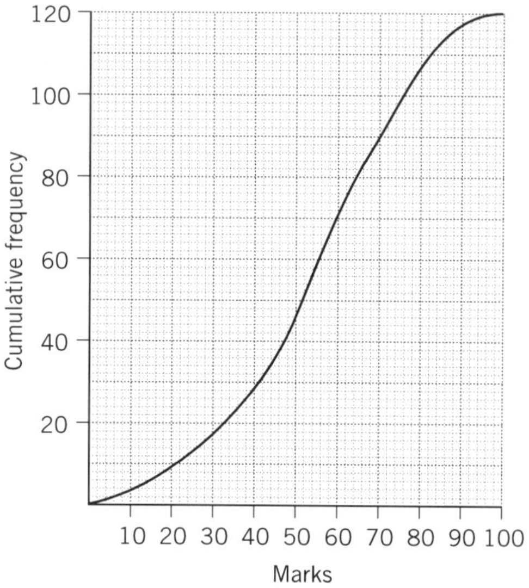

Here is an exam question

A wedding was attended by 120 guests.
The distance, d miles, that each guest travelled was recorded in the frequency table below.

Distance (d miles)	Number of guests
$0 < d \leqslant 10$	26
$10 < d \leqslant 20$	38
$20 < d \leqslant 30$	20
$30 < d \leqslant 50$	20
$50 < d \leqslant 100$	12
$100 < d \leqslant 140$	4

(a) Using the mid-interval values, calculate an estimate of the mean distance travelled.
(b) **(i)** complete the cumulative frequency table below.

Distance (d miles)	Number of guests
$d \leqslant 10$	26
$d \leqslant 20$	
$d \leqslant 30$	
$d \leqslant 50$	
$d \leqslant 100$	
$d \leqslant 140$	

  (ii) Draw a cumulative frequency graph to represent the information in the table.
(c) **(i)** Use the cumulative frequency graph to estimate the median distance travelled by the guests.
  (ii) Give a reason for the large difference between the mean distance and the median distance.

...and its solution

(a) $\dfrac{5 \times 26 + 15 \times 38 + \ldots\ldots\ldots.120 \times 4}{120}$

$= 3380 \div 120 = 28{\cdot}2$ miles

(b) **(i)** Cumulative frequencies
  = 26, 64, 84, 104, 116, 120.
  (ii)

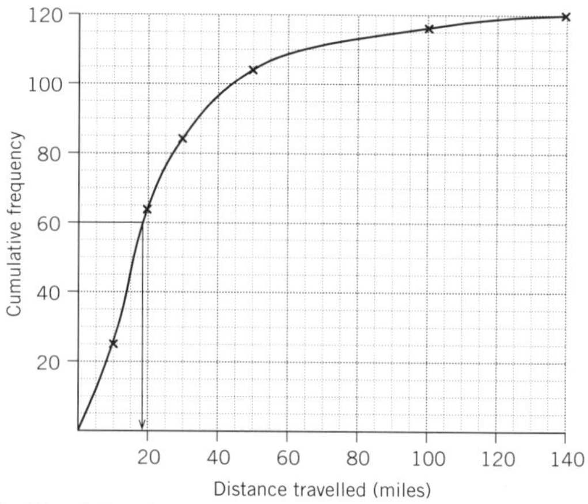

(c) **(i)** 19 miles.
  (ii) The mean is greatly affected by the guests who travel a long distance.

Now try these exam questions:

1 A class of 33 students sat a mathematics exam. Their results are listed below.

89	78	56	43	92	95	24	72	58	65	55
98	81	72	61	44	48	76	82	91	76	81
74	82	99	21	34	79	64	78	81	73	69

(a) Draw an ordered stem-and-leaf diagram for this information.
(b) Find the median mark.

2 A car dealer sold 120 new cars in August. He made a note of the colours of the cars and decided to draw a pie chart to illustrate the popularity of different colours.

(a) Copy and complete the table below to show the pie chart angles for each colour.

Car colour	Number of cars	Pie chart angle
Red	55	
Blue	32	
White	20	
Grey	13	
Total	120	

(b) Using a circle of radius 5 cm, represent this information on a pie chart.

3 The weight loss in pounds of each of 80 members of a slimming club is summarised in the table below.

Weight loss (w pounds)	$0 < w \leq 5$	$5 < w \leq 10$	$10 < w \leq 15$	$15 < w \leq 20$	$20 < w \leq 25$	$25 < w \leq 30$	$30 < w \leq 35$
Frequency	9	13	21	17	10	8	2

(a) (i) Copy and complete the cumulative frequency table.

Weight loss (w pounds)	$w \leq 5$	$w \leq 10$	$w \leq 15$	$w \leq 20$	$w \leq 25$	$w \leq 30$	$w \leq 35$
Cumulative frequency	9						

(ii) Draw the cumulative frequency graph for the weight loss of the club. Use a scale of 2 cm to 5 pounds on the horizontal axis and 1 cm to 10 members on the vertical axis.

(b) Use your graph to find **(i)** the median weight **(ii)** the interquartile range.
(c) The company running the club guarantees that everyone will lose at least 8 pounds. Use your graph to estimate how many achieve this target.
(d) The club's slimming champion lost 30% of his weight and and now weighs 84 kg. Calculate the champion's weight before he started slimming.

4 An orchard contains nine young apple trees. The table shows the height of each tree and the number of apples on each.

Height (m)	1·5	1·9	1·6	2·2	2·1	1·3	2·6	2·1	1·4
Number of apples	12	15	20	17	20	8	26	22	10

(a) (i) Draw a scatter graph to illustrate this information. Use a scale of 2 cm to 1 m on the horizontal axis and 2 cm to 10 apples on the vertical axis.
(ii) Comment briefly on the relationship between the height of the trees and the number of apples on the trees.
(iii) Add a line of best fit to your scatter graph.
(iv) Explain why it is not reasonable to use this line to estimate the number of apples on a tree of similar type but of height 4 m.

(b) The 150 apples were picked and weighed. Their weights are shown in the table below. Calculate an estimate of the mean weight of an apple.

Weight (w grams)	$50 < w \leq 60$	$60 < w \leq 70$	$70 < w \leq 80$	$80 < w \leq 90$	$90 < w \leq 100$
Number of apples	23	42	50	20	15
Mid-interval value	55				

Probability

Basic probability

- Probability can be expressed as fractions, decimals or percentages. All probabilities are between 0 and 1 inclusive.

  P(A does not happen) = 1 – P(A)
- For equally likely outcomes:

  $$P(A) = \frac{\text{number of ways A can happen}}{\text{total possible number of outcomes}}.$$
- **Mutually exclusive** outcomes are those which cannot happen together. If A, B and C are mutually exclusive outcomes covering all the possibilities, then P(A) + P(B) + P(C) = 1.

Never write probabilities as '1 in 5' or as a ratio '1 to 5' or 1 : 5. You will lose marks if you do. Instead, write $\frac{1}{5}$ or 0·2 (or 20% if the question uses percentages).

P(A) is a useful shorthand for the probability that A happens.

Example

If a bag contains just red, green and white balls and one is drawn out at random, P(red) + P(green) + P(white) = 1

Now try these:

1 If the probability that it will rain tomorrow is 0.7, find the probability that it will not rain tomorrow.

2 A bag contains just blue, green and yellow counters. A counter is taken out at random. The probability of getting a blue counter is 0·4 and of a yellow counter is 0·5.

(a) Find the probability of getting **(i)** a green counter, **(ii)** a white counter.

(b) There are 100 counters in the bag. How many of these are blue?

Relative frequency

- $$\text{Relative frequency} = \frac{\text{number of times event occurs}}{\text{total number of trials}}.$$
- When theoretical probabilities are not known, relative frequency can be used to estimate probability.
- The greater the number of trials, the better the estimate. The graph of relative frequency against the number of trials may vary greatly at first, but later 'settles down'.
- Relative frequency experiments may be used to test for bias, e.g. to see if a dice is fair.

Example

Sarah has a biased dice. This graph shows the relative frequency of throwing a 6, when Sarah threw her dice 1000 times.

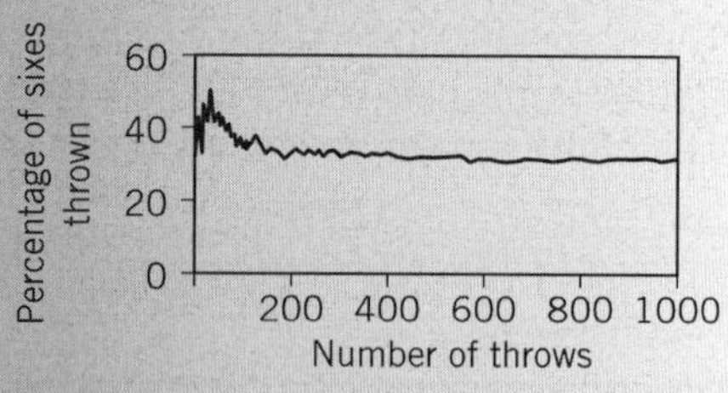

The graph shows that for this dice P(6) = 30% approx.

Now try these:

3 These are the results of 500 spins with a spinner.

No. on spinner	1	2	3	4	5
Frequency	106	92	74	127	101

Find as a decimal the relative frequency of scoring 3 with this spinner. Do these results suggest the spinner is biased? Explain your answer.

4 250 people were asked their favourite colour from a packet of sweets: 24 said mauve, 52 said yellow, 15 said brown, 72 said red, and 44 said green. The other colour was orange.

(a) How many said orange?

(b) Estimate the probability that the next person asked says red.

Combining probabilities

- Equally likely outcomes may be:
  - listed in a table
  - shown on a grid.
- When outcomes are not equally likely, use **tree diagrams**.
  Remember:
  - each set of branches shows the possible outcomes of the event.
  - the probabilities on each set of branches should add to 1.
  - when events are **independent**, the outcomes of the second event are not affected by the outcomes of the first event.
  - to find the probabilities of the combined events, multiply the probabilities along the branches.

Be systematic to make sure you don't miss out any possibilities.

Example

This shows the probabilities that Penny has to stop at lights or a level crossing on her way to work.

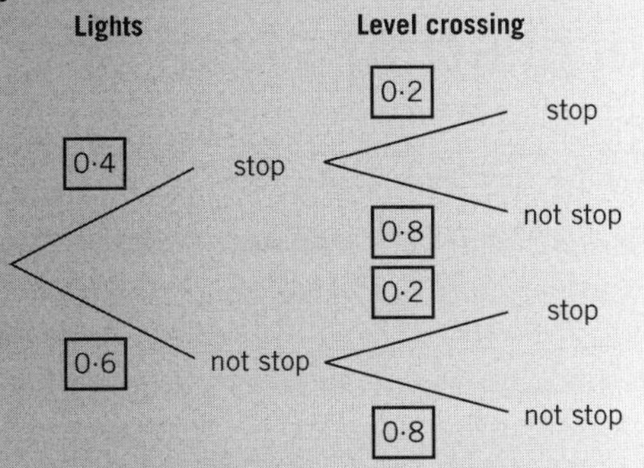

P(not stop at either) = 0·6 × 0·8 = 0·48

Now try these:

5 Jill offers her guests shepherd's pie or macaroni cheese for main course, and blackcurrant cheesecake, chocolate gateau or trifle for desert. List the possible two-course meals her guests could have.

6 Draw a grid, with axis marked from 1 to 4, to show the possible outcomes when a fair spinner numbered 1 to 4 is spun twice.
What is the probability of:
(a) getting 1 both times
(b) getting a total of 6?

7 A bakery makes doughnuts. Machine A fills them with jam. There is a probability of 0·03 that machine A misses a doughnut. Machine B coats them with sugar. The probability that machine B misses a doughnut is 0·02.
(a) Draw a tree diagram to show these probabilities, using the first set of branches for machine A.
(b) Calculate the probability that a doughnut has no jam inside and no sugar.
(c) Calculate the probability that a doughnut has just one of these faults.

Here is an exam question

Pete likes crisps. Without looking, he picks a bag out of an assorted pack. There are 12 bags of crisps in the pack. Two of these bags are ready-salted.
The manufacturers say that one bag in every hundred has a gold reward in it.
This is independent of the flavour of the crisps.
(a) Complete the tree diagram to show the probabilities.
(b) What is the probability that Pete picks a ready-salted bag with a gold reward in it?
(c) What is the probability that Pete picks either a ready-salted bag or one with a gold reward in it, but not both?

...and its solution

(a)

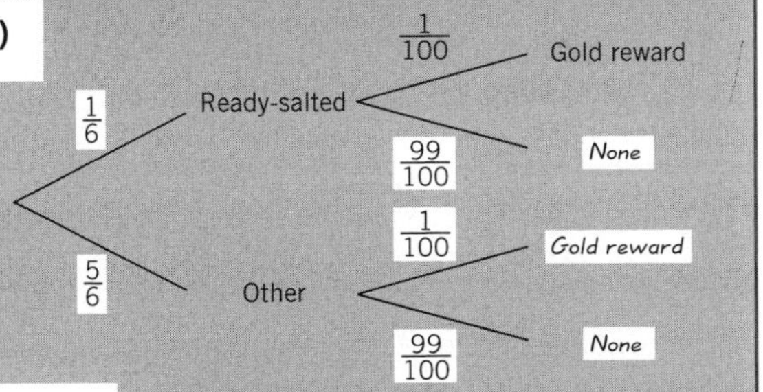

(b) $\frac{1}{600}$ $\quad \frac{1}{6} \times \frac{1}{100} = \frac{1}{600}$

(c) $\frac{13}{75}$ $\quad \frac{1}{6} \times \frac{99}{100} + \frac{5}{6} \times \frac{1}{100} = \frac{104}{600} = \frac{13}{75}$

Now try these exam questions:

1 Lynn buys a bag of 20 sweets for Joseph. The bag contains one orange, three white, four yellow, five green and seven red sweets.
Joseph takes one sweet out of the bag without looking. What is the probability that the sweet is:
(a) green **(b)** yellow or white **(c)** not green **(d)** black?

2 Ellen and Schweta are practising goal scoring in netball. When they each take one shot the probability that Ellen scores a goal is 0·7 and the probability that Schweta scores a goal is 0·8.
These probabilities are independent.

(a) Complete the tree diagram.

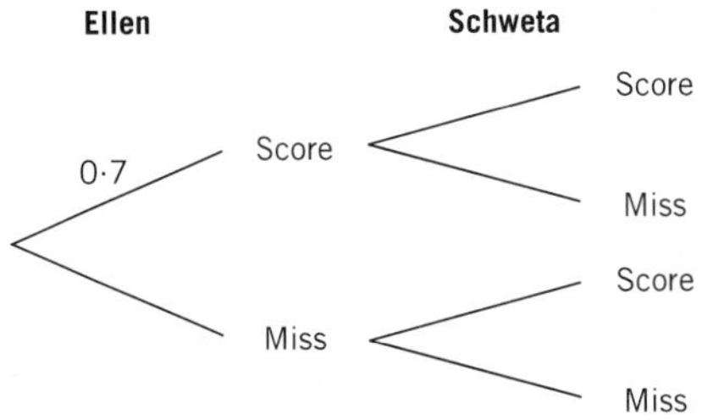

(b) Calculate the probability that, at their next attempt:
(i) both Ellen and Schweta score a goal
(ii) either Ellen or Schweta, but not both, score a goal.

Interpretation

Many GCSE Handling data questions require you to interpret diagrams and data. This section gives two examples. It is not new, as you have done all the calculations and drawing in earlier sections.

Interpreting stem-and-leaf diagrams

Example

The stem-and-leaf diagram shows the marks gained by pupils in a test.
Use the diagram to find:

(a) the number of pupils
(b) the mode
(c) the median.

Remember, the mode is the value that occurs most often.

4	3 8
5	0 4 4 7
6	4 7 9 9
7	1 3 3 5 8 8 8 9
8	0 0 4 5 6
9	0 1 1

Where 4|3 means 43

(a) 27
(b) 78, as there are three of them.
(c) The median will be the 14th, which is 73.

You could find all of this from the original data but is is quicker from the diagram.

Interpreting box-and-whisker diagrams

Example

The box-and-whisker diagram shows the number of fish caught by an angler on each of 15 days. Use the diagram to find:

(a) the range
(b) the median
(c) the interquartile range.

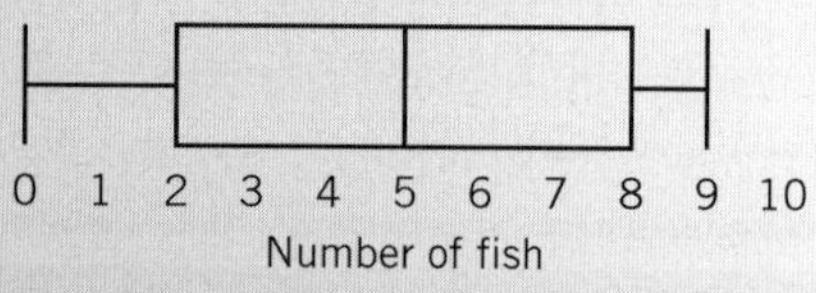

Notice that you cannot tell the total number of days from a box and whisker.

(a) 9 – 1 = 8 (b) 5 (c) 8 – 2 = 6.

Here is an exam question

The manager of the Metro cinema records the numbers watching each of two films for 25 days. The frequency diagram below is for Film A.

The table on the right shows the numbers of people who watched Film B. Compare the two distributions.

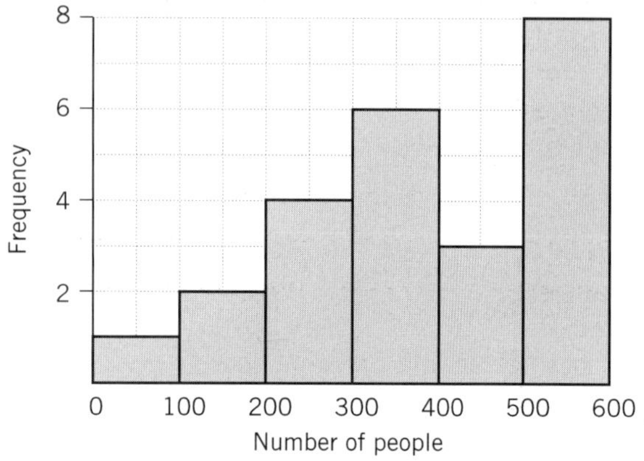

Number of people	Frequency
0–99	5
100–199	12
200–299	6
300–399	1
400–499	0
500–599	1

...and its solution

The average attendance at Film A was much higher, or more people watched Film A. The numbers attending Film A were more varied or the number watching Film B each night was more consistent.

Now try these exam questions

1 Bob and Eddie each collect pebbles from two different places on a beach. They measure the maximum diameter of 20 pebbles they have collected and record the data. All the measurements are in cm.

(a) Bob's measurements are given in this stem-and-leaf diagram:
Write down the range and the median diameter for Bob's pebbles.

Note that 1 | 9 means 1·9 cm.

1	9
2	0 1 2 2 5 5 7 8
3	0 0 1 1 3 4 7 8 9
4	0 6

(b) Eddie's pebbles have the following measurements:
Draw a stem-and-leaf diagram for Eddie's pebbles and find the range and the median.

1·2	5·5	2·2	2·1	3·4	1·8	4.5
3·2	3·0	1·4	3·3	4·9	2·1	2·1
2·8	4·8	4·2	1·9	3·8	1·1	

(c) Compare the two distributions.

2 Bob thinks there is a relationship between arm length and the length of the first finger of the writing hand. He measured these lengths for 14 pupils in his class. The measurements, in cm, are given in the table below.

Arm	56	65·5	73·5	64	64	81	58	60	69	53	65	72·5	58·5	74·5
Finger	6	6·5	7·5	7	6	8	6·5	6·5	7	6	7	7·5	7	7·5

(a) Draw a scatter graph to show this data.
(b) What does the graph show about any connection between the two lengths?
(c) Bob knows the arm length for a pupil is 68 cm. What would you expect the finger length to be?

3 A hospital recorded the birth weights, in kilograms, of 100 boys and 100 girls. The weights are summarised in the table on the right:
(a) Draw two box-and-whisker plots to show this information.
(b) Use your plots to compare the birth weights of boys and girls.

	Girls	**Boys**
Median	3·2	3·3
Lower quartile	2·6	2·3
Upper quartile	3·8	4·0
Minimum	1·2	1·2
Maximum	4·4	4·7

4 The data on the right show the time taken, in minutes, by 30 students to solve a puzzle.
(a) Draw a grouped frequency diagram to represent this data.
(b) What is the modal class?

3	6	14	18	20	14	6	16	13
7	15	8	15	10	14	10	15	5
4	9	16	9	15	12	14	10	6
13	15	12						

5 The prices, in £, of 108 three-piece suites (settee plus two arm chairs), offered by a furniture store are shown in the table on the left.
(a) Complete the cumulative frequency table on the right.

Price (£P)	**Number**
$400 \leqslant P < 500$	12
$500 \leqslant P < 600$	37
$600 \leqslant P < 700$	31
$700 \leqslant P < 800$	18
$800 \leqslant P < 900$	8
$900 \leqslant P < 1000$	2

Price (£P)	**Cumulative frequency**
$P < 400$	0
$P < 500$	
$P < 600$	
$P < 700$	
$P < 800$	
$P < 900$	
$P < 1000$	

(b) Draw on a grid the cumulative frequency curve.
(c) Use your graph to estimate:
(i) the median price
(ii) the percentage of suites that cost more than £800.

Answers

For full model answers to the exam questions, go to http://www.hoddermaths.co.uk.

Integers

Practice questions (pages 2–3)

1 **(a)** 4, 8, 12, 16, 20, 24
(b) 9, 18, 27, 36, 45, 54
(c) 15, 30, 45, 60, 75, 90

2 **(a)** 1, 2, 3, 4, 6, 8, 12, 24
(b) 1, 2, 4, 5, 8, 10, 20, 40
(c) 1, 2, 4, 8, 16, 32

3 **(a)** $2 \times 2 \times 3 \times 3$
(b) $2 \times 2 \times 5 \times 7$
(c) $2 \times 2 \times 3 \times 7$

4 **(a)** HCF = 3 LCM = 120
(b) HCF = 4 LCM = 120
(c) HCF = 9 LCM = 540

5 **(a)** $\frac{1}{5}$ **(b)** 9 **(c)** $1\frac{1}{3}$ **(d)** 5 **(e)** 0·4

6 **(a)** 2 **(b)** $^-1$ **(c)** $^-16$ **(d)** 11 **(e)** $^-15$ **(f)** 4 **(g)** $^-4$ **(h)** 24

Exam questions (page 3)

1 **(a)** 14
(b) 12 or 18
(c) 11, 13, 17 or 19

2 $2 \times 2 \times 2 \times 3 \times 11$ or $2^3 \times 3 \times 11$

3 HCF = 4 LCM = 48

4 HCF = 2 LCM = 60

5 $4 \times \frac{1}{4} = 1$

6 13

Powers and roots

Practice questions (pages 4–5)

1 81
2 1
3 $\frac{1}{9}$
4 1
5 216
6 $\frac{1}{8}$
7 5^{10}
8 6^3
9 $8a^9$
10 $6a^2b^{-1}$ or $\frac{6a^2}{b}$
11 c^{10}
12 $8x^{12}$
13 121
14 7
15 29·1
16 46 656
17 372 000
18 0·000 48
19 $5{\cdot}83 \times 10^{-5}$
20 $7{\cdot}56 \times 10^7$
21 $1{\cdot}2 \times 10^{14}$
22 $2{\cdot}5 \times 10^{10}$

Exam questions (page 5)

1 **(a)** 64 **(b)** $\frac{1}{16}$ **(c)** 1

2 9

3 **(a)** **(i)** 3^9 **(ii)** 3^2
(b) **(i)** 2 **(ii)** 18

4 **(a)** $1{\cdot}8 \times 10^8$
(b) $1{\cdot}2 \times 10^{-4}$

5 5·57

6 **(a)** 21·7
(b) **(i)** 5728·9761 **(ii)** 5730

7 $8{\cdot}75 \times 10^{-3}$

8 **(a)** $12a^3b^4$ **(b)** $7a^2b^{-1}$ or $\frac{7a^2}{b}$

9 **(a)** Botswana, Denmark, Australia, Egypt, China
(b) 18 to 2 s.f.

Fractions

Practice questions (pages 6–7)

1 $2\frac{3}{4}$
2 $3\frac{1}{5}$
3 $4\frac{5}{6}$
4 $\frac{7}{4}$
5 $\frac{19}{6}$
6 $\frac{35}{8}$
7 $\frac{11}{12}$
8 $\frac{11}{15}$
9 $5\frac{13}{24}$
10 $5\frac{7}{15}$
11 $\frac{1}{12}$
12 $\frac{3}{14}$
13 $1\frac{11}{20}$
14 $2\frac{17}{30}$
15 $\frac{23}{24}$
16 12
17 $\frac{3}{10}$
18 $10\frac{1}{2}$
19 $\frac{3}{10}$
20 $\frac{3}{8}$
21 $6\frac{2}{3}$
22 25
23 9
24 98
25 42

Exam questions (page 7)

1 **(a)** $\frac{5}{8}$ **(b)** $1\frac{1}{6}$

2 **(a)** $\frac{4}{15}$ **(b)** $3\frac{17}{20}$

3 **(a)** 15 **(b)** £22

4 **(a)** $\frac{3}{5}, \frac{5}{8}, \frac{7}{10}, \frac{3}{4}$ **(b)** $2\frac{27}{40}$

5 **(a)** $\frac{7}{8}$ **(b)** $\frac{5}{6}$

Decimals and percentages

Practice questions (pages 8–9)

1 **(a)** 34% **(b)** 27% **(c)** 35·6% **(d)** 142·8%

2 **(a)** **(i)** 0·6 **(ii)** 60%
(b) **(i)** 0·225 **(ii)** 22·5%
(c) **(i)** 0·625 **(ii)** 62·5%
(d) **(i)** $0{\cdot}\dot{4}$ **(ii)** $44{\cdot}\dot{4}\%$

3 35%

4 12·5%

5 60%

6 12·5%

7 **(a)** £7·20 **(b)** 17·02 m

8 **(a)** £89·88 **(b)** £6457·50

9 **(a)** £10·80 **(b)** £5723

10 £1714·75

11 60

12 £8200

13 £1200

Exam questions (page 9)

1 Loss = £800 Percentage loss = 14·3%

2 £8·17

3 84·7%

4 £80

5 **(a)** £629·30
(b) After 2 years = £440·51
After 3 years = £308·357
After 4 years = £215·8499
A quarter of £899 = £224·75

6 £329·60

Ratio

Practice questions (pages 10–11)

1 **(a)** 16 cm **(b)** 7 cm
2 **(a)** 75 g **(b)** 240 g
3 **(a)** 7·5 litres **(b)** 6 litres
4 **(a)** **(i)** 1 : 3 **(ii)** 8 : 3 **(iii)** 1 : 5 **(iv)** 2 : 5
(b) **(i)** 1 : 3 **(ii)** 1 : 0·375 **(iii)** 1 : 5 **(iv)** 1 : 2·5
5 £8, £10
6 21 litres
7 £25, £50, £75
8 125 m^2

Exam questions (page 11)

1 400 g
2 £18
3 **(a)** 100 ml **(b)** 300 litres
4 **(a)** 17·5 cm **(b)** 1 : 40 000
5 1200 ml

Mental methods

Practice questions (pages 12–13)

1 **(a)** ±11 **(b)** ±15 **(c)** ±8
2 **(b)** 15 **(b)** 365 **(c)** 121
3 **(a)** 124, e.g. because $11^2 = 121$ and $12^2 = 144$
(b) 200, e.g. because 200 = 2 × 100 and 2 is not a perfect square
4 **(a)** 5·4 **(c)** 0·31
(b) 12 **(d)** 45 000
5 **(a)** 20 **(c)** 0·7
(b) 100 **(d)** 1
6 **(a)** 4.6×10^4 **(c)** 3.6×10^6
(b) 4.84×10^{-2} **(d)** 5.965×10^3
7 **(a)** 8 000 000 **(c)** 77
(b) 9 400 **(d)** 0·000 303
8 **(a)** 41·6 **(b)** 2016 **(c)** 288
9 **(a)** 544 **(b)** 720 **(c)** 2288
10 **(a)** 4·606 **(c)** 460·6
(b) 46·06 **(d)** 0·046 06

Exam questions (page 13)

1 **(a)** 4·546 **(b)** 4·55
2 2 s.f.
3 2.4×10^{10}
4 8 640 000
5 **(a)** **(i)** 48 **(ii)** 8
(b) **(i)** 0·3318 **(ii)** 3318

Written methods

Practice questions (pages 14–15)

1 **(a)** $1\frac{1}{7}$ **(b)** $1\frac{3}{8}$ **(c)** 1·07
(d) 1·32 **(e)** 1·175
2 **(a)** $\frac{6}{7}$ **(b)** $\frac{5}{8}$ **(c)** 0·93
(d) 0·68 **(e)** 0·825
3 £179·20
4 31 888
5 **(a)** £2185·45 **(b)** £2687·83
6 £4331·93
7 £3145·73
8 11 975
9 **(a)** 0·5 hrs **(b)** 4 hrs **(c)** 5 hrs
10 **(a)** 150 ml of milk, 50 g of flour
(b) 900 ml of milk, 300 g of flour

Exam questions (page 15)

1 $450 \times 1.06^3 = 535.9572 = £535.96$
2 $160.48 \times 1.025^3 = 172.819... = £172.82$
3 $6 \div 4 = 1.5$
(a) No. of eggs = $2 \times 1.5 = 3$
(b) Amount of milk = $300 \times 1.5 = 450$ ml
(c) Amount of vanilla essence = $\frac{1}{2} \times 1.5 = \frac{3}{4}$ tsp
4 $300 \times 1.095^5 = 472.271... = £472.27$
5 **(a)** $100 \div 15 \times 24 = 160$ g
(b) $1000 \div 100 \times 15 = 150$ biscuits

Calculator methods

Practice questions (pages 16–17)

1 **(a)** $^{-}10$ **(d)** 36
(b) $^{-}9$ **(e)** 12
(c) $^{-}7\frac{1}{2}$ **(f)** $^{-}4$
2 **(a)** $\frac{4}{7}$ **(b)** $\frac{7}{9}$ **(c)** $\frac{31}{42}$
3 **(a)** $1\frac{7}{15}$ **(c)** $5\frac{1}{16}$
(b) $2\frac{7}{12}$ **(d)** $1\frac{1}{9}$
4 **(a)** £93 **(b)** 20
5 **(a)** $\frac{1}{8}$ or 0·125 **(c)** 25
(b) 1·25 or $\frac{1}{4}$ **(d)** $\frac{4}{11}$
6 **(a)** 625 **(c)** 3
(b) $^{-}2800$ **(d)** 3
7 **(a)** 43·35 **(c)** 25·26
(b) 2·32 **(d)** 4·00
8 **(a)** 7.31×10^{-5} **(b)** 1.37×10^{11} **(c)** 4×10^6
9 **(a)** 2·5 **(b)** 25·39 **(c)** 23·87

Exam questions (page 17)

1 **(a)** 120
(b) $\frac{19}{20}$
(c) £15·20
2 $0 \cdot \dot{1}\dot{1}$ or $\frac{1}{9}$
3 **(a)** 3·49 **(c)** 14·64
(b) 6·16
4 **(a)** 831·1
(b) 5·36
5 **(a)** 6.43×10^{10}
(b) 1.19×10^{17}
6 **(a)** 8·07
(b) 1·08

Solving problems

Practice questions (pages 18–19)

1 £6·24 **2** £27, £45 **3** £467·70
4 60 m.p.h. **5** 19·3 g/cm^3
6 220 000 to 3 s.f.
7 **(a)** $800 \div 20 = 40$ **(b)** $\frac{6000}{60 \times 20} = 5$
8 **(a)** 30·97 **(b)** 4·14 **(c)** 24·60
9 **(a)** 5350 **(b)** 61·4 **(c)** 3050
10 3·7 and 8·7 (or $^{-}3.7$ and $^{-}8.7$)

Exam questions (page 19)

1 £12·20
2 Special
3 (a) Must be more than $40 \times £20 = £800$
(b) 8%
4 (a) $4{\cdot}47 \times 10^7$ or $4{\cdot}5 \times 10^7$
(b) 310

Use of symbols

Practice questions (pages 20–21)

1 $3x + 4y$
2 $3ab - 2ac$
3 $a^2 + 2ab - 3b^2$
4 $2x + 3x^2 + 3x^3$
5 $8a^2 + a$
6 $6x - 14y$
7 $2x^2 + 21x$
8 $2x^2 - x$
9 $5(x - 5)$
10 $a(3b - 2c)$
11 $2ab(a - 3b)$
12 $2a(2bc - 4b + 1)$
13 $A = 6$
14 $B = 39$
15 $C = {}^-12$
16 $A = 16{\cdot}1$
17 $B = 60{\cdot}375$
18 $C = 63$
19 $8a^2b^3c^3$
20 $64a^6$
21 $\frac{7b^2}{a}$
22 $\frac{6b}{a}$

Exam questions (page 21)

1 $3pq(4p - 5q)$
2 $2x + 14$
3 (a) $8pq^3$
(b) $3a(a + 2b)$
4 (a) $v = 20$
(b) $2m - 6$
(c) $2a - b$
5 (a) $S = 65$
(b) $S = 40$
6 $6a^5$
7 (a) $F = 58$
(b) $F = 22$
8 (a) $12a^3b^4$
(b) $\frac{7a^2}{b}$
9 (a) $6a$
(b) $2a(2a - 1)$
10 $S = 3{\cdot}75$

Linear equations

Practice questions (pages 22–23)

1 $x = 5$
2 $p = 2$
3 $m = 3$
4 $y = 8$
5 $m = 9$
6 $p = 2$
7 $x = 8$
8 $x = {}^-3$
9 $x = 3$
10 $x = 2$
11 $x = \frac{1}{5}$
12 $x = {}^-4$
13 $x = {}^-18$
14 $m = 23$
15 $p = 42$
16 $x = 11$
17 $x = 16$
18 $x = 8$
19 $x = 1$
20 $x = 8$
21 $x = \frac{13}{9} = 1\frac{4}{9}$

Exam questions (page 23)

1 $x = \frac{1}{2}$
2 $p = 6$
3 $m = 12$
4 $y = 2$
5 $x = 3{\cdot}5$
6 $x = 1$
7 (a) $4x + 4 = 36$
(b) $x = 8$ cm
(c) Area = 80 cm^2
8 Tom 8, Maureen 3

Formulae

Practice questions (pages 24–25)

1 3
2 (a) 7·125 (b) ${}^-1\frac{7}{8}$ or ${}^-1{\cdot}875$
3 25
4 Let F = temperature in °F
Let C = temperature in °C
$C = \frac{5}{9}(F - 32)$
5 If U_n = nth term
(a) $U_n = n^2$ (c) $U_n = 3n - 1$
(b) $U_n = 3n^2$ (d) $U_n = 29 - 4n$
6 $c = y - mx$
7 $m = \frac{y - c}{x}$
8 $b = \frac{x + cd}{a}$
9 $c = \frac{ab - x}{d}$
10 $w = \frac{P - 2\ell}{2}$ or $\frac{P}{2} - \ell$
11 $h = \frac{3V}{\ell w}$
12 $r = \sqrt{\frac{A}{4\pi}}$
13 $r = \sqrt[3]{\frac{3V}{4\pi}}$
14 $x = \sqrt{y - a}$
15 $y = \frac{ax}{1 - b}$
16 $y = \frac{ax}{1 - a}$
17 $c = \frac{ab + bd}{a - d}$

Exam questions (page 25)

1 $n = \frac{C - 120}{4}$
2 $s = 144$
3 $y = \frac{30 - 5x}{6}$
4 $f = {}^-32{\cdot}3$ to 3 s.f.
5 $T = 20 + 30P$
6 $C = \frac{F - 30}{2}$ OR $C = \frac{F}{2} - 15$
7 $U_n = 3n - 2$
8 (a) $V = 1432{\cdot}2$ cm^3
(b) $y = \sqrt{\frac{x + 3}{4}}$
9 (a) $d = \frac{e - 3}{5}$
(b) $d = \frac{4e + 7}{3 - 5e}$
10 $v = \frac{fu}{u - f}$

Simultaneous equations and inequalities

Practice questions (pages 26–27)

1 (a) $x = 3, y = 2$ (b) $x = 6, y = {}^-5$ (c) $x = 2, y = {}^-1$
2 (a) $x < 2$ (b) $x < {}^-\frac{3}{5}$ (c) $x \geqslant \frac{1}{6}$
3 $x > 1$ so smallest value is 2
4 $x \geqslant 5$ or $x \leqslant {}^-5$
5 ${}^-6 < x < {}^-2$

Exam questions (page 27)

1 $x = 3, y = {}^-0{\cdot}5$
2 $x = {}^-1, y = 3$
3 (a) Replace x by 3 and y by 2
(b) $9p + 11q = 5$
(c) $p = 3, q = {}^-2$
4 $x > 2{\cdot}5$
5 $x < 5{\cdot}5$
6 3, 4, 5, 6, 7
7 ${}^-6 < x < 6$

Quadratic equations

Practice questions (pages 28–29)

1 $x^2 + 9x + 20$
2 $x^2 - 3x - 10$
3 $y^2 - 4y + 3$
4 $x^2 - 4$
5 $z^2 + 11x + 10$
6 $y^2 - 9$
7 $(x + 5)(x + 1)$
8 $(x - 5)(x + 5)$
9 $(x - 5)(x - 2)$
10 $(x - 6)(x - 3)$
11 $(x + 7)(x - 4)$
12 $(x - 6)(x + 5)$
13 $(y - 8)(y + 8)$
14 $(z + 1)(z + 6)$
15 $(x - 3)(x - 4)$
16 $(y + 7)(y - 6)$
17 $(x - 7)(x + 6)$
18 $(z + 3)^2$
19 3 or 6
20 $^{-}4$ or 1
21 $^{-}3$ or $^{-}7$
22 1 or $^{-}1$
23 $^{-}4$ or $^{-}1$
24 3 or 4
25 2 or $^{-}5$
26 $^{-}5$ or 6
27 3 or $^{-}3$
28 0 or 4
29 $x = {}^{-}2$ or $^{-}7$
30 $x = 8$ or $^{-}6$

Exam questions (pages 29)

1 $x = 2$ or 4
2 (a) $22x - 14$
(b) $x^2 - 9x + 20$
3 (a) $5x(x - 2y)$
(b) (i) $(x - 8)(x - 1)$ (ii) $x = 8$ or 1
4 (a) $x^2 - 12x + 35$
(b) (i) $(x + 5)(x - 2)$ (ii) $(x + 3)(x - 3)$
5 (a) $6x^2 + 9x - 42$
(b) $x = 6$ or $^{-}6$
6 (a) Length in m equals $22 - 2x$,
area in m^2 equals $x(22 - 2x) = 60$
so $22x - 2x^2 = 60$
so $11x - x^2 = 30$
so $x^2 - 11x + 30 = 0$ as required
(b) $x = 6$ or 5
(c) The pen is 6 m by 10 m or 5 m by 12 m.

Numerical methods

Practice questions (page 30)

1 $x = 1{\cdot}2$
2 $x = 3{\cdot}3$
3 $x = {}^{-}2{\cdot}3$
4 $x = {}^{-}3{\cdot}6$
5 $x = 1{\cdot}62$

Exam questions (page 31)

1 (a) Volume = $4x \times x \times (x + 1) = 200$
$4x^3 \times 4x^2 = 200$
$x^3 + x^2 = 50$
(b) $x = 3{\cdot}38$ to 3 s.f.
2 $x = 3{\cdot}8$ to 1 d.p.
3 $x = 2{\cdot}87$ to 2 d.p.
4 $x = 2{\cdot}41$ to 2 d.p.
5 (a) $x^3 - 8x + 5 = 0$
To show it has a root between 2 and 3. Try each and show they have different signs.
try $x = 2$ $x^3 - 8x + 5 = {}^{-}3$
try $x = 3$ $x^3 - 8x + 5 = 8$
(b) $x = 2{\cdot}4$ to 1 d.p.
6 (a)

x	1	2	3	4	5	6
V	7	32	81	160	275	432

(b) The dimensions are 4·4 cm by 4·4 cm by 10·4 cm.

Sequences

Practice questions (page 32)

1 6, 9, 12, 15
2 $5n - 3$
3 89, $6n - 1$
4 $44 - 4n$
5 $2n + 1$
6 $10n$
7 $5n - 9$
8 $35 - 3n$

Exam questions (page 33)

1 50th term = 248
Rule = $5n - 2$
2 Rule = $5n - 4$
3 (a) Rule = $7n - 5$
(b) If $7n - 5 = 300$ then $7n = 305$ and $n = 305 \div 7$.
Therefore $n = 43{\cdot}57$ i.e. n is not a whole number therefore 300 is not in the sequence.
4 (a) Rule = $4p + 1$ (b) Rule = $8p + 8$
5 (a) $c = 4t$ (b) $c = 2t + 2$

Graphs of linear functions

Practice questions (pages 34–35)

1 (a)

x	0	1	2
y	$^{-}2$	1	4

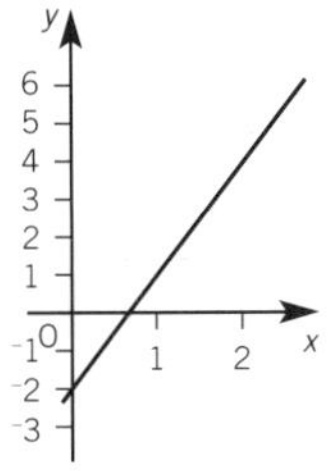

(b)

x	0	5	1
y	2	0	1·6

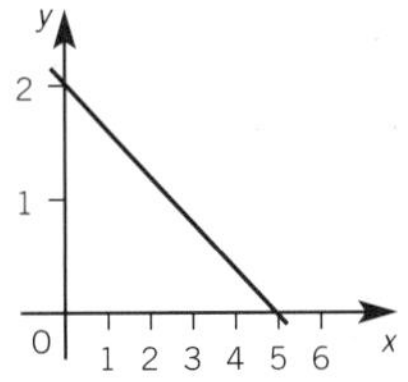

(c)

x	0	1	2
y	6	4	2

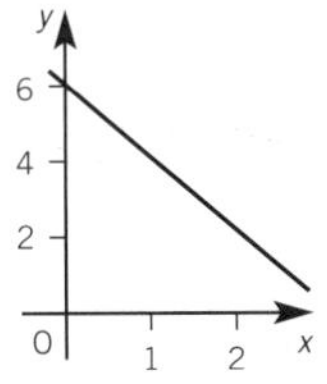

2 (a) Gradient = $^{-}1{\cdot}5$, y-intercept = 3
(b) Gradient = 2, y-intercept = 2
3 (a) $y = {}^{-}1{\cdot}5x + 3$ (b) $y = 2x + 2$
4 (a) $m = 4$, $c = {}^{-}1$ (d) $m = {}^{-}1$, $c = 4$
(b) $m = 2$, $c = 3$ (e) $m = 1{\cdot}5$, $c = 2$
(c) $m = 1$, $c = 0$ (f) $m = \frac{1}{4}$, $c = {}^{-}2{\cdot}5$
5 a, d and f are parallel
c and e are parallel

Exam questions (page 35)

1

x	0	1	2
y	$^{-}1$	2	5

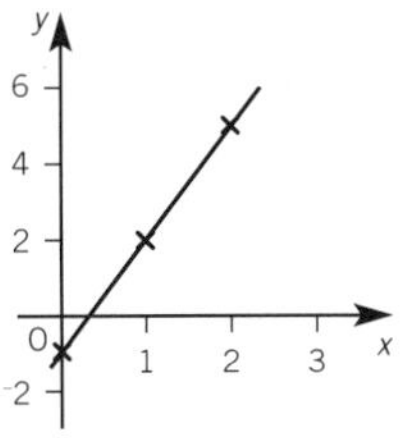

2 (a) Compare with $y = mx + c$

$m = {}^{-}2,\ c = 4$

(b) $m = {}^{-}2,\ c = {}^{-}1$

$y = {}^{-}2x - 1$

3 gradient $= \frac{^{-}5}{2} = {}^{-}2{\cdot}5$

Graphical solution of simultaneous equations and linear inequalities

Practice questions (pages 36–37)

1 (a) $y = 2x - 1$
$y = x + 2$

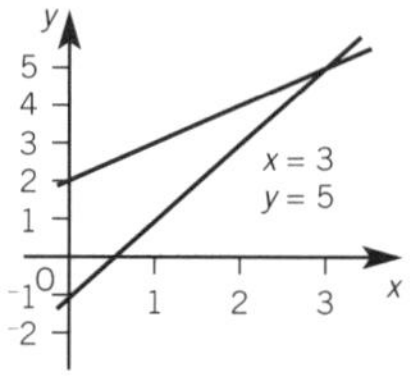

(b) $y = 2x - 5$
$2x + y = 3$

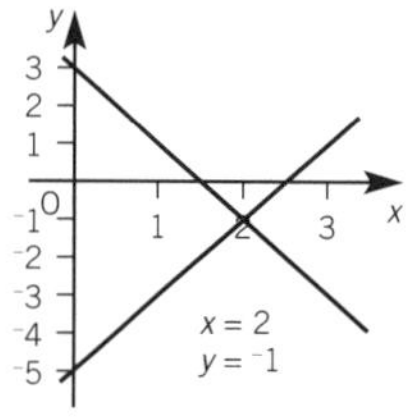

2 (a)

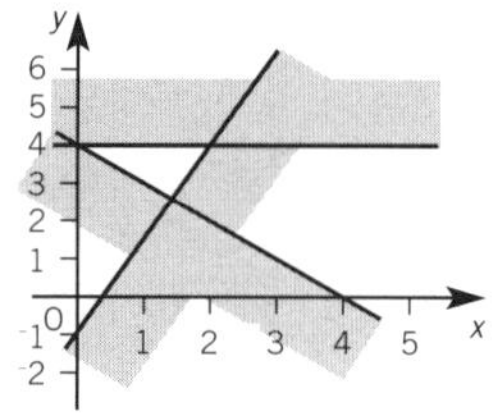

(b)

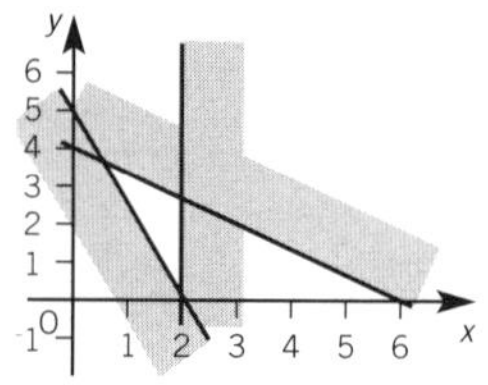

Exam questions (page 37)

1 $y = 3 - x$
$y = 3x - 2$

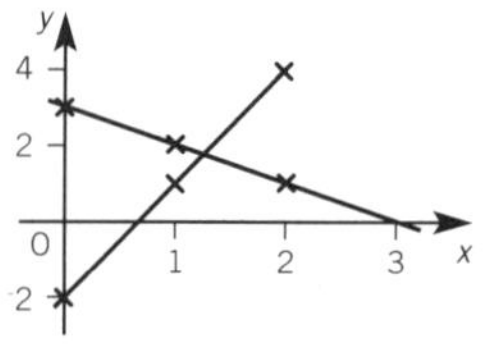

$x = 1{\cdot}25,\ y = 1{\cdot}75$

2 $y = 3x + 4$
$x + y = 2$

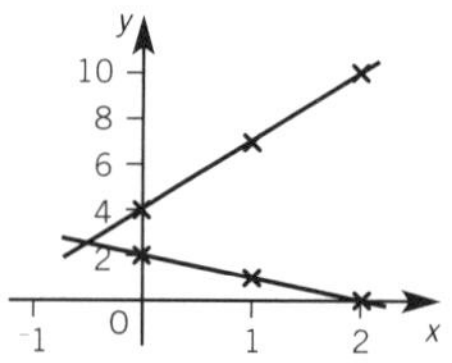

$x = {}^{-}0{\cdot}5,\ y = 2{\cdot}5$

3 $x + y = 5$
$y = 2x - 1$

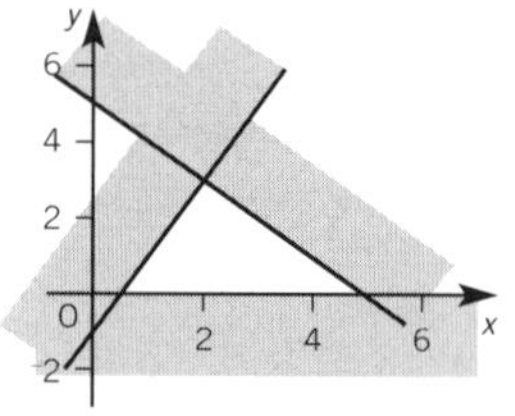

4 Choose (0, 1) to check lines

$y = x$	$1 \geqslant 0$	so $y \geqslant x$
$x + y = 3$	$1 + 0 \leqslant 3$	so $x + y \leqslant 3$
$x = {}^{-}2$	$0 \geqslant {}^{-}2$	so $x \geqslant {}^{-}2$

Interpreting graphs

Practice questions (pages 38–39)

1 (a) Accelerated at 0·8 m/s^2 for 25 seconds to 20 m/s.
Constant speed of 20 m/s for 15 seconds.
Retarded at 2 m/s^2 for 10 seconds to stop.

(b) Single tap filling at 4 litres/minute for 5 minutes followed by both taps filling at 8 litres/minute for $2\frac{1}{2}$ minutes. Constant at 40 litres for $12\frac{1}{2}$ minutes. Emptied at 8 litres/minute in 5 minutes

2

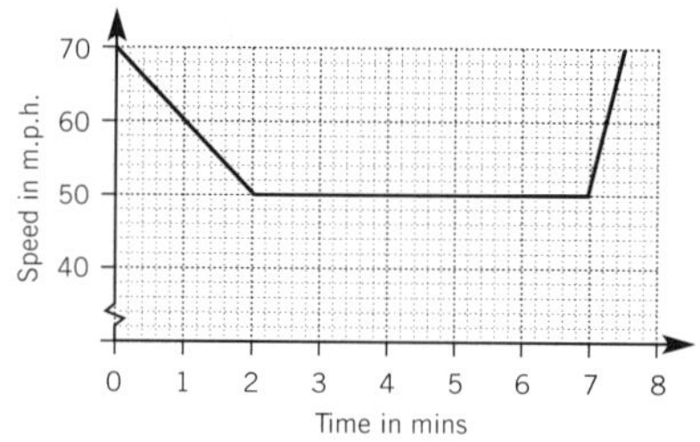

3 550 m

4

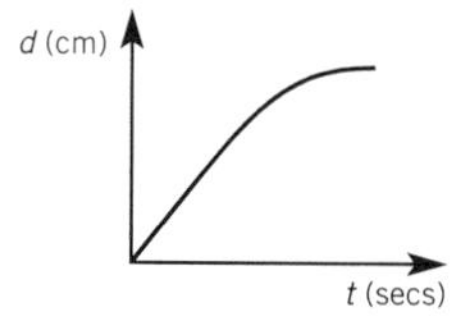

Exam questions (page 39)

1 (a)

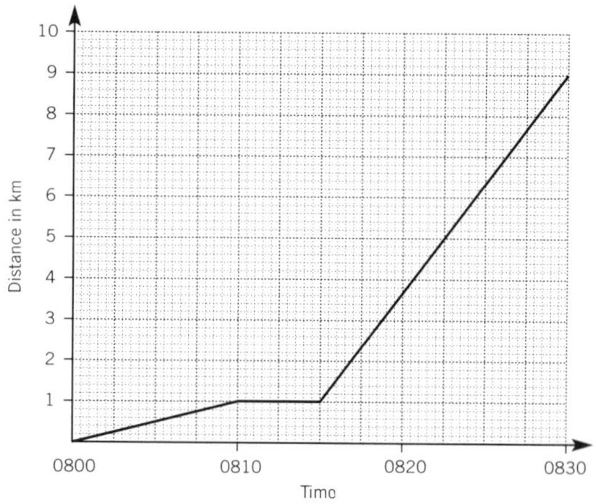

(b) $3\frac{2}{3}$ km or 3·7 km

2 e.g. A car accelerates and then travels at a steady speed and then stops suddenly (crashes etc.)

3 (a)

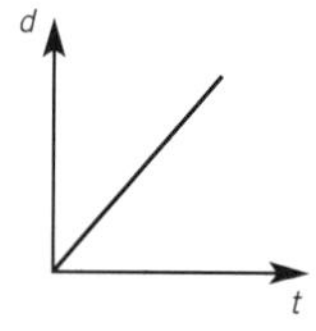

(b)

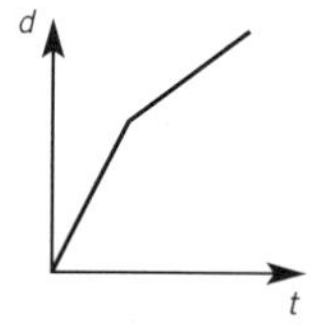

(c)

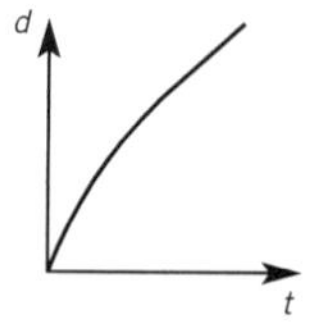

Quadratic and other functions

Practice questions (pages 40–41)

1 (a)

x	$^{-}1$	0	1	2	3	4	1·5
y	8	4	2	2	4	8	1·75

(b) So that the minimum point on the graph can be plotted accurately, 1·75.

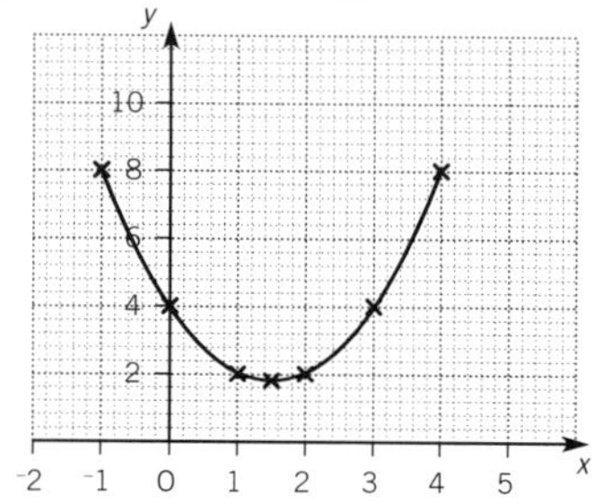

2

x	$^-2$	$^-1$	0	1	2	3	4	5
y	18	7	0	$^-3$	$^-2$	3	12	25

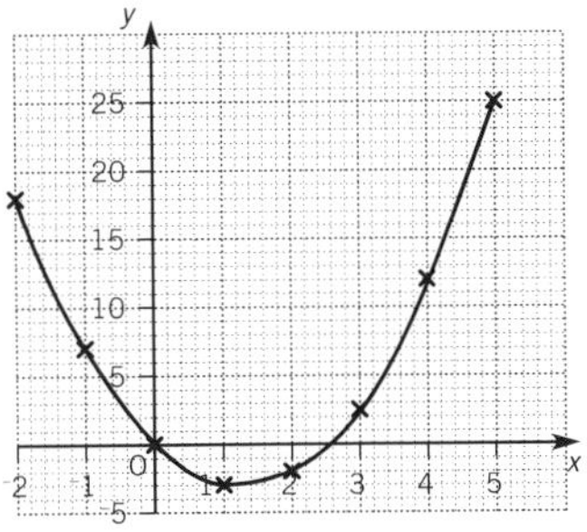

3 (a) $x = 0$ or 3

(b) $x = {}^-0{\cdot}8$ or $3{\cdot}8$ to 1 d.p.

4 (a) $x = 0$ or $2{\cdot}5$

(b) $x = 2{\cdot}3$ or $0{\cdot}2$ to 1 d.p.

5

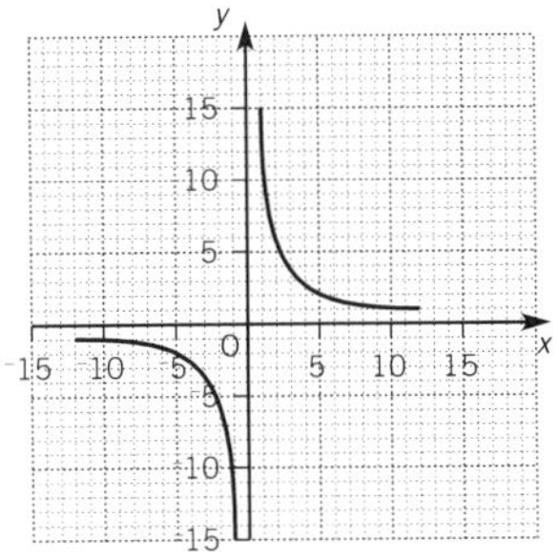

6

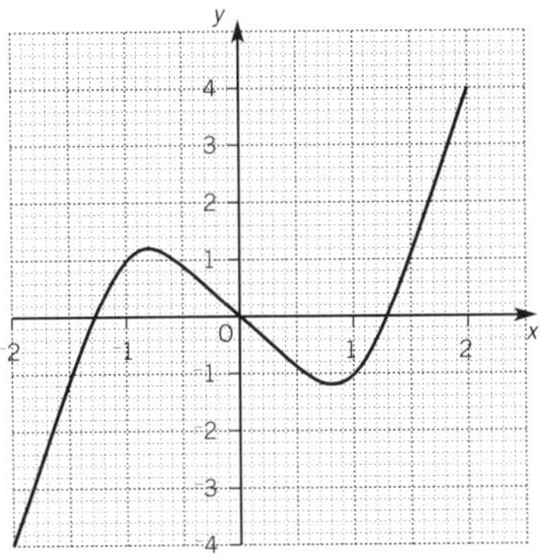

Roots $x = 0$ or $\pm 1{\cdot}4$ to 1 d.p.
Positive root $1{\cdot}41$ to 2 d.p.

Exam questions (pages 42–43)

1 (a)

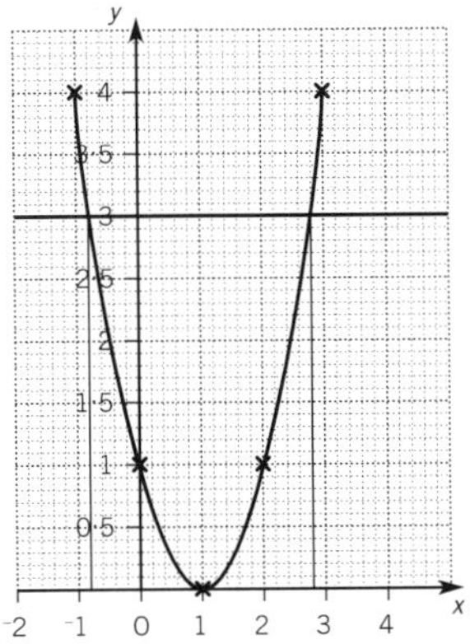

(b) $^-0{\cdot}7$ and $2{\cdot}7$

2 (a)

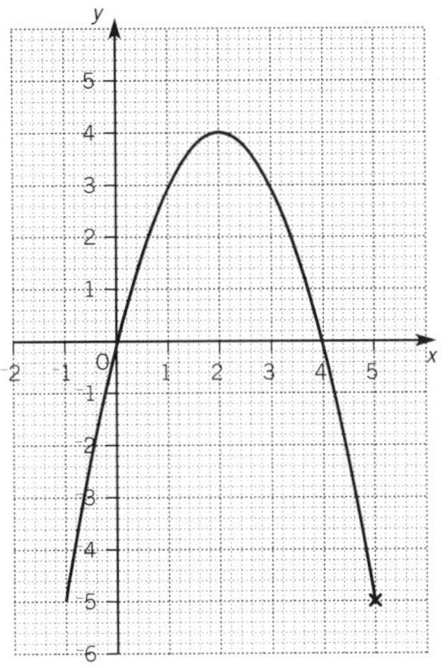

(b) (i) 2

(ii) $0{\cdot}6$ and $3{\cdot}4$

3 (a)

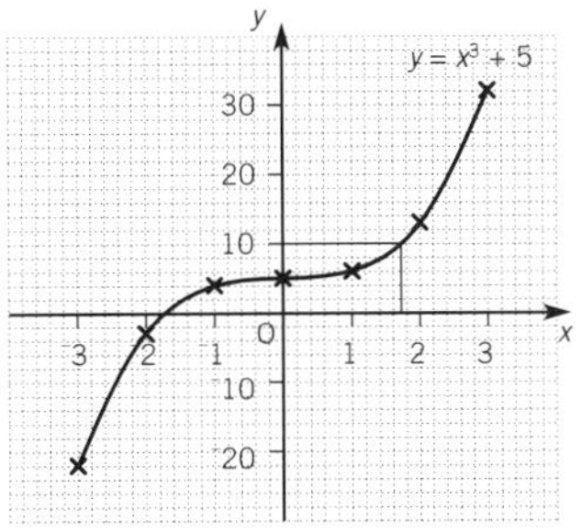

(b) $x = 1{\cdot}7$

4 (a) T **(b)** Q **(c)** U

5 (a) $V = x(x + 1)(x + 2)$

$= x(x^2 + 3x + 2)$

$= x^3 + 3x^2 + 2x$

(b)

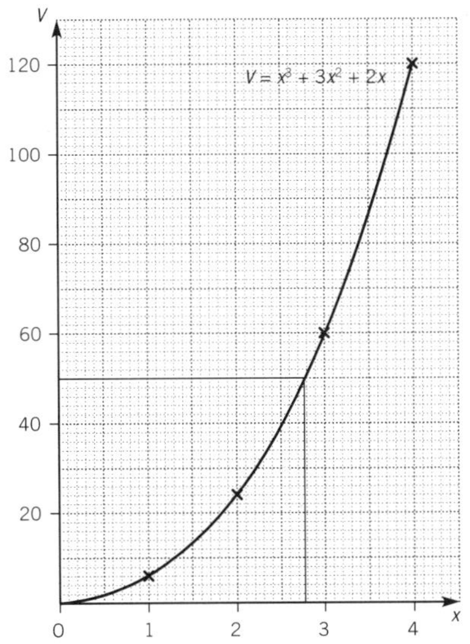

(c) $2{\cdot}8$ cm

6 (a)

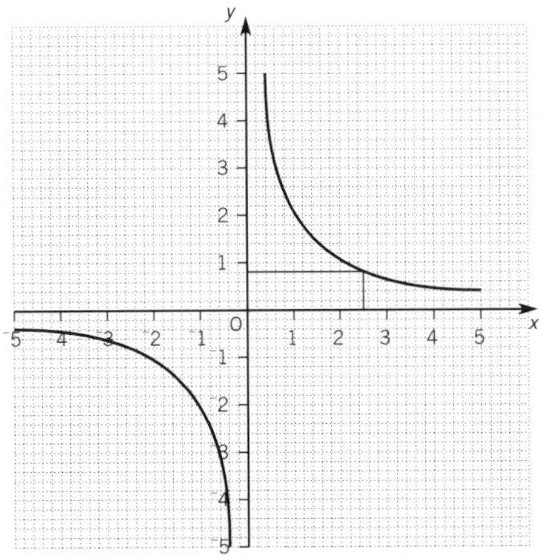

(b) $2{\cdot}5$

Properties of triangles and other shapes

Practice questions (pages 44–46)

1 $a = 63°$ vertically opposite angles are equal
$b = 63°$ alternate angles are equal, or corresponding angles are equal
$c = 49°$ vertically opposite angles are equal
$d = 49°$ alternate angles are equal, or corresponding angles are equal
$e = 112°$ vertically opposite angles are equal
$f = 112°$ corresponding angles are equal
$g = 68°$ angles on a straight line = 180°
$h = 36°$ alternate angles are equal
$i = 52°$ angles in a triangle = 180°
$j = 52°$ alternate angles are equal

2 **(a)** equal angles
(b) 3 cm

3 135°

4 104°

5 15 sides

6 102°

7 Rectangle, parallelogram, rhombus.

8 **(a)**
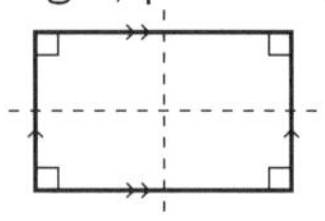

(c)
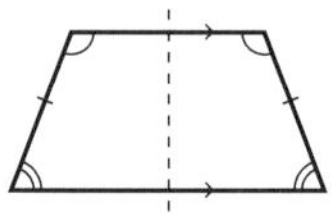

(b)
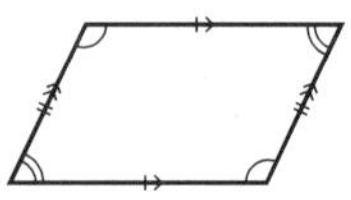

(d)
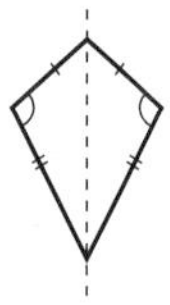

Exam questions (page 47)

1 **(a)** $x = \frac{360}{5} = 72°$
(b) Triangle OAB is isosceles.

2 **(a) and (b)**
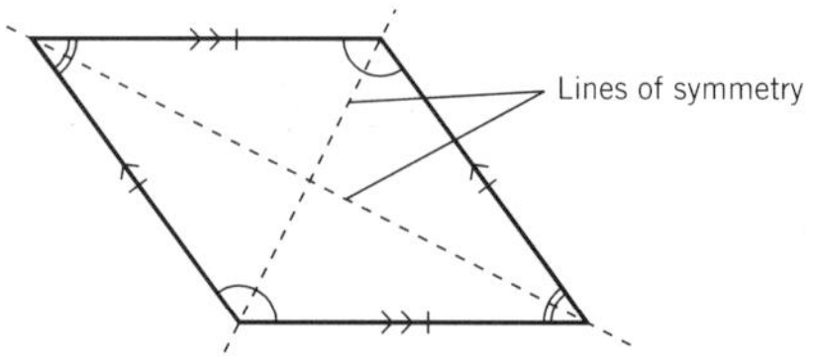

(c) Order of rotational symmetry is 2.

3 $x = 53°$ Corresponding angles are equal
$y = 84°$ Angles in a triangle = 180°

4 Hexagon: exterior angle $= \frac{360}{6} = 60°$
interior angle = 180 − 60 = 120°
n-sided polygon: interior angle = 120 + 48 = 168°
exterior angle = 180 − 168 = 12°
Number of sides $= \frac{360}{12} = 30$
$n = 30$

5 **(a)** $\frac{XC}{4{\cdot}2} = \frac{9}{3{\cdot}6}$ $\quad XC = \frac{9 \times 4{\cdot}2}{3{\cdot}6} = 10{\cdot}5$ cm
$\frac{DC}{2{\cdot}1} = \frac{9}{3{\cdot}6}$ $\quad DC = \frac{9 \times 2{\cdot}1}{3{\cdot}6} = 5{\cdot}25$ cm
(b) Angle BAX = angle DCX (corresponding angles in similar triangles). But these are alternate angles for AB and DC, making them parallel.

Pythagoras and trigonometry

Practice questions (pages 48–49)

1 $3\sqrt{6}$
2 $4\sqrt{2}$
3 $4\sqrt{10}$
4 $15\sqrt{10}$
5 4·5 cm
6 3·6 cm
7 13 cm
8 4·9 cm
9 6·13 cm
10 10·99 cm
11 11·47 cm
12 13·05 cm
13 39°
14 53°
15 60°
16 59°

Exam questions (page 50)

1 **(a)** = 4·7 cm
(b) $x = 62{\cdot}34°$ or 62°

2 $x = 5{\cdot}2$ cm
$y = 7{\cdot}89$ cm or 7·9 cm

3 3·91 m

4 **(a)** 4·57 m
(b) 66·8°

Properties of circles

Practice questions (pages 51–53)

1 17 cm
2 4·90 cm
3 50°
4 8·94 cm
5 20°
6 **(a)** 29° **(b)** 119°

7 Angle CDA = 65° (opposite angles of a cyclic quadrilateral)
Angle CDE = 180 − 65 = 115° (angles on a straight line)

8 Angle ADX = Angle BCX (angles in the same segment)
Angle DAX = Angle CBX (angles in the same segment)
Angle DXA = Angle CXB (vertically opposite angles)
(or any one of these replaced by 'angle sum of triangle')
Therefore triangles are similar (all angles are equal)

9 $a = 65°$, $b = 25°$, $c = 130°$

Exam questions (page 53)

1 Angle C = 53° (angle in a semicircle and angle sum of triangle)

2 $x = 36°$ (angles in the same segment)
$y = 72°$ (angle at centre = twice angle at circumference)
$z = 62°$ (radius at right angles to tangent)

3 **(a)** Angle OCB = 56°
(b) Angle CBT = 124°
(c) Angle CTA = 22°

4 **(a)** Angle ADE = $x°$
(b) Angle DAE = $90 - x°$
(c) Angle EAB = $x°$
(d) Angle AOE = $2x$

3D shapes

Practice questions (pages 54–55)

1 **(a)**
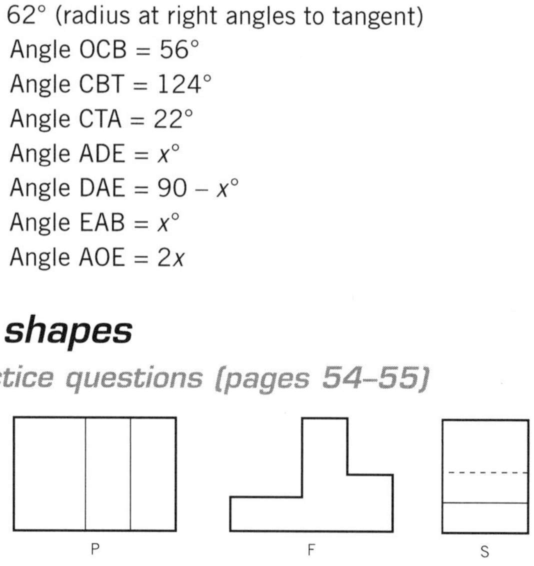

(b)

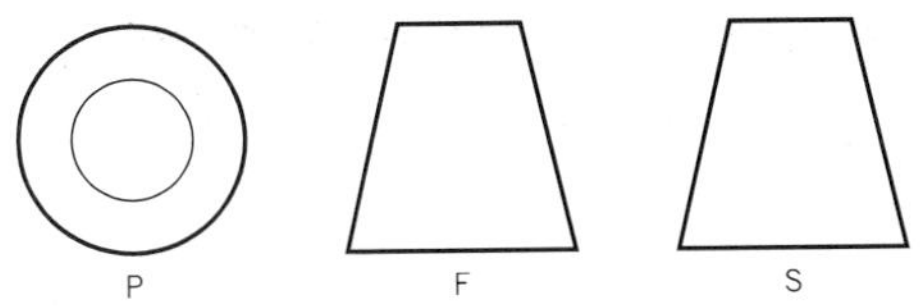

2 (a) Diagrams not to scale

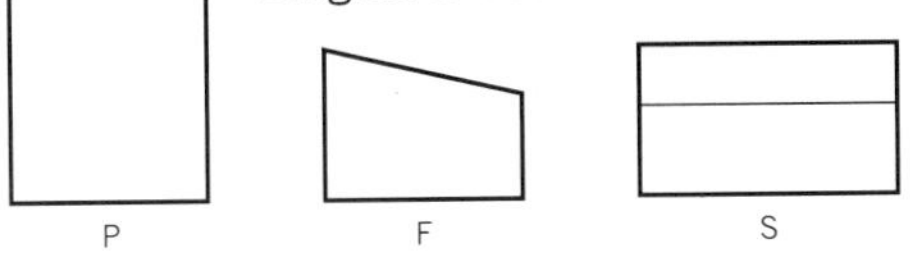

(b) $x = 4{\cdot}1$ cm

3 5 cm 4 265 cm^3 5 2 cm

Exam questions (page 55)

1

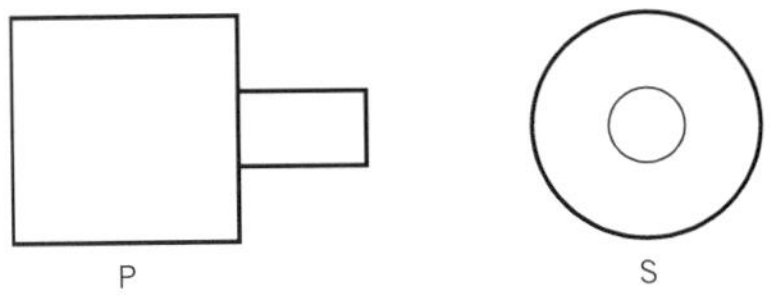

2 V = 1154·5 cm^3

3 V = 0·88 m^3

4 Surface area = 96 cm^2

Transformations, coordinates and vectors

Practice questions (pages 56–58)

1 (a) and (b)

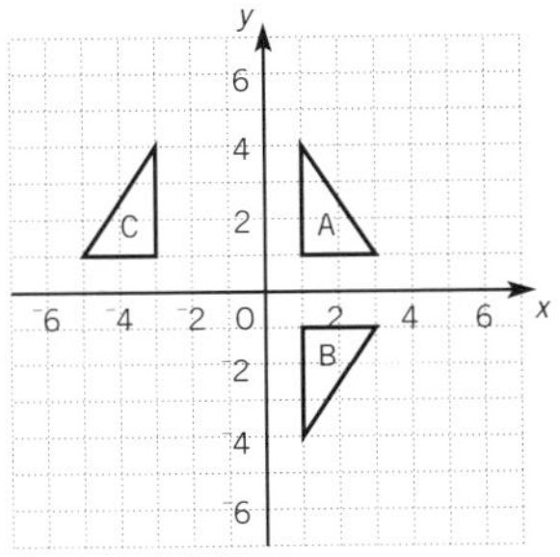

2 Reflection in line $y = x$

3 (a) and (b)

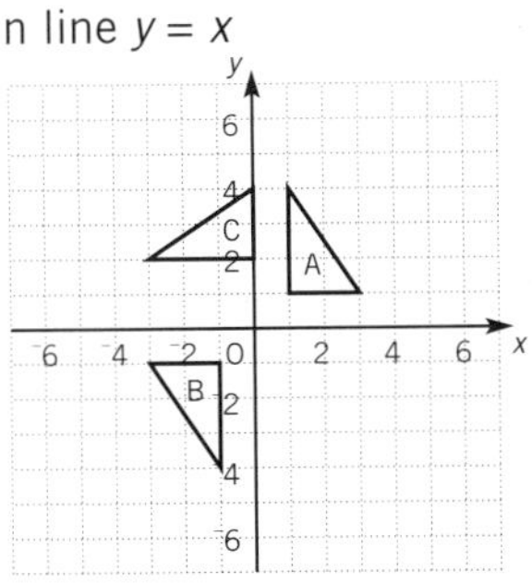

4 Rotation 90° anticlockwise about (3, 0)

5

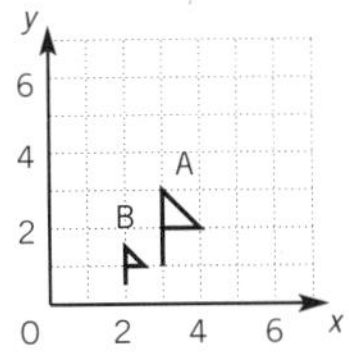

6 (4, 0); 3

7

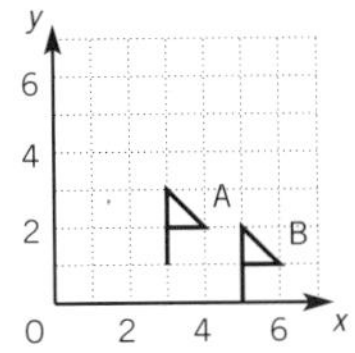

8 Translation by $\begin{pmatrix}4\\-1\end{pmatrix}$

9 Translation of $\begin{pmatrix}3\\1\end{pmatrix}$

10 Rotation through 180° about (3, 2)

11 Reflection in $y = x$

12 Reflection in $y = {}^{-}x$

13 (a) (i) (4·5, 4)
(ii) 8·06 to 2 d.p.
(b) (i) (3·5, $^{-}$2)
(ii) 12·04 to 2 d.p.
(c) (i) (1, $^{-}$1)
(ii) 10

14

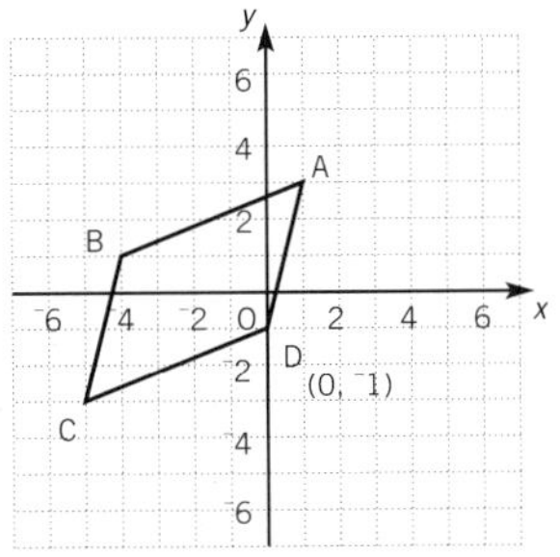

Exam questions (page 59)

1 (a)

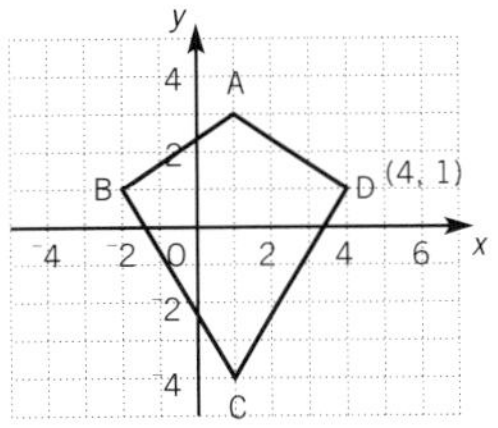

(b) ($^{-}$0·5, 1)
(c) 5·83 units to 2 d.p.

2 (a) (i) 2
(ii) (2, 2)

(b)

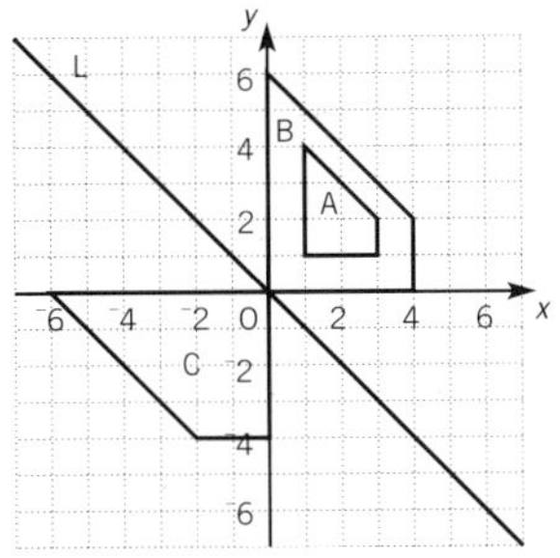

3 (a) Rotation through 90° clockwise about (0, 0).
(b) and (c)

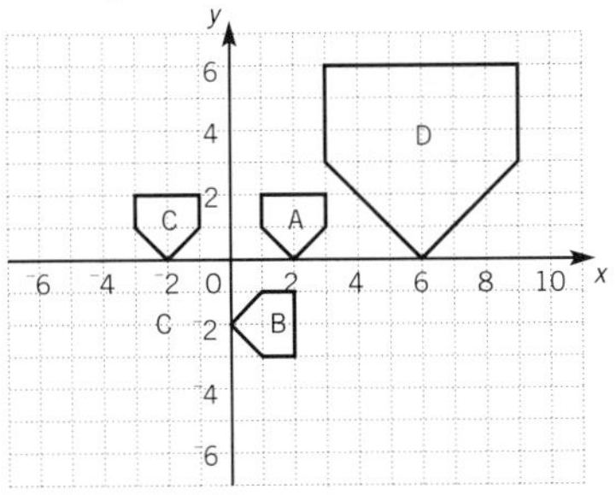

4 (a) Enlargement centre (0, 0), scale factor 0·5.
(b) Rotation through 180° about (4, 1).

Measures

Practice questions (pages 60–61)

1

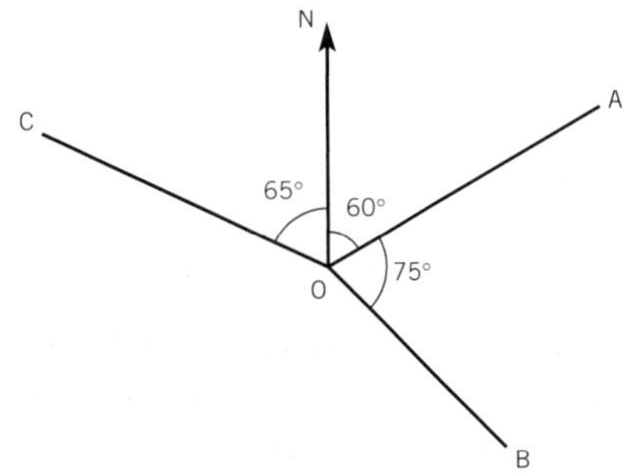

Diagrams are not full size.

2 307°

3 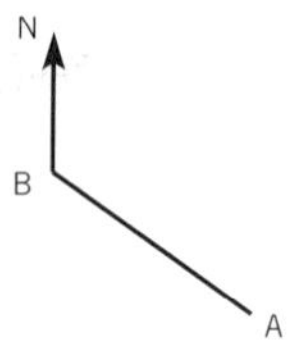

4 4 cm
5 1·5 m
6 1500 g
7 5 cm^2
8 5·254 m^3
9 52 000 ml
10 153 mm
11 1·465 kg
12 1·34 l
13 0·075 m
14 (a) 72·5 to 73·5 g
(b) 135 to 145 m
(c) 4·25 to 4·35 litre
(d) 46·5 to 47·5 cm
15 25·65 and 25·75 seconds

Exam questions (page 61)

When you have to take a measurement from your diagram, answers within 2 mm or 2° of the answer given below are acceptable.

1 (a) 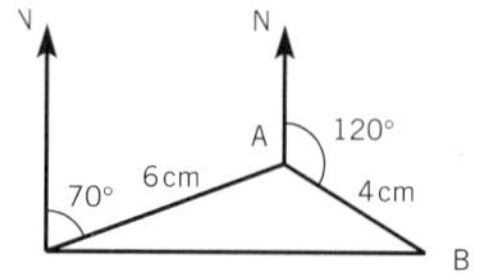

(b) Distance = 9·1 miles Bearing = 90°
2 (a) (i) Area = 22 656 cm^2
(ii) Area = 2·27 m^2 (to 3 s.f.)
(b) 3·535 to 3·545 and 63·5 to 64·5
3 (a) 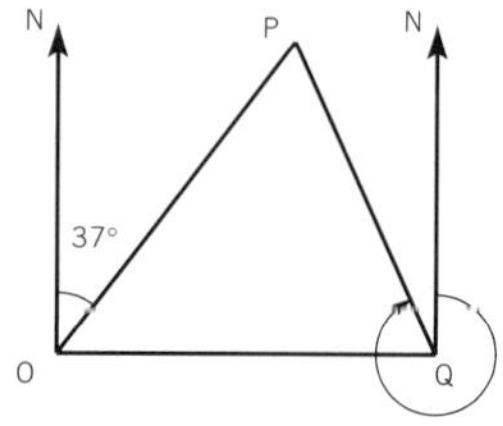

(b) (i) PQ measures 3·4 cm on the diagram so is 3·4 × 2 = 6·8 km.
(ii) Bearing is 341°.
4 1·15 to 1·25 million
5 (a) Bearing Coventry from Rugby is 285°.
(b) 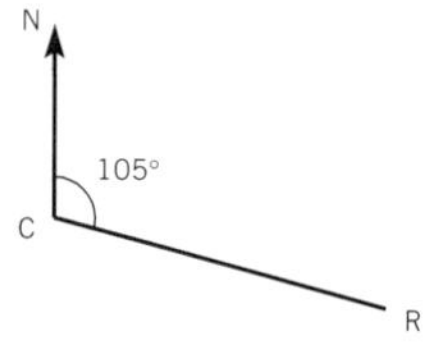

Constructions

Practice questions (pages 62–63)

Answers should be within ±1mm or ±1°.
1 5·4 cm, 85°, 45°
2 40°, 4·7 cm, 8·8 cm
3 118°, 36°, 26°
4 69°, 6·4 cm, 58°
5 5·74 cm
6 5·8 cm

Exam questions (page 63)

1 AX = 4·8 cm
2 MZ = 2·9 cm

Mensuration

Practice questions (pages 64–65)

1 42 cm^2
2 0·77 m^2
3 251·3 m^2
4 (a) area
(b) none, dimension is 4
(c) volume

Exam questions (page 65)

1 A = 15·7 cm^2
2 r = 6398 km
3 A = 445·8 m^2
4 A = 402 m^2
5 (a) and (d)

Loci

Practice questions (page 66)

1 Circle, centre P, radius 4 cm drawn.
2 (a) Perpendicular bisector of AB drawn.
(b) The side of it including A shaded.
3 Bisector of the angle drawn.
4 Shore line drawn running SE to NW.
Locus of boat drawn – a line parallel to the shore and 500 m from it.

Exam questions (page 67)

All diagrams are shown half-size.

1 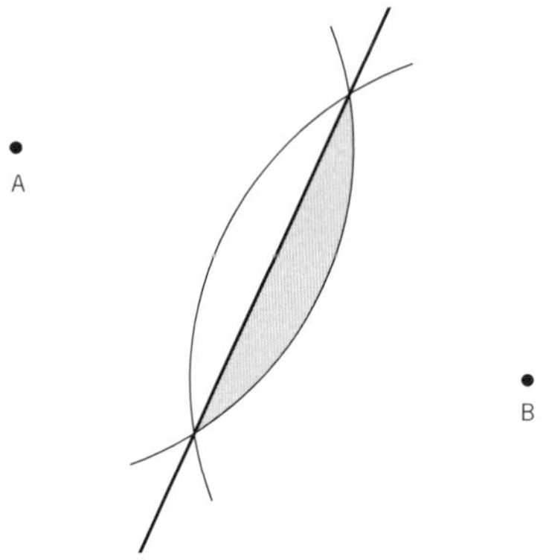

2 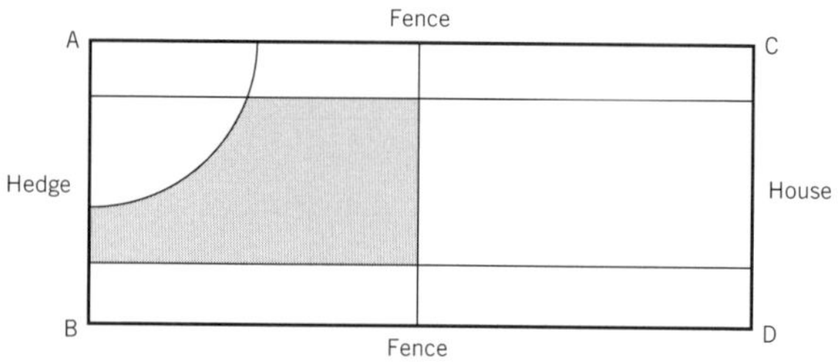

3 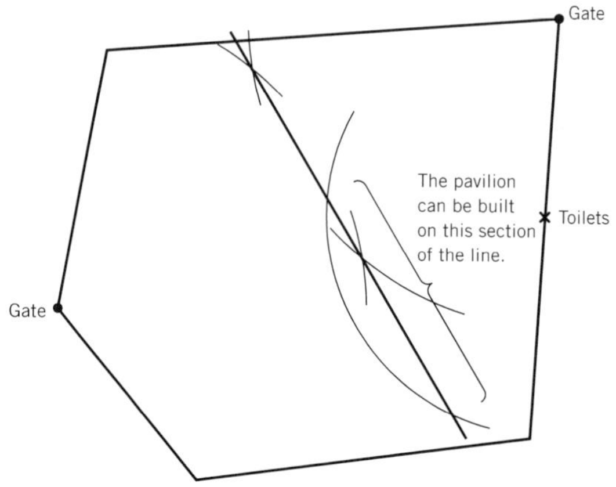

Identification and selection of data

Practice questions (pages 68–69)

1 **(a)** secondary **(c)** secondary
(b) secondary **(d)** primary

2 **(a)**, **(b)** and **(d)** are biased but **(c)** is not biased.

3 Method 2 is unbiased because this will not be influenced by location, age, sex, etc.

4 Examples:
How many hours per day do you watch TV?
Do you only watch TV in the evenings?
Do you watch soaps?
Do you watch comedies?
Do you watch sport?

Exam questions (page 69)

1 Possible answers are:
(a) because some people may be too embarrassed to answer.
(e) because someone who earns very little or is out of work might be too embarrassed to answer this.

2 Possible answers are:
only those people with a phone number in the phone book will be contacted;
only those who live in the town were asked and not people who may work in the town and live outside;
a week may not be a long enough period to find out the usage – people asked may have been away that week;
the question didn't mention the time.

Processing and representing data

Practice questions (pages 70–74)

1 **(a)**

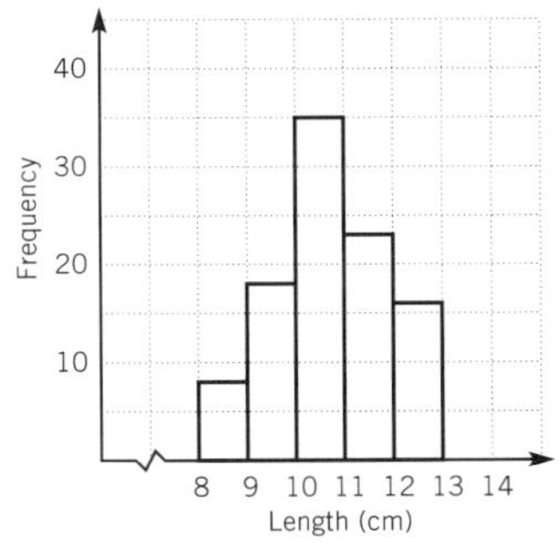

(b)

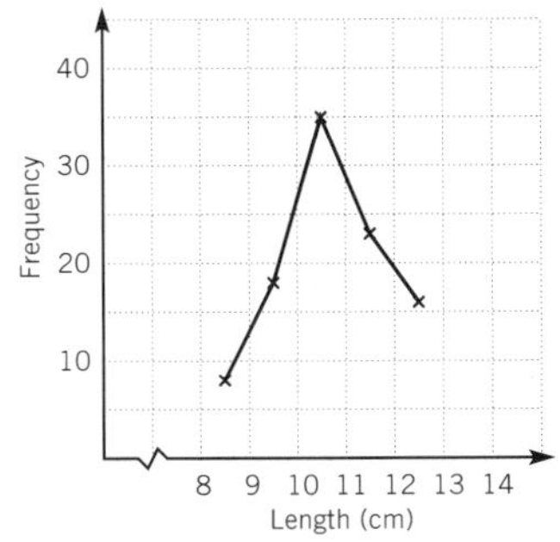

2

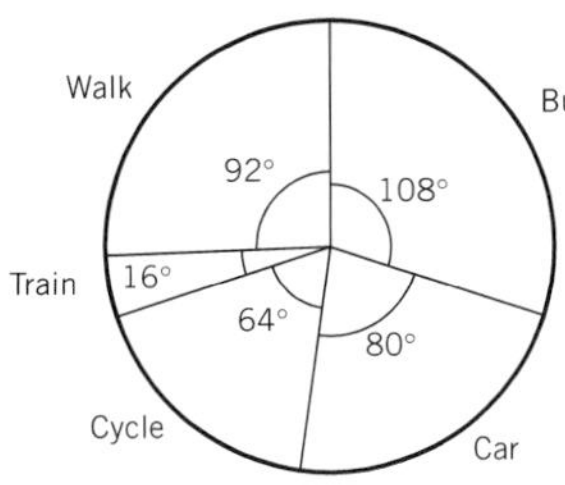

3 **(a)**, **(b)**

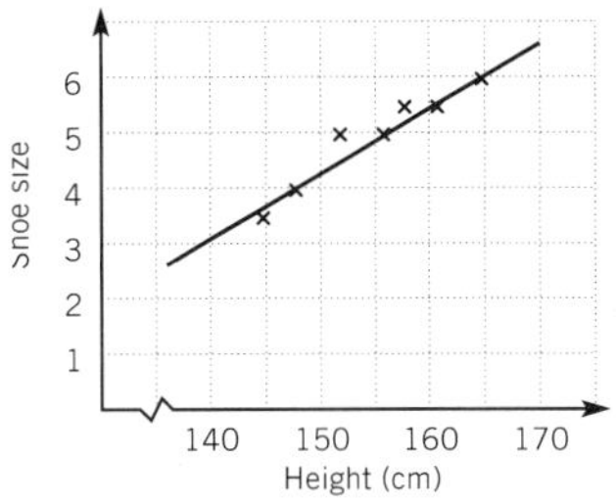

Fairly strong positive correlation

(c) $4\frac{1}{2}$

4 **(a)**, **(b)**

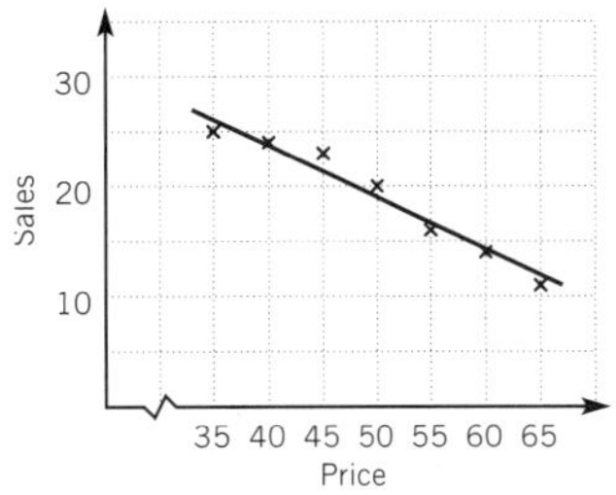

Fairly strong negative correlation

(c) 18 000

5 **(a)** **(c)**

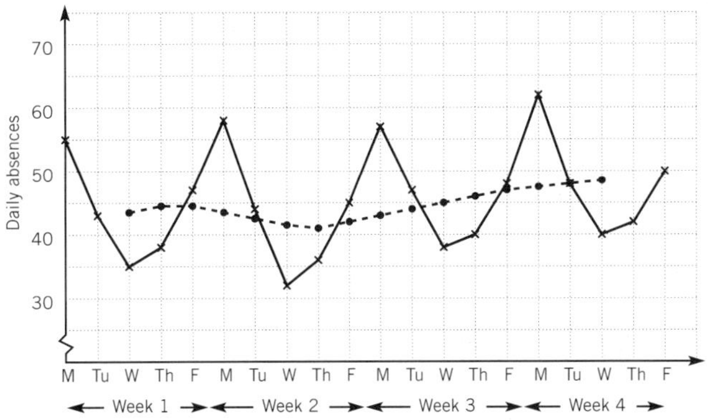

(b) Moving averages 43·6, 44·2, 44·4, 43·8, 43·4, 43, 42·8, 43·4, 44·6, 45·4, 46, 47, 47·2, 47·6, 48, 48·4.

(d) Highest always Monday followed by Friday. Lowest always Wednesday. General trend, fairly constant at first then a steady rise.

6 10·71

7

4	3 6 8 9
5	2 3 4 7 7 8 8
6	0 2 3 [5 6] 8
7	1 1 2 6 9 9
8	2 2 2 3 9
9	5 7

Key: 4 | 3 means 43

Median = 65·5

8 (a) Cumulative frequencies 8, 23, 56, 78, 95, 100.

(b)

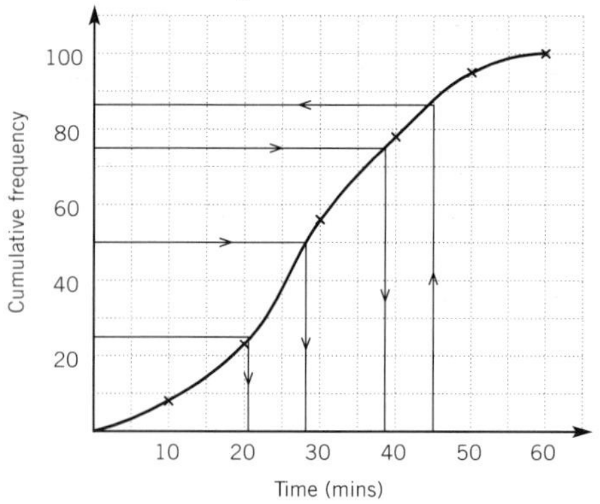

(c) (i) 13 **(ii)** 28 mins **(iii)** 18 mins

9 (a) 85

(b) Median = 56, interquartile range = 70 – 42 = 28

(c)

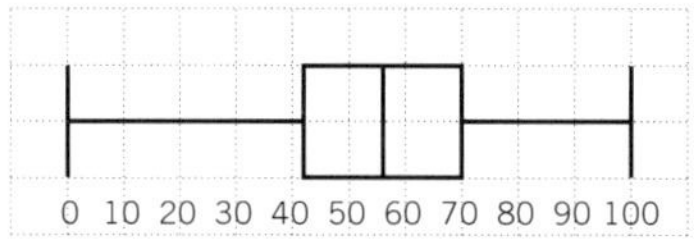

Exam questions (pages 74–75)

1 (a) Ordered

Key: 2 | 1 means 21

1	
2	1 4
3	4
4	3 4 8
5	5 6 8
6	1 4 5 9
7	2 2 3 [4] 6 6 8 8 9
8	1 1 1 2 2 9
9	1 2 5 8 9

(b) 74

2 (a) Angles: 165°, 96°, 60°, 39°.

(b)

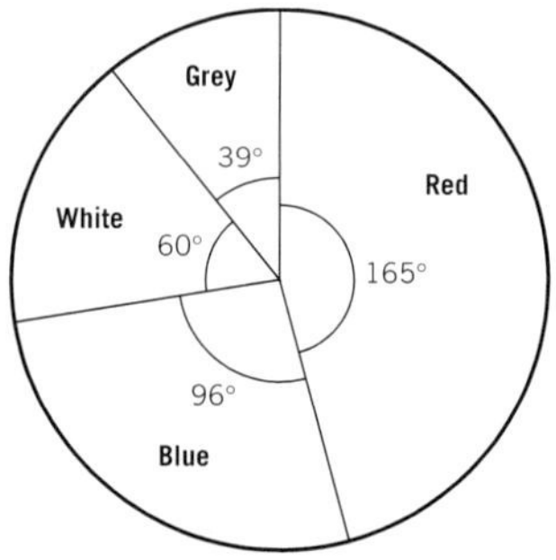

3 (a) (i) Cumulative frequency:
9, 22, 43, 60, 70, 78, 80.

(ii)

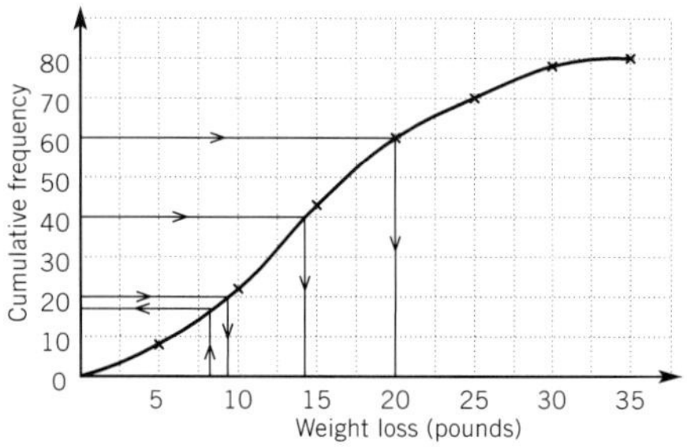

(b) (i) 14

(ii) 11 (10·5 to 11 is acceptable)

(c) 63 (63 to 65 is acceptable)

(d) 120 kg

4 (a) (i) and **(iii)**

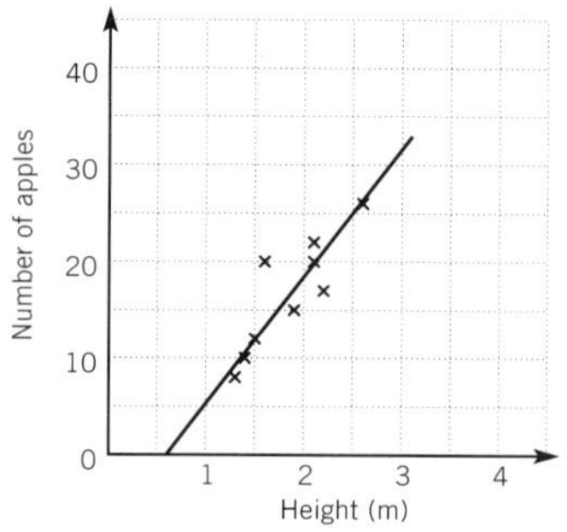

(ii) Positive correlation

(iv) 4 m is too far outside the range of the data

(b) Mid-interval values: 55, 65, 75, 85, 95
$w \times f$: 1265, 2730, 3750, 1700, 1425, 10 870.
Mean: 72·5 kg to 3 s.f.

Probability

Practice questions (pages 76–77)

1 0·3

2 (a) (i) 0·1 **(ii)** 0

(b) 40

3 0·148. Yes, there should be roughly the same frequency for each number, but there are nearly twice as many 4s as 3s.

4 (a) 43

(b) 0·288, given to 1 or more decimal places

5

Main course	Dessert
SP	BC
SP	CG
SP	T
MC	BC
MC	CG
MC	T

6

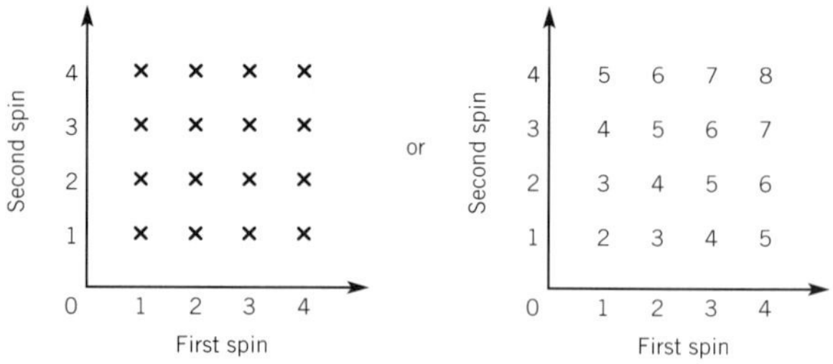

(a) $\frac{1}{16}$ **(b)** $\frac{3}{16}$

7 (a)

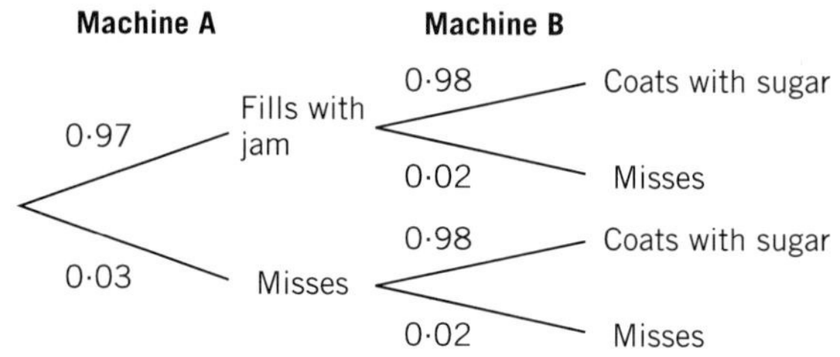

(b) 0·0006

(c) 0·0488

Exam questions (page 77)

1 **(a)** $\frac{1}{4}$ **(b)** $\frac{7}{20}$ **(c)** $\frac{3}{4}$ **(d)** 0

2 **(a)** 0·3 added to first set of branches, 0·8 and 0·2 to each of second sets.

(b) **(i)** 0·56

(ii) 0·38

Interpretation

Exam questions (page 79)

1 **(a)** Range = 2·7 cm Median = 3·0 cm

(b)

1	1 2 4 8 9
2	1 1 1 2 8
3	0 2 3 4 8
4	2 5 8 9
5	5

Range = 4·4 cm Median = 2·9 cm

(c) e.g. The pebbles in Eddie's set have a larger range and are more varied in size.

2 **(a)**

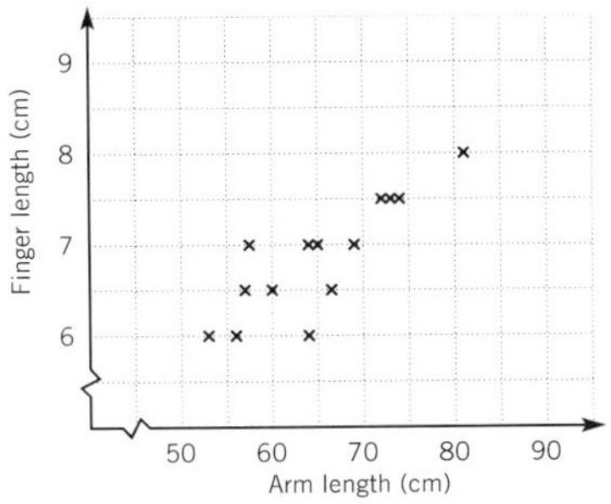

(b) Positive correlation – as arm length increases so does finger length.

(c) Between 6·8 cm and 7 cm

3 **(a)**

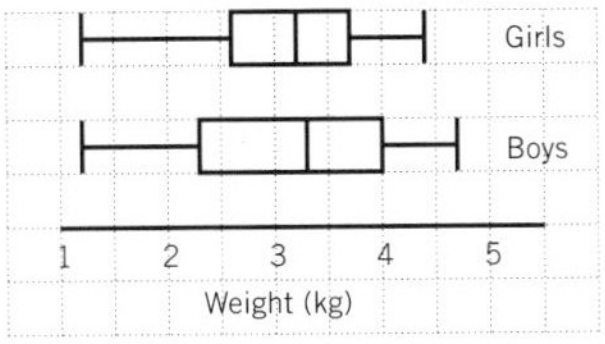

(b) For example: boys tend to be heavier;
the range for the girls is less;
the interquartile range for the girls is less;
25% of the boys weigh less than 2·3 kg,
25% of the girls weigh less than 2·6 kg,
so there are more boys with low weights;
girls' weights are more consistent, i.e. 50% of the girls have a weight between 2·6 kg and 3·8 kg but for the boys 50% weigh between 2·3 kg and 4·0 kg.

4 **(a)**

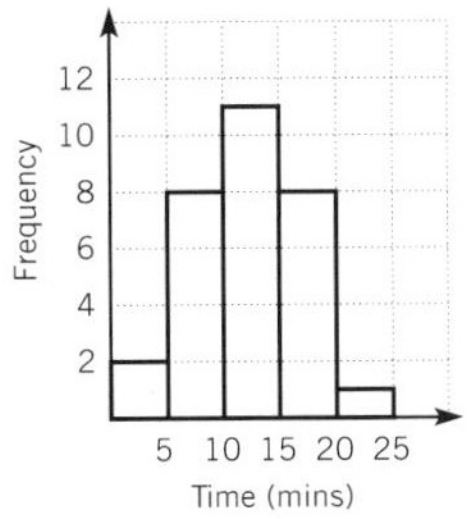

(b) The modal class is 10 – 15

5 **(a)** Cumulative frequencies:
0, 12, 49, 80, 98, 106, 108

(b)

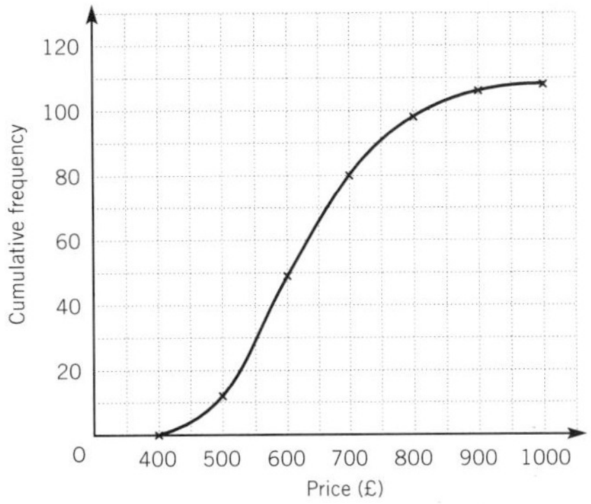

(c) **(i)** Median is between £610 and £625

(ii) At £800 the cumulative frequency is 98 therefore 10 cost more than £800.
The percentage = $\frac{10}{108} \times 100 = 9{\cdot}26\%$

Index